How to Study the Bible

Dr. J. L. Williams

How to Study the Bible

Copyright © 2011 by **Dr. J.L. Williams**

Published by:

Integrity Publishers Inc.
P.O. Box 789,
Wake Forest, NC 27588
U.S.A.
info@integritypublishers.org

ISBN 13: **978-0-9828630-4-6**

All Rights reserved. No portion of this book may be reproduced, stored in a retrieval system, or transmitted in any form by any means – electronic, mechanical, photocopy, recording, scanning or other – except for brief quotations in critical reviews or articles, without the prior written permission of the publisher.

Unless otherwise indicated, Scripture quotations are from *The New International Version*. ®. Copyright © 1973, 1978, 1984 International Bible Society. All italics, bold print, etc., are for the author's emphasis.

Printed in United States

TABLE OF CONTENTS

Why:

1. Perspective on the Word 11
2. Person of the Word 29
3. Purpose of the Word 43
4. Purity of the Word 55
5. Permanence of the Word 67
6. Proofs for the Word 77

How:

7. Prerequisites for Studying the Word 129
8. Principles for Interpreting the Word 139
9. Practical Steps for Studying the Word 179

Appendix:

I. Important New Testament Dates 197

II. Manuscript Evidence 201

III. The Dead Sea Scrolls: Content of Eleven Caves 211

IV. The KJV Translation Controversy 213

V. Dates of the New Testament Documents 223

VI. Biblical Timeline 225

VII.	New Testament to Old Testament Events	241
VIII.	The Error of the Documentary Hypothesis	243
IX.	Postmodernism and the Word	261
X.	Further Resources: Online Degree Opportunities	271

INTRODUCTION

In beginning this study of the Bible, I have chosen two verses to use as over-all texts. Many could have been chosen – but I have chosen one from the Old and one from the New Testament, as broad canopies for this study. Joshua 1:8 from the Old Testament:

> **"Do not let this Book of the Law depart from your mouth; meditate on it day and night, so that you may be careful to do everything written in it. Then you will be prosperous and successful"** (Josh. 1:8 NIV).

Of the over 16,000 Greek and Hebrew words used in the Bible, the Hebrew word for "success" is used only once – that being in the above quoted verse. *So here is the one place where God offers us a guarantee of success!* But the conditions on our side are plainly set forth.

1. Studying and storing up God's Word in our minds: **"Do not let this Book of the Law depart** (*'move'* or *'be removed'*) **from your mouth..."**

2. It shall become the fixed point of our thought and meditation: **"...meditate on it day and night..."**

3. Knowledge must lead to obedience: **"...so that you may be careful to do everything written in it..."**

After these conditions are met God says: "...**Then you will be prosperous and successful.**" In a world that is obsessed with success and *"formulas for success"* – here is *"God's guaranteed program of success!"* Most of man's plans and programs of success do not work or are only temporarily successful at best. Here is God's program that is proven with time – and is as certain and absolute as He is! Tragically, most people are either ignorant of it – or, *are not willing to meet the conditions* that God has laid down. This study is designed to challenge people to *"find success and prosperity God's way!"*

The New Testament text is II Timothy 2:15:

> **"Study to shew thyself approved unto God, a workman that needeth not be ashamed, rightly dividing the word of truth"** (King James Version).

> **"Do your best to present yourself to God as one approved, a workman who does not need to be ashamed and who correctly handles the word of truth"** (New International Version).

Not only will most people – even most Christians – not find prosperity and success, but most will stand unapproved and ashamed one day before God because of their lack of diligent study, and corresponding sloppy and incorrect handling of God's Word! *Every great heresy in the history of the Christian church has been started by someone mishandling and incorrectly interpreting God's Word.* Jesus said that "...**scripture cannot be broken**" (John 10:35) – but Peter said that it could be twisted (II Peter 3:16)! That realization brings us to one of the rather disturbing principles of this study:

PROBLEMATIC PRINCIPLE: *"Because of laziness and ignorance, the lovers of the Bible have done – and continue to do – more harm than the haters of the Bible!"*

The Bible is, therefore, the most *quoted* and *misquoted* book in the world. It is my prayer that this book will not produce guilt, but rather motivation and practical skills to help God's people get into, understand

and apply His Word to their lives. Then and only then will they be able to enter into the experience of what Jesus said: "**and you will know the truth, and the truth will make you free**" (John 8:32).

J.L. Williams

JL, Patt & Friends, Inc.

> "The Bible is the most realistic book ever written. It not only describes God as He really is, but us as we really are."
> Paul Little

Part 1
Why

PERSPECTIVE ON THE WORD

In any study of the Bible, there are many terms and concepts with which one needs to become familiar. Here are a few of the basic ones.

1. **Bible**: The word "Bible" comes from the Greek word "biblia" (plural) or "biblos" (singular), meaning book. Biblos comes from "byblos". *In ancient times papyrus was used in making paper from which books were made.* The papyrus reed grew in Egypt and Syria, and large shipments of papyrus were sent through the Syrian port of Byblos. The Greek word for books – biblos – probably comes from the name of this port.

   The word is used in Daniel 9:2 for the Scriptures. By about the 5th century, the Greek Church Fathers applied the term "biblia" to the whole of Christian Scriptures. It later passed to the Western Church and then into all Christendom.

2. Throughout this study I will be using abbreviations for certain translations of the Bible, and will abbreviate "Old Testament" to O.T. and "New Testament" to N.T.

> KJV = King James Version
> RSV = Revised Standard Version
> NASB = New American Standard Bible
> NIV = New International Version

3. **Old and New Testaments**: The Bible is divided into "*Old*" and "New Testaments". These terms have been used since the close of the 2nd century to distinguish the *Jewish* and *Christian Scriptures*. "Testament" is used in the KJV New Testament to render the Greek word "*diatheka*" (Latin: "*testamentum*") which meant "*a will*". But in the Septuagint (see page 5, number 6A) – it was used to translate the Hebrew word "*berith*" meaning "*a covenant*". Strictly speaking, "**Old**" and "**New Testament**" means "**Old**" and "**New Covenant**".

4. The Old Testament was originally written on scrolls or rolls. These were made by gluing sheets of papyrus (made from the papyrus plant) together and then winding these long strips around a stick. In order to make reading easier, the codex or book form was created in the 2nd century. This method is like ours today, making it possible to use both sides of the paper.

Christianity then, and its need of Scriptures, was the prime reason for the creation of the codex or book method of binding. You can quickly see the necessity of the codex form of writing and binding for Christian Scriptures when you realize that the Gospel of Matthew took a scroll about 30 feet long!

5. **Chapters and Verses**: The Bible is made up of 1189 chapters

and 773,746 words. The Old Testament has 929 chapters and the New Testament has 260 chapters. It is hard for us to think of the Bible without reference to chapter and verse. Yet the ***original Scriptures had no such divisions***. For example, the first five books of the Old Testament (Genesis to Deuteronomy – the Pentateuch) comprise one scroll and are thus referred to as *The Book of Moses*. Until A.D. 1200 no copies of Scripture had these divisions. The beginning of this practice of division is traced to Cardinal Lugo, who was the first to divide the Old Testament into chapters to go along with a concordance he prepared. Stephen Langton, Archbishop of Canterbury, who died in 1228, made the chapter divisions we use today. The New Testament was similarly divided by Hugo de St. Cher about 1240. The further division of the Old Testament chapters into verses came about 300 years later by Rabbi Mordecai Nathan in order to aid the study of the Hebrew Bible. The division of the New Testament into its present verses is found for the first time in an edition of the Greek New Testament published in 1551 by the Paris printer, Robert Stephens. The division of the Old Testament was adopted by Robert Stephens in his edition of the *Vulgate Version* in 1555 and transferred to the KJV in 1611. Stephens supplied the verse divisions for the New Testament which were transferred to the first English version in Geneva in 1560.

Problem: *Though this division into chapters and verses may on the surface appear to be helpful – it has serious drawbacks! Sometimes carelessness characterizes the chapter divisions. Many times thought patterns are broken – thus making it difficult to grasp the writer's message. A couple of the many examples are as follows*:

A. A false division occurs in Genesis 1 and 2 between the six working days and the Seventh Day of Rest.

B. The formation of chapter 9 of Isaiah from two incongruous prophecies makes these sections difficult to understand. A better division should have been to begin the new chapter at verse 8 of chapter 9.

C. The two books of Samuel, Kings and Chronicles were originally one book each with no chapter and verse divisions. Now the separation of them tends to destroy the natural connection and flow between them.

A real danger exists in studying the Bible by chapter divisions! You tend to deal with each chapter as a separate entity rather than as a part of a greater whole. (**Note**: There are several Bibles on the market now that have been printed without chapter and verse divisions, so they can be read and studied as a flowing narrative. These are a good investment for any serious Bible student. For new or young students of the Bible, *The Message* by Eugene Peterson is a good beginning study.)

6. **Early Translations of the Bible**:

   A. The ***Septuagint*** (LXX or 70): The first and most important of the ancient translations of the Hebrew O.T. into Greek. It probably originated out of a need by Alexandrian Jews. They no longer spoke Hebrew and needed the Scriptures in their mother tongue of Greek. It has the name *LXX* for 70 because the first five books (Genesis to Deuteronomy) supposedly were translated by 72 men – six from each of the 12 tribes. Therefore, they are called "the seventy." It was picked up by Christians as their Bible, and for that reason largely dropped by the Jews about 100 A.D. – and so it became primarily a Christian book. The oldest copies of the LXX came from three great Greek manuscripts of the Bible from the 4th and 5th centuries A.D.:

   (1) **Codex Sinaiticus**: (350 A.D.) This manuscript contains almost all of the N.T. (except Mark 16:9-20; John 7:53-8:11) and over half of the O.T. It was discovered in a wastebasket in the Mount Sinai (thus "Sinaiticus") Monastery in 1844, and is housed in the British Museum.

(2) ***Codex Vaticanus***: (325-350 A.D.) Housed in the Vatican Library, it contains almost all of the Bible – and is one of the most valuable and important Greek translations.

(3) ***Codex Alexandrinus***: (400 A.D.) It also contains almost the entire Bible. Many scholars believe that it was written in Egypt. It is likewise housed in the British Museum.

B. The Bible was also soon ***translated into other languages***, from the original Hebrew, Aramaic and Greek. These translated versions give us other important tools of comparative Biblical study.

{
- Syriac Version
- Coptic (Egyptian) Version
- Latin Version (Vulgate)
- Armenian
}

Some Basic Facts:

1. It should clearly be noted that the **Bible does claim to be the "Word of God"**. Over 2,000 times in the Old Testament alone the phrase "**Thus says the Lord**..." or its equivalent occurs. In the New Testament, the Old Testament is usually referred to as "**the Scriptures**" (Matt. 21:42; 22:29; Lk. 24:32; Jn. 5:39; Acts 18:24). Other terms used are "**Scripture**" (Acts 8:32; Gal. 3:22), "**the Holy Scriptures**" (Rom. 1:2; II Tim. 3:150, and "**sacred writings**" (II Tim. 3:15).

2. The Bible was written over an approximate 1600 year period – or 60 generations.

3. It was written by over 40 authors from every walk of life: *kings, peasants, philosophers, fishermen, poets, statesmen, scholars*, etc.:

        Moses..Political Leader

Peter..Fisherman
Amos..Herdsman
Joshua..Military General
Nehemiah...Cupbearer
Daniel...Prime Minister
Luke...Doctor
Solomon..King
Matthew..Tax Collector
Paul..Rabbi

4. It was written in *different places*:

Moses...Wilderness
Jeremiah...Dungeon
Daniel...Hillside and Palace
Paul..In Prison
Luke...Traveling
John...Banishment

5. It was written under *different circumstances*:

David..Times of War
Solomon..Times of Peace

6. It was written under *different moods*:

Philippians..Joy
Jeremiah...Sorrow

7. It was written on *three different continents*:

$\Bigg[$ Asia
Africa
Europe

8. It was written in three languages:

   Hebrew: The language of the Israelites in Canaan before their Babylonian captivity. After their "return" this gave way to a related dialect spoken in the area – *Aramaic*. It should also be noted that the Hebrew text of the Bible consisted only of *consonants* since the Hebrew alphabet has no written vowels. The vowel signs were invented and added later by the Jewish *Masoretic* scholars in the 6th century and later.

   Aramaic: (Ezra 4:8-7:18; 7:12-26; Jer. 10:11; Dan. 2:4-7; 28);

   Greek: Except for a few words and sentences the entire New Testament was written in *Koine* Greek, the common language of the Hellenistic world of the day.

9. The Old Testament can conveniently be divided into:

   A. The Law
   B. The Prophets } Composing 39 books and 929 chapters
   C. The Writings

10. The Old Testament begins with *God*. The New Testament begins with *Jesus Christ*. From Adam to Abraham we have the story of the human race – from Abraham to Christ we have the history of the *chosen race*, or Israel. From Christ on we have the history of the *church* or the New Israel. The Old Testament is primarily the account of a *nation* – and the New Testament is the account of a man – Jesus!

11. Bible history takes us back into the unknown of *eternity past* – while much of Bible prophecy takes us into the unknown of *eternity future*. Genesis, the first book of the Bible, is a book of *beginnings* – and Revelation, the last book of the Bible, is a book of *endings*!

12. And, the subject matter of all the books between Genesis and Revelation *covers practically every known controversial subject* – but they do so with *harmony, continuity and lack of contradiction when properly interpreted and understood!*

Conclusions

The conclusion to which any unbiased reader is driven is that the Bible *literally has no peer.* Two scholars summarized the Bible's uniqueness this way:

"Comprised as it is of 66 books, written over a period of some fifteen hundred years by nearly forty authors in several languages containing hundreds of topics, it is more than accidental that the Bible possesses an amazing unity of theme – Jesus Christ. One problem, sin – and one solution, the Savior – unify its pages from Genesis to Revelation." [1]

As J.B. Phillips put it, *"The New Testament given a fair hearing does not need me or anyone else to defend it. It has the proper ring for anyone who has not lost his ear for truth."* [2]

Rousseau justly remarked: *"It is more inconceivable that several men should have united to forge the Gospel than that a single person should have furnished the subject of it. The Gospel has marks of truth so great, so striking, so perfectly inimitable, that the inventor of it would be more astonishing than the hero."* [3]

C.S. Lewis said this of the Bible: *"If any message from the core of reality ever were to reach us, we should expect to find in it just that unexpectedness, that willful, dramatic intricacy which we find in the Christian faith. It has the Master touch – the rough, male taste of reality, not made by us, or indeed, for us, but hitting us in the face."* [4]

---

1   Normal L. Geisler and William E. Nix, *From God to Us: How We Got Our Bible.* Quoted by Wally Kroeker's in "How We Got The Bible," *Moody Monthly,* April 1975, p. 27.
2   J. B. Phillips, *The Ring of Truth,* New York: The Macmillan Co., 1967, p. 20.
3   J.N.D. Anderson, *Christianity: The Witness of History,* London: The Tyndale Press, 1969, p. 35.
4   Clyde S. Kilby, ed. *A Mind Awake, An Anthology of C. S. Lewis,* New York: Harcourt, Brace, and World, Inc., 1968, p. 49.

It is just that "ring of truth" or "sound of reality" that convinced Tatian (c. 110-172), who became a Christian apologist, to say; *"I happened to meet with certain barbaric writings, too old to be compared with the opinions of the Greeks, and too divine to be compared with their errors; and I was led to put faith in these by the unpretending cast of the language, the inartificial character of the writers, the foreknowledge displayed of future events, the excellent quality of the precepts, and the declaration of the government of the universe as being centered in one Being."*[5]

Lewis S. Chafer, the founder and former president of Dallas Theological Seminary, put it this way: *"The Bible is not such a book a man would write if he could, or could write if he would."*[6]

The apologist Josh McDowell said this of the Bible in contrast to other popular writings: *"The Bible deals very frankly with the sins of its characters. Read the biographies today, and see how they try to cover up, overlook, or ignore the shady side of people. Take the great literary geniuses; most are painted as saints. The Bible does not do it that way. It simply tells it like it is."*

Finally, I will conclude this section with a very humorous – but true – statement by Martin Luther concerning the Bible: *"To try to compare our wisdom, insight and understandings to God's revelation in scripture is like a donkey singing a duet with a nightingale."*

A BRIEF OVERVIEW OF THE NEW TESTAMENT

1. The New Testament is composed of 27 short *Greek* writings (260 chapters) commonly called "books".

2. The first four are the *Gospels or "Good News" that God has revealed Himself in Jesus Christ for*

> "Religions are man's search for God; the Gospel is God's search for man There are many religions, but only one Gospel."
> - E. Stanley Jones

---

[5] William Barclay, *The Making of the Bible*, "Tatians Address to the Greeks 29", New York: Abingdon Press, 1965, p. 41.

[6] Josh McDowell, *More Evidence that Demands a Verdict*, Vol. 1, Arrowhead Springs, CA: Campus Crusade for Christ, Inc., 1972, p. 25.

the purpose of redeeming mankind. These are not *biographies* in the popular sense of the word – but narratives. The first three (Matthew, Mark, Luke) are called *Synoptic* – meaning *"see together"*.

Comparison of Synoptic Gospels

Mark This is the earliest Gospel and is – according to the tradition of *Papias* (c. 60-130 A.D.) – *from the preaching and teaching of Peter*, whose personality is seen on every page! Mark has been called the *"moving picture"* of the life of Christ. It is characterized by *rapidity of movement and action*. Words like *"immediately,"* and *"straightforth,"* are constantly noticed. **It was written in *Rome primarily for Romans*.** Therefore, there is very little O.T. quotation or Jewish overtones, as is found in Matthew. Mark pictures Christ as a Conqueror – which would have interested the Romans. Christ conquers *disease, demons and death*! However, Christ is also seen as a Servant – but throughout as the Son of God. That title is given Him in the very first verse of the Gospel: **"The beginning of the gospel about Jesus Christ, the Son of God"** (Mk. 1:1). Near the end the centurion makes the same affirmation: **"Surely this man was the Son of God"** (Mk. 15:39).

There are 661 verses in this shortest Gospel. Of them:

> found...606 are found in Matthew
>
> ...380 are found in Luke

Conclusion: Since there are only 31 verses in Mark that are not found in either Matthew or Luke, *those writers must have had Mark's account before them as they wrote their accounts.*

Matthew Matthew was obviously *written by a Jew for Jews*. It is thoroughly interlaced with references and allusions to the O.T. It begins with a *genealogy* (unlike Mark) that traces

Christ's ancestry back to Abraham and David. These two men represent the theme of Matthew's portrait of Jesus: David was the great King of Israel – and Jesus is David's greater Son who is "**King of the Jews**". Abraham is remembered for the almost sacrifice of his son, Isaac. Jesus was the Son of God who was sacrificed for our sins.

Whereas Mark has only 31 verses unique to itself – Matthew has 300 verses found only in this Gospel. Many of these are quotations from the O.T.

Luke Whereas Matthew begins his genealogy of Jesus with the two greatest Jews, David and Abraham, Luke traces Christ's ancestry back to *Adam*. Here is the key to interpreting this Gospel. It was written by "Doctor Luke", a Gentile, who was writing to present Christ as the *universal Man*. This "***Gospel to the Gentiles***" presents the Christ who is the Universal Savior for all men!

Luke has 520 verses not found in the other Gospels. These are primarily the sayings of Jesus. This has also been called the "*Gospel for Women*" because in it we see and learn of the women who loved and followed Christ and ministered to Him.

The importance of Luke for history is also significant because he alone, of the Gospel writers, places the events he records within the context of their contemporary world history. This gives us an ability to *accurately date much New Testament activity*.

3. ***The Fourth Gospel***: Unlike Matthew and Luke, we find the key to the fourth Gospel at the "back door" or end of the Gospel instead of at the beginning or "front door". There John clearly sets forth his purpose in writing: "**...these are written that you may believe that Jesus is the Christ, the Son of God, and that by believing you may have life in His name**" (John 20:31). Rather than begin with human genealogies like Matthew or Luke, John presents the *pre-existence of Christ* as the Word (logos) of God.

Also, because of the fact that John mentions three Passovers (2:26; 6:4; 11:55) – and perhaps a fourth (5:1) it is possible for us to safely assume that Christ's public ministry lasted at least three years.

4. **The Book of Acts**, or Acts of the Apostles, is the fifth book of the N.T. It is really a continuation of the Third Gospel written by the physician Luke. It gives an account of the growth of Christianity after the resurrection and ascension of Christ. Its historical trustworthiness is beyond serious criticism. F. F. Bruce wrote: *"The confirmation of historicity is overwhelming...Roman historians have long taken it for granted."*[7] In addition to what we learn in it of the growth of the early church, we secondarily learn a great deal about the then Roman world. A Lord Chief Justice of England said of it 50 years ago:

> "...the best short general picture of the Pax Romana and all that it meant – good roads and posting, good police, freedom from brigandages and piracy, freedom of movement, toleration and justice – is to be found in the experience, written in Greek, of a Jew who happened to be a Roman citizen – that is, in the Acts of the Apostles."

5. Twenty-one of the rest of the N.T. documents are letters – 13 of which bear the name of Paul:

...nine are addressed to *specific churches*:

Romans
I and II Corinthians
Galatians
Ephesians
Philippians
Colossians
I and II Thessalonians

---

7   F. F. Bruce, "Are the New Testament Documents Still Reliable?" *Christianity Today*, Oct. 20, 1978, p. 30.

...four are addressed *to friends or working companions of Paul*:

> *I and II Timothy*
> *Titus*
> *Philemon*

6. **Hebrews** is anonymous – but often associated with Paul, and sometimes with Apollos. It was written to a community of Jewish Christians in Italy.

7. **James** and **Jude** were written by brothers of Jesus.

8. **I** and **II Peter** were written by the "big fisherman" who was a member of the inner circle of three disciples (Peter, James and John).

9. **I, II** and **III John** bear no name but because of their close affinity with the Fourth Gospel, they have been accepted since early days as Epistles of John, the "Beloved Disciple".

10. **Revelation** is an apocalyptic writing also by John who was banished on the Isle of Patmos (Rev. 1:9).

See the Appendix for Chapter One (page 146-150) for Important New Testament Related Dates, and Dates of the New Testament Documents to compare the gap between historic events and their being written down.

---

8   F. F. Bruce, "Are the New Testament Documents Still Reliable?" *Christianity Today*, Oct. 20, 1978, p. 32.

Summary Chart

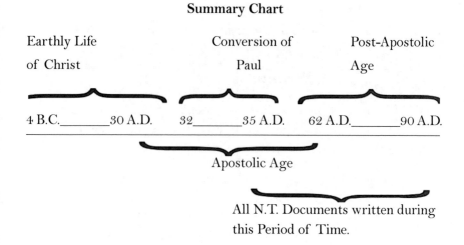

Conclusions

From the preceding chart you can readily see that the time between the biblical events themselves and their being written down is actually very short. F.F. Bruce said: "*...the time elapsing between the evangelistic events and the writing of most of the New Testament books was, from the standpoint of historical research, satisfactorily short.*"[9]

Paul's whole argument in I Corinthians 15 is based on the veracity of these many eyewitnesses of the death and resurrection of Christ. There he recounts the many people that Christ appeared to after His resurrection: "**...that He was buried, that He was raised on the third day according to the Scriptures, and that He appeared to Peter, and then to the Twelve. After that, He appeared to more than five hundred of the brothers at the same time, most of whom are still living, though some have fallen asleep. Then He appeared to James, then to all the apostles; and last of all He appeared to me also, as to one abnormally (untimely, NASB) born**" (I Cor. 15:4-8).

Did you catch the thrust of Paul's argument? In essence he is saying

---

9   F. F. Bruce, *The New Testament Documents: Are They Reliable?* Downers Grove, IL: InterVarsity Press, 1960, p. 14.

this: *"If you do not believe me when I say that Christ was literally raised from the dead – go check out the many other eyewitnesses!"* He then says that there are over 500 who are still alive who saw Jesus after His resurrection. That's certainly a large enough number to substantiate any historical event! Paul wrote those words in I Corinthians 15, about 25 years after the event. That gap of 25 or so years between the actual historical events and their being written down is not a seriously long one.

As F.F. Bruce said: *"It is comparable to the gap separating us today from the events of World War II. No one, writing an account today of those events, could hope to get away with it if he misrepresented them in terms which could be refuted by many people's recollection of them: they would certainly say to him, 'You are wasting your breath! I remember it as if it were yesterday!'"* [10]

The combination of the **large number of living eyewitnesses with the short span in time between the actual events and their being written down** – is a double check for accuracy and authenticity! You can lie in a written account and perhaps get by with it if there are no longer any eyewitnesses alive to correct you. But you could not hope to pull off a misrepresentation when there were still over 500 eyewitnesses alive to refute your error!

And then there is the occasion when Paul was making his defense before Festus, he clearly reminded him that the things he was speaking about were historical and not mythological. He reminds Festus of his own knowledge of these things – regardless of whether or not he would acknowledge them. Paul says to Festus: **"The king is familiar with these things, and I can speak freely to him. I am convinced that none of this has escaped his notice, because it was not done in a corner"** (Acts 26:26).

Paul reminds Festus that Christianity and the events surrounding it are historical! *Nothing was done behind closed doors or in secrecy – but out in the open for all to observe.* There are many that do not believe – but

---

10 F. F. Bruce, *The New Testament Documents: Are They Reliable?* Downers Grove, IL: InterVarsity Press, 1960, p. 30.

few are there among unbelievers who have really objectively studied the historical facts. In essence Paul said to Festus, *"Disbelieve you may – but ignore the historical facts you cannot! They are clearly there for everyone to examine!"* Never forget that Christianity is historical! That is what the Apostle John was reminding his readers when he wrote:

"That which was from the beginning, which we have heard, which we have seen with our eyes, which we have looked at and our hands have touched – this we proclaim concerning the Word of life. The life appeared; we have seen it and testify to it, and we proclaim to you the eternal life, which was with the Father and has appeared to us. We proclaim to you what we have seen and heard, so that you also may have fellowship with us. And our fellowship is with the Father and with His Son, Jesus Christ" (I John 1:1-3).

Notice that neither John nor Paul was writing primarily about some emotional experience – but about *historical, verifiable facts.* Facts that can be *observed, touched,* and then *accurately testified to*! **OUR FAITH IS IN THOSE FACTS!**

But you might want to challenge me with something like: *"Can I trust them in what they reported?"* It is really a matter of authority. You see, everything you believe in, you believe on the basis of someone's authority. We should not be afraid of this fact.

As C.S. Lewis said: *"Believing things on authority only means believing them because you have been told them by someone you think trustworthy. Ninety-nine percent of the things you believe are believed on authority. I believe there is such a place as New York. I have not seen it myself. I could not prove by abstract reasoning that there must be such a place. I believe it because reliable people have told me so. The ordinary man believes in the Solar System, atoms, evolution, and the circulation of the blood on authority – because the scientists say so. Every historical statement in the world is believed on authority. None of us has seen the Norman Conquest or the defeat of the Armada. None of us could prove them by pure logic as you prove a thing in mathematics. We believe them simply because people who did see them have left writings that tells us about them: in fact, on authority. A man who jibbed at authority in other things as some people do in religion would have to be content to know nothing all his life."*[11]

As Christians then we can rely on the authority of the New Testament witnesses. History, archaeology and personal experience have done nothing for 2,000 years but verify that our faith is sound! The Biblical record is absolutely trustworthy!

Quotations for Further Reflection

- *Both the Old and the New Testaments proclaim the mercy of God, but the Old has more than four times as much to say about it as the New. We should banish from our minds forever the common but erroneous notion that justice and judgment characterize the God of Israel, while mercy and grace belong to the Lord of the Church. Actually **there is in principle no difference between the Old Testament and the New.** In the New Testament Scriptures there is a fuller development of redemptive truth, but one God speaks in both dispensations, and what He speaks agrees with what He is…We who feel ourselves alienated from the fellowship of God can now raise our discouraged heads and look up…As we approach the Garden, our home before the Fall, the flaming sword is withdrawn. The keepers of the tree of life stand aside when they see a son of grace approaching.*[12]

---

11 Clyde S. Kilby, ed., *A Mind Awake, An Anthology of C. S. Lewis*, New York: Harcourt, Brace, and World, Inc., 1968, p. 135.
12 A. W. Tozer, *The Knowledge of the Holy*, New York, NY: HarperCollins, 1961, pp. 91, 96.

PERSON OF THE WORD

It can be emphatically stated that Jesus Christ is the focal point of the entire Bible! He is what some theologians have called, the "Scarlet Thread" that runs through the Bible from Genesis to Revelation. As C.S. Lewis once said:

> *"Understanding the true meaning of Christ is not learning a 'Subject' but rather 'steeping ourselves in a Personality, acquiring a new outlook and temper, breathing a new atmosphere, suffering Him, in His own way, to rebuild in us the defaced image of Himself.'"*[13]

As Lewis said, the Bible is not a completion of theological subjects we learn – but the revelation of a Person to whom we submit our entire life! That's why if we only learn "theology" and Bible facts and not bow at His feet and call Him Lord - we have missed the real purpose of the Bible. The purpose of Scripture is to point you to the Person of Scripture! Jesus Christ is the very zenith of God's self-revelation. Therefore, the Bible is His Story. As Henrietta C. Mears put it:

> *"The Old Testament is an account of a nation...The New Testament is*

---

13 Clyde S. Kilby, *The Christian World of C. S. Lewis*, Grand Rapids: Wm. B. Eerdmans Publishing Co., 1964, p. 152.

an account of a Man...The nation was founded and nurtured of God in order to bring the Man into the world...The Old Testament sets the stage for it. The New Testament describes it."[14]

The Bible As His Story

When properly understood ***Jesus Christ is the theme of each book of the Bible***. We could summarize each book as it relates to Christ as follows:

Old Testament

Genesis	Jesus Christ, our Creator God
Exodus	Jesus Christ, our Passover Lamb
Leviticus	Jesus Christ, our Sacrifice for sin
Numbers	Jesus Christ, our "Lifted up One"
Deuteronomy	Jesus Christ, our True Prophet
Joshua	Jesus Christ, Captain of our Salvation
Judges	Jesus Christ, our Deliverer Judge
Ruth	Jesus Christ, our Kinsman-Redeemer
I & II Samuel	Jesus Christ, our King
I & II Kings	Jesus Christ, as King
I & II Chronicles	Jesus Christ, as King
Ezra & Nehemiah	Jesus Christ, our Restorer
Esther	Jesus Christ, our Advocate
Job	Jesus Christ, our Redeemer
Psalms	Jesus Christ, our All in All
Proverbs	Jesus Christ as our Wisdom
Ecclesiastes	Jesus Christ, the End of all Living
Song of Solomon	Jesus Christ, the Lover of our souls

---

14 Henrietta Mears, *What the Bible is all About*, Glendale, CA: Gospel Light Publications, 1966, p. 12.

Isaiah	Jesus Christ as the Messiah
Jeremiah	Jesus Christ, the Righteous Branch
Lamentations	Jesus Christ, the Righteous Branch
Ezekiel	Jesus Christ, the Son of Man
Daniel	Jesus Christ, the Smiting Stone
Hosea	Jesus Christ, Healer of the Backslider
Joel	Jesus Christ, the Restorer
Amos	Jesus Christ, the Heavenly Husbandman
Obadiah	Jesus Christ, our Savior
Jonah	Jesus Christ, Resurrection and Life
Micah	Jesus Christ, Witness against rebellious nations
Nahum	Jesus Christ, Stronghold in the day of trouble
Habakkuk	Jesus Christ, God of our salvation
Zephaniah	Jesus Christ, our Jealous Lord
Haggai	Jesus Christ, the Desire of all nations
Zechariah	Jesus Christ, the Righteous Branch
Malachi	Jesus Christ, the Son of Righteousness

Christ is in the Old *concealed*…and in the New *revealed*!

New Testament

Matthew	Jesus Christ, the Promised Messiah
Mark	Jesus Christ, the Servant of God
Luke	Jesus Christ, the Son of Man
John	Jesus Christ, the Son of God
Acts	Jesus Christ, the Living Lord

Romans	Jesus Christ, our Righteousness
I Corinthians	Jesus Christ, our Lord
II Corinthians	Jesus Christ, our Sufficiency
Galatians	Jesus Christ, our Liberty
Ephesians	Jesus Christ, our All in All
Philippians	Jesus Christ, our Joy
Colossians	Jesus Christ, our Life
I Thessalonians	Jesus Christ, the Coming One
II Thessalonians	Jesus Christ, our Returning Lord
I Timothy	Jesus Christ, our Teacher
II Timothy	Jesus Christ, our Example
Titus	Jesus Christ, our Pattern
Philemon	Jesus Christ, our Lord and Master
Hebrews	Jesus Christ, our Intercessor at the Throne
James	Jesus Christ, our Pattern
I Peter	Jesus Christ, Precious Cornerstone of our Faith
II Peter	Jesus Christ, our Strength
I, II, III John	Jesus Christ, our Life, Truth, the Way
Jude	Jesus Christ, our Keeper
Revelation	Jesus Christ, our Triumphant King

The Bible then is the prism by which the light of Jesus is broken into its many radiant and redemptive colors:

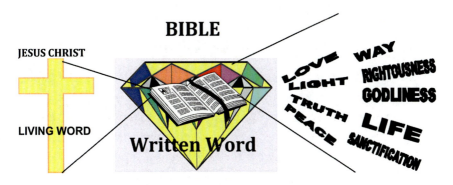

Jesus Himself clearly taught that He was the key to understanding the Scriptures because they all speak of Him. Look at the following examples:

- "But blessed are your eyes because they see, and your ears because they hear. For I tell you the truth, many prophets and righteous men longed to see what you see but did not see it, and to hear what you hear but did not hear it" (Matt. 13:16-17).

- "You diligently study the Scriptures because you think that by them you possess eternal life. These are the *Scriptures that testify* about Me" (Jn. 5:39).

- "And beginning with Moses and all the Prophets, He explained to them what was said in all the Scriptures concerning Himself...He said to them, 'This is what I told you while I was still with you: Everything must be fulfilled that is *written about Me in the Law of Moses, the Prophets and the Psalms*'" (Lk. 24:27, 44).

The other New Testament writers clearly testified to the same thing:

- "*All the prophets testify about Him* that everyone who believes in Him receives forgiveness of sins through His Name" (Acts 10:43).

- "Brothers, children of Abraham, and you God-fearing Gentiles, it is to us that this message of salvation has been sent. The people of Jerusalem and their rulers did not recognize Jesus, yet *in condemning Him they fulfilled the words of the prophets that are read every Sabbath*" (Acts 13:26-27).

- "But their minds were made dull, for to this day the same veil remains when the old covenant is read. It has not been removed, because only in Christ is it taken away. Even to this day when Moses is read, a veil covers their hearts. *But whenever anyone turns to the Lord, the veil is taken away.* Now the Lord is the Spirit, and where the Spirit of the Lord is, there is freedom" (II Cor. 3:14-17).

So apart from an *understanding of* and *relationship with Jesus Christ* – you cannot properly interpret the Scriptures. Let me share several examples that show how Christ is the Key to understanding the Scriptures.

"Then the Lord sent venomous snakes among them; they bit the people and many Israelites died" (Num. 21:6).	Jesus Christ as the serpent lifted up by Moses.	"Just as Moses lifted up the snake in the desert, so the Son of Man must be lifted up" (Jn. 3:14).
"The animals you choose must be year-old males without defect…Take care of them until the fourteenth day of the month, when all the people of the community of Israel must slaughter them at twilight. Then they are to take some of the blood and put in on the sides and tops of the doorframes of the houses where they eat the lambs" (Ex. 12:5-7).	Jesus Christ as "Paschal Lamb"	"Get rid of the old yeast that you may be a new batch without yeast – as you really are. For Christ, our Passover Lamb, has been sacrificed" (I Cor 5:7).

"Then Moses raised his arm and struck the rock twice with his staff. Water gushed out, and the community and their livestock drank" (Num. 20:11).	Jesus Christ as "Smitten Rock"	"They all ate the same spiritual food and drank the same spiritual drink; for they drank from the spiritual rock that accompanied them, and that rock was Christ" (1 Cor. 10:3-4).

The Scriptures then, with solidarity and unity, point to Christ and Christ in turn points to the Scriptures. From the above several examples we can see that His life and teachings are inseparably connected to Scripture. Let's take a further moment then to look at Christ's use of Scripture. How He approached and used Scripture should be our "Master key" of understanding how we should approach and apply it.

1. Jesus clearly taught the ***divine origin and permanence of the Word***:

    - "**Do not think that I have come to abolish the Law or the Prophets; I have not come to abolish them but to fulfill them. I tell you the truth, until heaven and earth disappear, not the smallest letter, not the least stroke of a pen, will by any means disappear from the Law until everything is accomplished**" (Matt. 5:17-18).

    - "**David himself, speaking by the Holy Spirit, declared: 'The Lord said to my Lord: 'Sit at My right hand until I put Your enemies under Your feet'''** (Mk. 12: 36).

    - "**It is easier for heaven and earth to disappear than for the least stroke of a pen to drop out of the Law**" (Lk. 16:17).

    - "**If he called them 'gods,' to whom the word of God came – and the Scripture cannot be broken…**" (Jn. 10:35).

2. Secondly, Jesus used the Scriptures as His chief weapon in ***His temptation***. Both His offense and defense in each temptation were the Scriptures: "***It is written…***" (Matt. 4:4, 7, 10). However, a

note of warning needs to be sounded here! You see, Satan also used Scripture – or should I say, *abused* Scripture! As soon as Christ quoted a Scripture to Satan as His defense against the first temptation, Satan picked up on this and then sought to twist Scripture to his own advantage. He did not fool Christ – but he does fool many of us with his tactics. Tragically Satan knows the Bible better than most Christians! He has prompted the origin of every ancient heresy and contemporary cult by the use of twisted Scripture! If you are to be successful against the enemy, you must know and use your weapons better than he does! And, armed with a correct understanding of God's Word, you – like Christ – can cut the ground from beneath your adversary!

3. Thirdly, we see that Jesus constantly used Scriptures in His teaching ministry. Let's look at just a couple of examples.

   A. **Divorce**

   Christ said: "**Haven't you read…that at the beginning the Creator 'made them male and female,' and said, 'For this reason a man will leave his father and mother and be united to his wife, and the two will become one flesh'?**" (Matt. 19:4-6).

   B. **Traditions of man**

   "**The Pharisees and some of the teachers of the law who had come from Jerusalem gathered around Jesus and saw some of His disciples eating food with hands that were "unclean," that is, unwashed. (The Pharisees and all the Jews do not eat unless they give their hands a ceremonial washing, holding to the tradition of the elders. When they come from the marketplace they do not eat unless they wash. And they observe many other traditions, such as the washing of cups, pitchers and kettles.) So the Pharisees and teachers of the law asked Jesus, 'Why don't Your disciples live** according to the tradition of the elders instead of eating their food with 'unclean' hands?' He replied, 'Isaiah was right when he prophesied about you hypocrites; as it is written:

> 'These people honor Me with their lips,
> but their hearts are far from Me.
> They worship Me in vain;
> their teachings are but rules taught by men.'

You have let go of the commands of God and are holding on to the traditions of men.' And He said to them: 'You have a fine way of setting aside the commands of God in order to observe your own traditions! For Moses said, 'Honor your father and your mother,' and, 'Anyone who curses his father or mother must be put to death.' But you say that if a man says to his father or mother: 'Whatever help you might otherwise have received from me is Corban' (that is, a gift devoted to God), then you no longer let him do anything for his father or mother. Thus you nullify the word of God by your tradition that you have handed down. And you do many things like that'" (Mark 7:1-13).

C. Resurrection from the dead

The Sadducees, "who say there is no resurrection" questioned Jesus. He said: "Are you not in error because you do not know the Scriptures or the power of God?" (Mk. 12:24).

D. Violence

Concerning the use of violence Christ said: "**Put your sword back in its place...for all who draw the sword will die by the sword. Do you think I cannot call on**

My Father, and He will at once put at My disposal more than twelve legions of angels? But how then would the Scriptures be fulfilled that say it must happen in this way?" (Matt. 26:52-54)

This list could be multiplied many times – you can see that the teaching of Christ was filled with Scripture, and it was His constantly-used touchstone for authority. It is also very instructive to note that from the 39 books of the Old Testament, Jesus used extracts from 24. He also quoted from Isaiah 40 times; Psalms 36 times; and Daniel 22 times. So since Scripture was so vital to the teaching of Christ, can it play any less important role in the teaching and preaching ministry of the Church today?! I think not!

4. Fourthly, one of Christ's most pointed and directed attacks was against the *"traditions of man"* or the *"traditions of the elders"*. It was this as much as any one thing that kept Him in conflict with the Jewish authorities – and ultimately led to His crucifixion. But just what were the "traditions of man?" *A tradition develops when man either adds to God's Word – or takes the liberty of interpreting the mind and will of God to a particular situation.*

Let's take a few moments to contrast the difference between man's traditions and God's laws. I think that you will see that the difference and distinction is very crucial. I will list several principles and the verses they are derived from.

Traditions of Man vs. The Word of God

A. Man constantly exchanges his precepts for God's *principles.* He substitutes his "traditions" for God's laws:

   "These people honor Me with their lips, but their hearts are far from Me. They worship Me in vain; their teachings are but rules taught by men" (Matt. 15:8-9; c.f. Mk. 7:7).

B. This is really man attempting to interpret the mind and will of God – and thus these traditions become *a religion of man's creation rather than a religion of God's revelation.* The traditions of man always stand against the revelation of God in some way:

"**And why do you break the command of God for the sake of your tradition?...you nullify the word of God for the sake of your tradition**" (Matt. 15:3, 6: c.f. Mk. 7:8,13).

C. Man's traditions always become harder to bear than God's laws. They ultimately become *"laws of bondage"* rather than *"principles of liberty"* as God's laws are:

"**The teachers of the law and the Pharisees sit in Moses' seat...they do not practice what they preach. They tie up heavy loads and put them on men's shoulders...**" (Matt. 23:2-4; c.f. Lk. 11:54).

Note: Many of the burdensome *Sabbath day observances* of Christ's day are other good examples of traditions that ultimately destroy man rather than edify him. Jesus and His disciples were constantly breaking these contrived rules (See: Matt. 12:1-14; Mk. 2:23-28, etc).

D. St. Paul likewise warned: "**See to it that no one takes you captive through...human tradition...**" (Col. 2:8). He said that before his conversion to Christ "**I was advancing in Judaism beyond many Jews of my own age and was extremely zealous for the traditions of my fathers**" (Gal. 1:14). So, whereas the "traditions of man" will victimize you and bring you into bondage; ***God's laws result in fulfillment and freedom.*** Jesus said:

"**Come to Me, all you who are weary and burdened, and I will give you rest. Take My yoke upon you and learn from Me, for I am gentle and humble in heart, and you will find rest for your souls. For My yoke is easy and My burden is light**" (Matt. 11:29-30).

The best summary then of the fruit of living by Jesus' principles of freedom are His own words: "**...you will know the truth, and the truth will set you free...if the Son sets you free, you will be free indeed**" (Jn. 8:32-36).

At this point it might be helpful to list some of the "**traditions of the elders**" that we have surrounded Christianity with today. We have a great tendency to look back on the scribes and Pharisees with scorn for their traditions while ignoring our own! We need to honestly face the fact that we have established and encased the Christian faith today with almost as many traditions as the Judaism of Christ's day. Let's look at just a few:

(1) The fact that we worship at 11:00 a.m. on Sunday morning;

(2) Our various liturgical traditions and forms that we employ in our services;

(3) The institution of the Sunday school;

(4) The acceptable and unacceptable types of clothes for "worship service";

(5) The various committees that we have established to govern the church;

(6) Our denominational structure and programs – and even denominations themselves;

(7) The role of church buildings as essential to the growth of the Church;

(8) The establishment of a "religious professional" or "ecclesiastical caste system" that divides the clergy and laity with unscriptural divisions; etc. – the list could go on and on!

> "Christ in the heart and the Bible in the hand are adequate guides for the ordinary Christian."
> Carl H. Lundquist

SUMMARY

Jesus Christ is the Person of the Bible! History is His story and the Bible records that story. He is the Incarnate Word and the Bible is the Inscripturated Word. Both are divine in origin and nature. Therefore, since Christ clearly endorsed the Scriptures as inerrant and authoritative – and since the Bible clearly sets Him forth as God's incarnate Son of God – HIS AUTHORITY AND THE AUTHORITY OF THE BIBLE STAND OR FALL TOGETHER!

Let me close with the following very important quotation concerning Jesus Christ:

"This Jesus of Nazareth, without money and arms conquered more millions than Alexander, Caesar, Mohammed, and Napoleon. Without science and learning, He shed more light on things human and divine than all philosophers and scholars combined; without the eloquence of schools, He spoke such words of life as were never spoken before or since, and produced effects which tie beyond the reach of orator or poet; without writing a single line, He set more pens in motion, and furnished themes for more orations discussions, learned volumes, works of art, and songs of praise than the whole army of great men of ancient and modern times." [15]

Quotations for Further Reflection

- *Jesus was utterly delightful. He enjoyed people...Children loved Him. Adults were affected so much by Him that some just wanted to touch His clothes. Why? They saw that Jesus loved them. His love was extravagant, almost reckless – never cautious or timid. And He talked of His Father's endless love...In Jesus' case we have the story of the holiest Man who ever lived, and yet it was the prostitutes and lepers and thieves who adored Him, and the religious folk who hated His guts.* [16]

- *...most important, among all the people described in the Bible, the leading*

---

15 Philip Schaff, *"The Person of Christ"*, American Tract Society, 1913.
16 Rebecca Manley Pippert, *Out of the Salt Shaker and into the World*, Downers Grove, IL: InterVarsity Press, 1999, pp. 32-33, 36.

character throughout is the one, true, living God made known through Jesus Christ. Consider first the Old Testament: The Law provides the "foundation for Christ," the historical books show "the preparation" for Christ, the poetical works aspire to Christ, and the prophecies display an "expectation" of Christ. In the New Testament, the Gospels record the historical manifestation of Christ, the Acts relate the propagation of Christ, the Epistles give the interpretation of Him, and in Revelation is found the consummation of all things in Christ. From cover to cover, the Bible is Christocentric. [17]

- *Who you decide Jesus Christ is must not be an idle intellectual exercise. You cannot put Him on the shelf as a great moral teacher. That is not a valid option. He is either a liar, a lunatic, or the Lord. You must make a choice...The evidence is clearly in favor of Jesus as Lord. However, some people reject the clear evidence because of the moral implications involved. There needs to be a moral honesty in the above consideration of Jesus as either liar, lunatic, or Lord and God.* [18]

---

17 Josh McDowell, *The New Evidence that Demands a Verdict*, Nashville: Thomas Nelson Publishers, 1999, p. 6.
18 Ibid., p. 163.

PURPOSE OF THE WORD

"We do, however, speak a message of wisdom among the mature, but not the wisdom of this age or of the rulers of this age, who are coming to nothing. No, we speak of God's secret wisdom, a wisdom that has been hidden and that God destined for our glory before time began. None of the rulers of this age understood it, for if they had, they would not have crucified the Lord of glory. However, as it is written: 'No eye has seen, no ear has heard, no mind has conceived what God has prepared for those who love Him' but God has revealed it to us by His Spirit. The Spirit searches all things, even the deep things of God" (I Cor. 2:6-10).

"...men ought to regard us as servants of Christ and as those entrusted with the secret things of God" (I Cor. 4:1).

What the Apostle Paul is saying here is that what the world *does not know and cannot know* about God because of the limitations of the fallen human finite condition – *God has taken the initiative in making known through revelation.* A study of revelation is crucial to any study of the Word.

Purpose of Revelation

Let's begin with a definition. Most simply put, the purpose of revelation is to *"get the mind of God into the actions of man."* Or, *"to communicate God's Being, Word and Will to fallen men."* This is **"revelation."**

Since all action springs from thinking; and, since man in his fallen condition is incapable of right spiritual thinking - he desperately needs to receive a new nature and a new mind whereby he once again can think God's thoughts after Him and thereby get God's actions into his everyday experience.

This Divine way of thinking and acting is what the Bible variously calls **"godliness"**, **"sanctification"**, **"walking by the Spirit"**, **"righteousness"**, etc. (see Jn. 17:17; Gal. 5:16, Rom. 8:1-10, etc.)

Look at the following illustration to see how *natural man* is not able to apprehend the mind of God – whereas *regenerate man* is able to receive revelation, and move in obedience towards godliness.

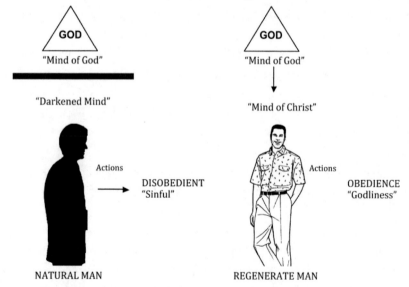

Reason and Revelation

As you can infer from the illustration, since man's mind is darkened (Rom. 1:21; Eph. 4:17-18; Col. 1:21) he is incapable of *thinking God's thoughts*. He therefore cannot achieve or attain a true knowledge of God through philosophy, reason or research – but only by revelation. So where human reason leaves off, Divine revelation must step in.

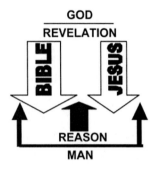

Job 11:7
"Can you find out the deep things of God?"
(RSV)
"Can a man by searching find God?"
(KJV)

Nature of Revelation

There are at least 6 things you need to understand about the nature of revelation.

1. **The nature of revelation is the "history of salvation."**

    German thinkers have long been very influential in the field of theology. A word that they have used to express the Nature of Biblical Revelation is *Heilgeschichte*. It simply means: "story of salvation." That means that the Bible is not primarily a scientific book, history book, philosophy book, geography book – but rather a book about salvation! It is a history of the salvation story. This story of salvation *was conceived in eternity past...achieved at a historical point in time...worked out in human history...and will be consummated in eternity future!*

2. **This revelation is inspired – "God-breathed"**

    One of the great verses of scripture we must look at in this regard is II Timothy 3:16: "**All scripture is inspired by God and profitable for teaching, for reproof, for correction for training in righteousness**" (NASB).

Let's break this verse down to try and get the full impact of what Paul is saying.

A. First he deals with the **origin of scripture**. He says: "**All Scripture is God-inspired...**"

   (1) First, I want you to note that the Greek word Paul uses here for *inspired* is a word used only once in the Bible. It was a word coined by Paul under the inspiration of the Holy Spirit to describe the completely unique event of **God revealing Himself to man**. It is the word "theopneustos" meaning "God breathed" or "God-spirited". So all Scripture, says the Apostle Paul is *"breathed out by God"*.

   (2) The logical question is "What was Paul meaning by the phrase *'all scripture?'* What does that *'all'* include?"

   First, the "sacred writings" – which was the Old Testament;

   Secondly, "his own words." Paul believed that his writings were inspired. He clearly said on a number of occasions that his words were God's – and he was therefore speaking in the name and authority of Christ:

   - "**For we are not peddlers of God's word like so many; but in Christ we speak as persons of sincerity, as persons** *sent from God and standing in His presence*" (II Cor. 2:17 NASB).

   - "...since you are demanding proof that *Christ is speaking through me*...This is why I write these things when I am absent...in my use of authority – the *authority the Lord gave me*..." (II Cor. 13:3, 10).

   - "...it was because of an illness that I first preached

the gospel to you. Even though my illness was a trial to you, you did not treat me with contempt or scorn. Instead, you welcomed me as if I were an angel of God, as if I were *Christ Jesus Himself*" (Gal. 4:13-14; c.f. I Thess. 2:13; II Thess. 3:6, 12; I Cor. 2:12-13; I Cor. 14:37).

Thirdly, it is important to note that Paul's writings were read in Christian meetings by his instructions along with the Old Testament:

- "**I charge you before the Lord to have this letter read to all the brothers**" (I Thess. 5:27).

- "**After this letter has been read to you, see that it is also read in the church of the Laodiceans and that you in turn read the letter from Laodicea**" (Col. 4:16).

Fourthly, Paul also took the liberty to put Old Testament quotations together with the words of Christ:

- "**For the Scripture says, 'Do not muzzle the ox while it is treading out the grain,'** (Deut. 25:4) and, '**The worker deserves his wages**' (Lk. 10:7)" (I Tim. 5:18).

Fifthly, it is also important to realize that Peter viewed Paul's writings as scripture:

- "**Bear in mind that our Lord's patience means salvation, just as our dear brother Paul also wrote you with the wisdom that God gave him. He writes the same way in all his letters, speaking in them of these matters. His letters contain some things that are hard to understand, which ignorant and unstable people distort, as they do the other Scriptures, to their own destruction**" (II Pet. 3:15-16).

So we can see from the above what Paul meant when he used the phrase "*all Scripture*". That "all" clearly included what we today understand as the Old and New Testaments.

B. Paul tells us the **purpose of Scripture**. Because they are all God-breathed, he says that they have a three-fold purpose:

   (1) "*Instruct you in salvation through faith which is in Christ Jesus*" (II Tim. 3:15b);

   (2) "**...Profitable** (because it is "God Breathed") *for teaching, reproof, correction, training in righteousness*" (3:16);

   (3) *Bring you to maturity:* "**...that the man of God may be adequate, equipped for every good work**" (3:17 NASB).

All Scripture

Instruction	Profitable	Maturity
"for salvation through faith in Christ Jesus"	"teaching, reproof, correction, training in righteousness"	"that the man of God may be complete, equipped for every good work."

Thus far concerning the nature of revelation, we have seen that it is first of all *heilgeschichte* or a "story of salvation." However, this is not a story of salvation concocted by man - so secondly, we have seen that this is an inspired revelation. As Paul said: "**All scripture is inspired by God...**"

3. The third thing I want you to note about the nature of revelation is that it is consistent. It only stands to reason that the nature of revelation is consistent with the nature of the Revealer! Let's take a moment then to look at some of the attributes of God:

   (1) **Holy** (Rom. 1:2)

   (2) **Unchanging** (Ja. 1:17; Heb. 13:8) (Immutable)

   (3) **Eternal** (Deut. 33:27) "**The eternal God is your refuge...**"

(4) **Consistent** (II Tim. 2:13) "**If we are faithless, He will remain faithful...**"

(5) **Grace** (I Pet. 5:10) "**The God of all Grace...**"

(6) **Love** (I Jn. 4:8) "**God is Love**"

(7) **Judgment** (Heb. 10:30-31; 12:29), etc.

So these attributes of God are also attributes of His Word.

4. Fourthly, concerning the nature of revelation you need to realize that it is **incomplete**. That simply means that the Bible contains "true truth" but not exhaustive truth – i.e., its communication to us is true communication but not exhaustive communication. We do not have exhaustive knowledge at any point – because man in his fallen and finite state is incapable of handling exhaustive truth. There are many areas about which God has not given us exhaustive knowledge. For example:

> *... creation*
> *... origin of evil*
> *... problem of pain*
> *... angels*
> *... eschatology – or "end times"*
> *... Trinity, etc.*

As Moses said: "**The secret things belong to the Lord our God...**" (Deut. 29:29). Therefore, as Paul said: "**...we know in part**" (I Cor. 13:9). The apostle John explained it this way: "**Jesus did many other things as well. If every one of them were written down, I suppose that even the whole world would not have room for the books that would be written**" (Jn. 21:25).

So the Bible does not tell us everything we want to know – but it does tell us everything we need to know! Mark Twain said *"Most people are bothered by those passages of Scripture which they* cannot understand, but as for me, I have always noticed that the passages in Scripture that trouble me most are those I do understand."

5. Fifthly, revelation is both **unified and progressive**. As Isaiah said: **"So then, the word of the Lord to them will become: Do and do, do and do, rule on rule, rule on rule; a little here, a little there…"** (Isa. 28:13 NIV).

Even though God's revelation to man has been progressive – it has never been contradictory. The progression in revelation has not been from error to truth – but from truth to more truth:

$$\text{Revelation} \neq \text{Error} \longrightarrow \text{Truth}$$

But

$$\text{Revelation} = \text{Truth} \longrightarrow \textbf{TRUTH}$$

We can see a **logical progressive revelation** from the Old Testament to the New Testament…from the Old Covenant to the New Covenant… from the Old Israel to the New Israel, etc…

Principle
The Old is revealed in the New and the New concealed in the Old

---

This principle teaches us that *God gives light in the Old Testament that He releases in the New.* We might further express it this way: The Old Testament gave man what he needed to know from the Fall to the *First Advent*; the Old and the New together tell man what he needs to know from the First Advent to the *Second Advent*. We can see this unity through a study of the Scriptures: the Epistles drive us back to the Gospels – which in turn drive us back to the Old Testament.

Old Testament ← Gospels ← Epistles

There is then a progressive unity of Revelation in Scripture – the Bible is organically One!

PROGRESSIVE REVELATION

"In Scripture God's revelation is verbalized, and in nature it is visualized."

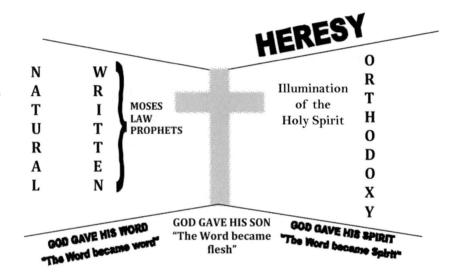

There is *fresh illumination* – but not new revelation.

6. The final thing that I want you to understand is the **relationship between** *revelation and illumination*. As Christians, we do not believe that God continues to give new revelation. After He has perfectly revealed Himself in His Son – and inspired a written record of that revelation in the Bible – all revelation has ceased! As the old hymn "How Firm a Foundation" says "...What more can He say than to you He has said..."

When God has completely revealed Himself to us – what more can He reveal? Now, I am quite confident that there is more to know of God than He has presently revealed to us through Christ and Scripture – but within the limitations of this life we are incapable of receiving it! Obviously, the finite cannot completely comprehend the Infinite! But all that we are capable of understanding of God – and even more (the Trinity) – He has revealed to us. When we are in our glorified state after this life, I am sure there will be more to learn – but until then we have both *all we need* and *all we can comprehend*! Therefore God gives no further revelation! **He completed His self-revelation in His Son, Jesus Christ**! As Paul said: "**For in Christ all the fullness of the Deity lives in bodily form**" (Col. 2:9).

It is important to understand that every ancient heresy and contemporary cult deviates from orthodoxy at this point. All of them come along offering what they believe to be "further revelations from God." So when you hear that – *be alert*!

However, even though God does not give further revelation – His Holy Spirit working through His Word does continue to give ***further illumination***. "**For with You is the fountain of life; in Your light we see light**" (Ps. 36:9).

So as we walk in the light we have received we receive *further* light. It is a basic scriptural principle: "Light begets light." If I am obedient to the illumination I have received I will receive more. I often find that much of my illumination of God's revelation is during the night. Often, when my conscious mind is turned off in sleep, my subconscious mind – guided by the Holy Spirit – receives important illumination concerning some portion of God's Word. That is why **it is important to read and meditate on God's Word before bedtime**. Read the Psalms and see how David practiced this (Ps. 63:6; 77:11, etc).

So we must receive God's *illumination* through His Holy Spirit of His *revelation* if we are to properly understand it. Let me share just a couple of verses that demonstrate this fact.

- "The Spirit searches all things, even the deep things of God...no one knows the thoughts of God except the Spirit of God. We have not received the spirit of the world but the Spirit who is from God, that we may understand what God has freely given us...The man without the Spirit does not accept the things that come from the Spirit of God, for they are foolishness to him, and he cannot understand them, because they are spiritually discerned" (I Cor. 1:10-14).

- "Then He (Jesus) **opened their minds so they could understand the Scriptures**..." (Lk 24:45; c.f. Acts 16:14).

In the above verses we can see the important role of the Holy Spirit illuminating the hearts and minds of individuals so they could understand the Scriptures and spiritual reality. We might put it into a formula like this:

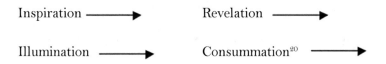

SUMMARY

Let's take a moment to review this important chapter. We have seen that the purpose of God's Word is to *make known His will*, or "to get the mind of God into the actions of man." We also saw that man in his fallen and finite condition is incapable of receiving this revelation from God. The darkened mind of man (Eph. 4:18) is incapable of receiving the light of God (I Cor. 2:14). Therefore we must receive the "**mind of Christ**" (I Cor. 2:16). What the darkened, fallen, finite reason cannot achieve through its best efforts – God makes known to the believer through revelation.

---

20 When we speak of *consummation*, we mean that it must be fulfilled both *in our lives and in history*. The Bible begins with a revelation of *Creation* – and ends with a consummation in *re-creation*!

We also saw that there were at least 6 important things to understand about the nature of revelation. We could summarize those things with the following sentences:

1. The nature of revelation is Heilgeschichte or "history of salvation."

2. It is also unique in inspiration, or *"breathed out by God."*

3. There is a consistency between the nature of the revelation and the Revealer.

4. Our revelation is incomplete, i.e. we have "true truth" but not "exhaustive truth."

5. It is unified and progressive; "the Old is revealed in the New and the New is concealed in the Old."

6. Revelation has ceased because it is complete in Christ and the Scriptures – but illumination of that revelation continues.

Quotations for Further Reflection

- *God does not intend His Word to be used as an encyclopedia or an encyclical – but as a system of truth that we are to steep ourselves in its tone or temper and so learn its overall message.* (C.S. Lewis)

- *I prayed for Faith, and thought that some day Faith would come down and strike me like lightning. But Faith did not seem to come. One day I read in the tenth chapter of Romans, '**Now faith cometh by hearing, and hearing by the Word of God.**' I had closed my Bible, and prayed for Faith. I now opened my Bible, and began to study, and Faith has been growing ever since.* (D. L. Moody)

- **"Send forth Your light and Your truth, let them guide me; let them bring me to Your holy mountain, to the place where You dwell. Then will I go to the altar of God, to God my joy and my delight"** (Ps. 43:3-4).

PURITY OF THE WORD: INERRANCY OF SCRIPTURE

In this section, I want to briefly discuss the matter of inerrancy. Put most simply, the doctrine of inerrancy says that "***the Bible is free from errors.***" As the theologian, Charles Hodge, put it in his well known classic, Systematic Theology: *"The Bible is all from God; it is the Word of God in toto, and there is no admixture of human error in its production."* However, for many people the inerrancy of scripture seems quite impossible to hold to because of the matter of human fallenness and fallibility. Therefore, many people consider it a *human book* rather than a divine book. Dr. Donald G. Barnhouse deals with this objection as follows:

> *"It is objected by some that the marks of human personality upon the writings of the various human authors indicate that the Bible is a human book. We would answer this with an analogy. The angel who announced to Mary that she would become the mother of the Messiah, heard the Virgin ask, 'How shall this be seeing that I know not a man?' The answer came: 'The Holy Spirit shall come upon thee, and the power of the Highest shall overshadow thee; therefore that thing which shall be born of thee shall be called the Son of God' (Luke 1:35). So the baby was born. He was the second Person of the Trinity, the Son of God...Just as the Holy Spirit came upon the womb of Mary, so He came upon the brain of a Moses, a David, an Isaiah, a Paul, a John, and the rest of the writers of the divine library. The power of the Highest overshadowed them, therefore that holy thing which was*

born of their minds is called the Holy Bible, the Word of God. The writings of Luke will, of course, have the vocabulary of Luke, and the works of Paul will bear the stamp of Paul's mind. However, this is only in the same manner that the Lord Jesus Christ might have had eyes like His mother's, or hair that was the same color and texture as hers. He did not inherit her sins, because the Holy Spirit had come upon her. If we ask how this could be, the answer is that God says so. And the writings of the men of the Book did not inherit the errors of their carnal mind, because the writers were conceived by the Holy Spirit and born out of their personalities without partaking of their fallen nature. If we ask how this could be again the answer is that God says so."[21]

Barnhouse is not setting forth some kind of "dictation theory" of inspiration whereby the Biblical writers were reduced to nothing more than robots. In the process of using them, **God did not destroy their humanity – but fully used it.** These men were "**carried along by the Holy Spirit**" (II Pet. 1:21).

Inerrancy is the heated theological battlefront of the day. Martin Luther said: *"If I profess with the loudest voice and clearest exposition every portion of the truth of God except precisely that little point which the world and the devil are at that moment attacking, I am not confessing Christ, however boldly I may be professing Christ. Where the battle rages, there the loyalty of the soldier is proved, and to be, steady on all the battle front besides is mere flight and disgrace if he flinches at that point."*[22]

That issue where the battle is raging today is the matter of inerrancy. This subject is being debated not only among those who hold a more liberal view of Scripture – but also among conservatives. Dr. Harold Lindsell wrote a book entitled *Battle For The Bible*. That book seemed to draw up the battle lines and divide the camp into several theological groups. Some think that the division is good because it is "flushing out" the ones they consider to be theological turn-coats in the conservative

---

21 Donald Grey Barnhouse, *The Invisible War*, Grand Rapids: Zondervan Publishing House, 1965, pp. 44-45.
22 Francis Schaeffer, "Schaeffer on Scripture", *Christianity Today*, August 29, 1975, p. 29.

PURITY OF THE WORD: INERRANCY OF SCRIPTURE

ranks. Others feel it is very tragic that the evangelical part of the Body of Christ is being further divided at a time when their collective impact was being felt as never before.

A conference was held in Chicago to discuss, clarify, and defend the doctrine of inerrancy. It was called *"The International Council on Biblical Inerrancy"* or ICBI. It was headed by such theologians as J. I. Packer, James M. Boice, Edmund P. Clowney, R. C. Sproul and others. This transdenomination group affirmed their belief in inerrancy, by saying:

> *"We affirm that the whole of Scripture and all its parts, down to the very word of the original, were given by divine inspiration...Being wholly and verbally God-given, Scripture is without error or fault in all its teaching, no less in what it states about God's acts in creation and the events of world history, and about its own literary origins under God, than in its witness to God's saving grace in individual lives."* [23]

These theologians further clarified their belief in inerrancy by the following summary statements:

1. God, who is Himself Truth and speaks truth only, has inspired Holy Scripture in order thereby to reveal Himself to lost mankind through Jesus Christ as Creator and Lord, Redeemer and Judge, Holy Scripture is God's witness to Himself. [24]

2. Holy Scripture being God's own Word, written by men prepared and superintended by His Spirit, is of infallible divine authority in all matters upon which it touches; it is to be believed as God's instruction, in all that it requires; obeyed, as God's command, in all that it requires; embraced, as God's pledge, in all that it promises.[25]

3. The Holy Spirit, its divine Author, both authenticates it to us

---

[23] Kay Oliver, "Summit '78 Takes Stand on Inerrancy", *Moody Monthly*, Dec. 1978, p. 12.
[24] Ibid., p. 12.
[25] Connie Oliver, "Pinnock Speaks on Biblical Inerrancy", *Perspective*, May/June 1976, p. 8.

by His inward witness and opens our minds to understand its meaning. [26]

4. The authority of Scripture is inescapably impaired if this total divine inerrancy is in any way limited or disregarded, or made relative to a view of truth contrary to the Bible's own; and such lapses bring serious loss to both the Individual and the Church.[27]

I personally think that is a very good summary of the doctrine of inerrancy and its importance for the church. However, not all conservative, evangelical Christians would agree. We now have those on the one side who would say that the Bible is completely error free – even in details. On the other hand we have those evangelical scholars represented by someone like Dr. Clark Pinnock, who would say, "*The Bible contains errors but teaches none.*" That there are some problems in Scripture no one can honestly escape. As Pinnock would say, "*Belief in inerrancy of detail is possible only for those...who do not take the difficulties of the Bible seriously.*" As a *Christianity Today* editor said: "*There exists difficult problems of apparent discrepancies. There is no advantage to pretending that difficulties do not exist or are of no consequence. They must be recognized, admitted, and honestly studied.*"[28] Some would say that these difficulties concerning conflicting details are not crucial because "*Historical, chronological and geographical data are never in themselves the object of the witness of the Holy Spirit.*" Scholars who hold to that viewpoint would affirm Scriptural inerrancy concerning doctrine but not *detail*. In other words, the Bible is inerrant concerning matters essential to the faith – but possibly errant in some details and factual matter. However, even then they would say that it was still inerrant in intent if not so in actuality.

There are yet others who are seeking to avoid conflict and division by redefining the word "*inerrant*" to make it more inclusive. However, for many that is an unacceptable alternative. One such theologian who

---

26 Normal L. Geisler, "The Nature of Scripture", *Christianity Today*, Feb. 24, 1978, p. 34.
27 "Inerrancy Matters", *Christianity Today*, Oct. 1978, p. 10.
28 "Inerrancy Matters", Christianity Today, Oct. 1978, p. 10.

cannot accept this type of solution is John Warwick Montgomery, who wrote:

> "*Whenever we reach the point of affirming on the one hand that the Bible is infallible or inerrant and admitting on the other hand to inerrant contradictions or factual inaccuracies within it, we not only make a farce of language, promoting ambiguity, confusion, and perhaps even deception in the church; more reprehensible than even these things, we in fact deny the plenary inspiration and authority of Scripture, regardless of the theological formulae we may insist on retaining.*"[29]

All evangelical Christians do agree, though, on the fact that inerrancy holds only for the original autographs. However, we now have enough manuscripts to support our belief that **the current translations of the Bible we have today are close to 98% inerrant.** Dr. Walter Martin said:

> "*The inspiration of the Bible...only refers to the autographs of the Old Testament and the New Testament. Through the centuries since then, He (God) has preserved His message in the thousands of copies of those very manuscripts with less than four percent error. The errors are the result of poor copies or copyists – not the result of an errant original. Through the science of textual criticism, we are able easily to determine the original contents in almost all of the questioned sections. Those questioned portions that remain involve mainly punctuation and spelling problems and in no way affect any article of Christian faith.*"[30]

The big question is *"Why would God make an error-free original and yet permit errors in the copies?"* The only logical answer to that is that God chose to use man as the recipient and transmitter of His revelation – and man is now a fallen creature. By a disobedient exercise of his free will, man rebelled against God and as a result, sin and corruption entered both the universe and man's own life. *"This corruption tainted all of the descendants of Adam, some of whom later copied and recopied the*

---

29 John Stuart Mill, "Three Essays on Religion", quoted by J.N.D. Anderson in Christianity: *The Witness of History*, London: The Tyndale Press, 1969, p. 38.
30 Walter Martin, *The Christian Research Institute Newsletter*, Third Quarter, 1977, p. 2.

Divine record. Except for the initial use of the initial writers of the Word, the imperfections of a fallen humanity were allowed to touch the perfect record." [31]

I personally must keep referring to Christ's view of Scripture. His view must determine mine. I still feel that it is rather absurd to call Him "Lord" and then hold a view of Scripture lower than His! That to me is calling into question His Lordship, authority and knowledge concerning Scripture. For many involved in this inerrancy debate, Christ's view of Scripture is their final appeal and highest argument. Again I quote John Montgomery:

> "The doctrine of Biblical inerrancy derives from the attitude of Scripture toward itself, and in particular the attitude of Christ toward Scripture. What we must recognize is that Scripture and its Christ do not give us an open concept of inspiration that we can fill in as the extrabiblical methodologies of our time appear to dictate, To the contrary, the total trust that Jesus and the apostles displayed toward Scripture entails a precise and controlled hermeneutic. They subordinated the opinions and traditions of their day to Scripture; so must we. They did not regard Scripture as erroneous or self-contradictory; neither can we. They took its miracles and prophecies as literal fact; so must we. They regarded Scripture not as the product of editors and redactors but as stemming from Moses, David, and other immediately inspired writers we must follow their lead. They believed that the events recorded in the Bible happened as real history; we can do no less."[32]

Montgomery then concludes his argument on inerrancy with the following analogy:

> "I must not tolerate for a moment the argument that because the Trinity is nowhere set forth by name in the Bible, evangelicalism mustn't be divided over the doctrine. Biblical inerrancy, though the expression does not appear in Scripture, is nevertheless Christ's view; and He must

---

31 Ibid., p. 2.
32 John Warwick Montgomery, "*History and Christianity*", *His*, Jan. 1965, pp. 38-42.

be my Lord in this as in all other areas. If He is not Lord of all, He is not Lord at all."[33]

When we happen upon what we believe is an error or contradiction in God's Word, we do well to heed the timely advice of Augustine:

> *"If you chance upon anything in Scripture that does not seem to be true, you must not conclude that the sacred writer made a mistake; rather your attitude should be: the manuscript is faulty, or the version is not accurate, or you yourself do not understand the matter."*[34]

You and I need to be assured then, that we will never come up with a question or problem in Scripture that has not been raised a thousand times before – and reasonably answered![35] If you still think you have found one, then wisdom and history would strongly suggest that you place your doubt, skepticism and agnosticism in your question – and not in the Bible! As you will see in this book, over and over again scholars thought the Bible contained historical inaccuracies, factual contradictions and inconsistencies – but **time, further study and later archaeological discoveries have consistently confirmed Scripture**. Therefore, we do well to leave some questions open ended and allow more time for further research and study before jettisoning the Scriptures! The creedal statement of one seminary I think expresses this attitude very well. Concerning the harmonizing of apparent contradictions, it says:

> *"Harmonization of apparent scriptural difficulties should be pursued within reasonable limits, and when harmonization would pass beyond such boundaries the interpreter must leave the problem open rather than by assuming error, impugn the absolute trustfulness of God, who inspires all Holy Scripture for our salvation and learning."*[36]

---

33 Ibid., p. 42.
34 "Letters of St. Augustine LXXXII," No. 3, quoted by Harold Lindsell, "The Infallible Word", *Christianity Today*, Sept. 15, 1972, p. 16.
35 Note: There are many good books on the market that deal with these questions, difficulties and reputed contradictions. I would highly suggest books by W.F. Arndt and F. W. Gingrich - Compilers of one of the most prevalent Greek-English lexicon used today. Arndt has written a book on *Bible Difficulties* that you will find very helpful.
36 "Melodyland School of Theology's Doctrinal Statement" quoted by John Warwick Montgomery in "Whither Biblical Inerrancy?" *Christianity Today*, July 29, 1977, p. 42.

Now, this kind of attitude toward the Bible is not Biblioatry. We do not so inseparably associate God with His Word that we end up either worshipping His Word above, or along with, Him! No, as Billy Graham rightly put it:

> *"I am not advocating Bibliolatry. I am not suggesting that we should worship the Bible...any more than a soldier worships his sword or a surgeon worships his scalpel. I am, however, fervently urging a return to Bible-centered preaching, a gospel presentation that says without apology and without ambiguity,* **'Thus saith the Lord.'**"[37]

No minister, evangelist, or Christian will ever stand up and clearly say **"Thus saith the Lord"** if inside he deeply questions the accuracy and trustworthiness of God's Word. That is one of the problems with so much preaching and teaching in the church today! Many ministers had their belief in the Bible subtly eroded during their seminary days – and their preaching has had little or no power or authority since then! It is still a basic principal of life that *"an ambiguous heart sends out an ambivalent flow!"* There is no way that I can preach and teach authoritatively if I have no authority! I personally stand with those who affirm the inerrancy of Scripture! I do recognize the legitimate problems involved – but I think the better part of wisdom is to leave some things open ended for further research and study. Man's basic tendency is to jump too quickly to the wrong conclusions! For me, the problems with admitting errors in the Bible are several:

1. Once you begin to admit errors and contradictions of the Bible, there is no logical stopping point. It is the case of the proverbial camel's nose in your tent – you have the whole camel, and no tent!

2. Secondly, there is no way I can reach those conclusions unless I make myself an authority over the authority of the Scriptures. As one person put it: *"To the extent that you weaken inerrancy, to that extent you weaken inspiration; to the extent that you weaken inspiration, you have a garbled revelation; to the extent that you have a garbled*

---

[37] Billy Graham, "Biblical Authority in Evangelism", *Christianity Today*, Oct. 22, 1976, p. 15.

revelation you have a weakened authority; and when you weaken the authority of the Bible you launch upon a shifting sea of uncertainty."[38]

3. Finally, in the process of accepting the errancy of Scripture, we must also lower our view of the character of God. Why? Because if God was involved in the composition of the Bible – then any mistakes must be chargeable to God Himself.

SUMMARY

The doctrine of the inerrancy of Scripture is not of secondary importance! It seems to me that we cannot continue the Reformation maxim of *Sola Scriptura* without inerrancy. It is essential for the authority of preaching and teaching – and therefore crucial both for evangelism of the church and the edification of the church! As one writer concluded: "There is little doubt that any marked departure from the historic view of the Church on this matter leads to further heresies and finally to apostasy."

Sola Scriptura! *Our faith is based on the Bible alone.*

"The words of the Lord are pure words; as silver tried in a furnace on the earth, refined seven times" (Ps. 12:6).

Quotations for Further Reflection

- *In the Book of Acts, we find the early Christians presenting reasoned answers to a variety of charges made against Christianity. To the Jews the church pointed out that Christ was the fulfillment of Old Testament prophecy (Acts 3:17-26). To the Gentiles the church argued that God*

---

[38] Earl Radmacher, "Inspiration of Scriptures" tape series, Conservative Baptist Theological Seminary, Denver, Colorado.

was calling them to turn from superstitious religions to the true God revealed in Jesus Christ (19:1-22). In all their apologetics, the early church emphasized the undeniable event of the resurrection of Christ (4:10; 17:31). And, unlike some Christians today, the early church was not plagued by the disease "non-rock-a-boatus"; indeed, the early Christians defended the faith whenever and wherever the opportunity arose. We must commit to doing the same.

Far from being some abstract discipline or quaint pastime for a select few (such as theologians and ministers), apologetics is in reality an immensely practical tool for every single member of the body of Christ. And the need for apologetics today is critical. Believers must realize that we are living in a post-Christian era, with a host of religions, cults, and occultic systems vying continuously for people's commitments and, indeed, for their very lives. We must face these challenges head-on.

Using apologetics, equipped Christians can show that the Christian world view is consistent, coherent, and corresponds to reality over and above all other competing world views. Apologetics also shows that Christianity is both spiritually and intellectually fulfilling, and that Christianity is nothing less than the truth (John 17:17). (That Christianity has an intellectual or rational element is clear in Jesus' words about loving God not only with all our heart, soul, and strength, but also with all our mind; Mark 12:29.)...the number of people hungry for sound answers is anything but diminishing...Is apologetics still relevant today? In my thinking, apologetics has never been more relevant than it is today...May God continue to sustain all those committed to standing for truth.[39]

- The character of God Himself proves the inerrancy of Scripture:

  1. *Sovereign:* *A sovereign God is able to preserve the process of inspiration from error.*

  2. *Righteousness:* *A righteous God is unable to inspire error.*

---

39 Hank Hanegraaf "Apologetics – Still Relevant Today?" *Crosswalk.com* [August 13, 2003]

3. *Just:* A just God could not be untruthful in asserting His word is inerrant. He would be unjust if He bore witness to errant Scripture as holy and true.

4. *Love:* A loving God would adequately provide for the spiritual health and safety of His people by inspiring an inerrant Word.

5. *Eternal:* An eternal God has had forever to determine the canon and means of inspiration (e.g., verbal, plenary) for His Word.

6. *Omniscient:* An omniscient God knows every contingency that might arise to inhibit inerrancy.

7. *Omnipotent:* An omnipotent God can effectively respond to every contingency and also preserve the transmission of His Word.

8. *Omnipresent:* An omnipresent God can initially reveal and inspire His Word and later illuminate it.

9. *Immutable:* An immutable God could never change His Word.

10. *Veracity:* A truthful God would not lie when He testifies about the inerrancy of His Word.

11. *Merciful:* A merciful God would not be unmerciful inspiring both truth and error and then having His people vainly attempt to find the parts that are true. He would not leave His people to such subjectivism and uncertainty.

12. *Personal:* A personal God can inspire, verbally, with words, to insure effective communication.[40]

- Since God is the Author, the Bible is authoritative. It is absolute in its authority for human thought and behavior. **"As the Scripture has said"** is a recurring theme throughout the New Testament…New Testament writers, following the example of Jesus Christ, built their theology on the Old Testament. For Christ and the apostles, to quote the Bible was to settle an issue…Because its source is God, the Bible

---

40 John Ankerberg and John Weldon, *The Facts on the King James Only Debate*, Eugene, OR: Harvest House Publishers, 1996. Pp. 39-39.

is trustworthy in all its parts so that all parts form a harmonious unity...New Testament authors quoted from every section of the Old Testament, and from almost every book of the Old Testament.[41]

---

41 J. Robertson McQuilkin, *Understanding and Applying the Bible*, Chicago: Moody Press, 1983, pp. 19-20.

PERMANENCE OF THE WORD

PERSECUTION OF THE WORD

The Bible is unquestionably the most persecuted book of history! It has no rival either historically or contemporarily when it comes to either the amount or variety of persecution. It has been persecuted politically, socially, academically, literally, and religiously. It has been attacked from every conceivable angle by emperors, kings, governors, scientists and  theologians! Because of the nature of its message man either loves it or hates it. Therefore, it has been banned, burned, and *banished over and over again in history!* Bernard Ramm put it this way:

> *"A thousand times over, the death knell of the Bible has been sounded, the funeral procession formed, the inscription cut on the tombstone, and the committal read. But somehow the corpse never stays put!"*[42]

Let's take a moment to look back at some of the earlier attempts to destroy the Bible.

---

[42] Josh McDowell, *Evidence that Demands a Verdict, Vol. 1,* Arrowhead Springs, CA: Campus Crusade for Christ, Inc., 1972, p. 23.

- When God's Word came to King Jehoiakim of Judah, he would not repent but "**stiffened his neck**" (Jer. 17:23). God dictated His words to Jeremiah who in turn dictated them to his scribe, Baruch. When the king heard it read, he was so angered that he took his penknife and cut the scroll off section by section as it was read to him and then threw it into the fire (Jer. 36:22-24). However, God always protects His Word. So again He dictated it to Jeremiah who had Baruch write it down again on another scroll (36:27-32)!

  > In 2000, Jiang Zemin of China was reported as saying, "*The enemy of the people is not those who hold guns in their hands, but those who hold the Bible in their hands.*"

- In A.D. 303 the Roman Emperor, Diocletian (245-313) issued an edict to destroy Christians and their sacred book. Christians were killed, churches razed to the ground and Bibles burned. He felt he had succeeded in this area and even erected a monument: "*Extincto nomene christianorum*" (the name of Christians is extinguished). He was a genius as an organizer and many of his administrative measures lasted for centuries in Rome – but not this one! His successor, Constantine, publicly converted to Christianity in 312 A.D., and decreed full legal toleration for Christianity (*Edict of Milan*) which historically testifies to the folly of Diocletian's attempt!

- King Henry V considered Bible reading a crime and passed a law to punish offenders – but like Diocletian, he could not succeed.

- Thomas Payne in his famous Age of Reason scoffed at the Bible – but now the Bible's truths scoff at the folly of his reasoning!

- The French skeptic philosopher, Voltaire, said arrogantly: "Another century and there will not be a Bible on earth." He is dead but God's Word lives and prospers – far more than his works! In fact, only 50 years after his death, the Geneva Bible Society used his press and house to produce stacks of Bibles!

As Dr. A.Z. Conrad said:

> "*Empires rise and fall and are forgotten – there it stands;*
> *Dynasty succeeds dynasty – there it stands;*
> *Kings are crowned and uncrowned – there it stands...*
> *It outlives, outfits, outloves, outreaches, outranks, outruns, all other books.*
> *Trust it, love it, obey it, and Eternal life is yours.*"[43]

> **"The Bible is an anvil that has worn out many hammers!"**

The Bible's permanence in the face of such long, unrelenting opposition is something which every honest Bible opponent must honestly face. As Dr. J. B. Phillips said:

> "*Critics of Christianity have somehow got to explain this if they are to have a leg to stand on. Let them read these Letters for themselves and attempt to explain these transformations of character. No one had anything to gain in those days from being a Christian; indeed there was a strong chance that the Christian would lose security and property and even life itself. Yet, reflected in the pages of these Letters, both men and women are exhibiting superb courage and are growing as naturally as fruit upon a tree, those qualities of the spirit of which the world is so lamentably short. To my mind we are forced to the conclusion that something is at work here far above and beyond normal human experience, which can only be explained if we accept what the N.T. itself claims, that is, that ordinary men and women had become, through the power of Christ, sons and daughters of God.*"[44]

Historical Criticism of the Bible[45] was written by Eta Linnemann – but it is not about criticism of the Bible throughout history! Historical criticism is a method of studying or interpreting the Bible. This book is about the theology of university, Bible college and seminary professors

---

43 Josh McDowell, *Evidence that Demands a Verdict*, Vol. 1, Arrowhead Springs, CA: Campus Crusade for Christ, Inc., 1972.
44 J. B. Phillips, *New Testament Christianity*, New York: The Macmillan Co., 1957, pp. 11-12.

who have – in the name of "scholarship" – built a philosophical house of cards upon a foundation that the Bible is not the Word of God. With smoke and mirrors, and unproven premises, they have decided some of the Bible is more reliable... provable...divine than other parts. Worse, these teachers pass along these heresies to students, who become pastors and writers. How could Ms. Linnemann speak so ably against these academic arguments and modern-day Pharisees? She was once one of those professors! She proudly wrote and taught those heresies in her classroom at a German university – until the veil was lifted, and she was called to repentance.

What did she do? She threw the books and papers she had written into the trash, and asks others to throw her previous writings into the trash as well! She writes: *"I am so grateful that Jesus' blood has washed away my errors!"* Here are some quotes from her book – and if you have an opportunity to read the book in its entirety, it is a fantastic resource!

- *In the face of attack from the world, we Christians have adopted a defensive posture in the area of Christian belief...It would be more appropriate to the situation, however, to take up a position of criticism based on God's Word with respect to the world we confront. Since the rise of humanism we have become accustomed to having our faith criticized from every quarter of academic learning...the best defense is a good offense (p. 55).*

- *The Bible is a very old book, and today what is old no longer commands respect...Today, that which is old is generally considered to be outmoded. What counts is what is modern: the latest technological conveniences, the newest scientific findings, the latest news, the new fashions, and other trappings of modern living (p. 72).*

- *Lines are drawn through parts of God's Word. Some of what it says is no longer believed, and its power is accordingly no longer experienced as it was before...the authority of God's Word is thereby called in question. It loses its binding character, as becomes swiftly evident with*

---

45 Eta Linnemann, *Historical Criticism of the Bible: Methodology or Ideology?*, Grand Rapids, Michigan: Baker Book House, 1990.

respect to those passages which make us uncomfortable. Let us make no mistake; even a mouse hole can endanger a dike. That becomes clear when a storm brings high water (p. 88).

- *Overwhelmed by the "expertise" of theologians, the student or the person being confirmed or the church member loses all confidence of being able to personally understand God's Word. Another loss, typically, is the joy the Christian once had in the Bible (p. 95).*

PERSEVERANCE OF THE WORD

"The grass withers and the flowers fall, but the word of our God stands[46] forever" (Isa. 40:8; I Pet. 1:24-25).

For any Christian, what Jesus said about the Bible must be conclusive. A number of times Jesus clearly taught that the Scriptures were divine and therefore eternal:

- "**I tell you the truth, until heaven and earth disappear, not the smallest letter, not the least stroke of a pen** ("jot or tittle" KJV[47]), **will by any means disappear from the Law until everything is accomplished**" (Matt. 5:18); or "**It is easier for heaven and earth to disappear than for the least stroke of a pen to drop out of the Law**" (Lk. 16:17).

- "**Heaven and earth will pass away, but My words will never pass away**" (Matt. 24:35; Mk. 13:31; Lk. 21:33).

- "**…the Scripture cannot be broken**" (Jn. 10: 35).

It is interesting to note that the very books of the Old Testament that are contested by liberal scholarship and higher criticism are the ones most quoted by Christ Himself:

---

[46] The Hebrew word is *yagum* meaning *"rises to stand."* It describes something that is beaten and battered, *yet rises to stand.*

[47] *"Jot"* is the smallest letter in the Hebrew alphabet and almost identical with our apostrophe sign. *"Tittle"* is a small horn-shaped mark used to differentiate similar letters in Hebrew.

- Books of Moses
- Isaiah
- Jonah
- Daniel

For the Christian, **Christ's quotation of them substantiates their authority and trustworthiness forever!** Therefore, as Francis Schaeffer has said: *"It is sheer folly and presumptive arrogance for any professing Christian to have a view of Scripture that is either lower or contradictory to that of Christ."*

Conclusions

The authority of Christ and the authority of the Bible stand or fall together. You cannot have a high view of one and a low view of the other! It is not without significance that those scholars who hold a lower view of the *written word* usually likewise hold a lower view of the Incarnate Word. So it seems to be both academically and emotionally true that one cannot have a low view of Scripture and a high view of Christ! **Both Jesus Christ and the Bible testify to each other and are inseparably connected in *origin, nature, and therefore in authority*.**

Let's look at the following similarities of Jesus Christ, the *Incarnate Word* – and the Bible, the *Inscriptured Word*.

Comparison

INCARNATE WORD
(Jesus Christ)

1. Jesus Christ was conceived by the Holy Spirit (Mtt. 1:20; Lk. 1:35).

2. Jesus Christ came through the human instrumentality of Mary with either destroying her full humanity on the one hand – or infecting Christ with her sinful nature on the other – thus the virgin birth (Isa. 7:14; Lk 1:27; Matt. 1:23). **"Therefore the child to be born will be called holy..."** (Lk. 1:35)

2. So Jesus, the Incarnate Word, is the perfect God-Man – fully God and fully man. Never ever less than God – never ever more than man.

INSCRIPTURED WORD
(Bible)

1. The Bible was conceived ("inspired") by the same Holy Spirit (II Pet. 1:21)

2. The Bible likewise came through human instrumentality without either destroying the full humanity of the writers or infecting their writing with their own sin or imperfections: **"...the Gospel of God, which He promised beforehand through His prophets in the holy scriptures, the gospel concerning His Son..."** (Rom. 1:2).

3. The Bible, the Inscripturated Word, is likewise the perfect Divine-Human Book – fully divine and yet fully human. It is the "Word of God" through the "words of man."

Therefore, if you inscripturated the Living Word (Jesus) you would have the Written Word (Bible); and if you Incarnated the Written Word (Bible) you would have the Living Word (Jesus).

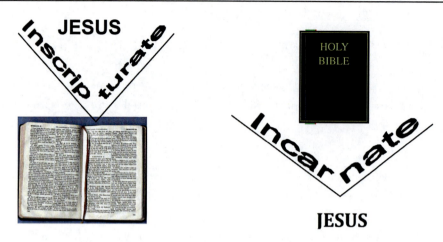

So since Jesus is the eternal Word of God and will last forever; and since His written Word is likewise eternal – everyone who places full faith in one is led to faith in another and that person also becomes eternal:

- "For you have been born again, not of perishable seed, but of imperishable, through the living and enduring word of God" (I Pet. 1:23);

- "The world and its desires pass away, but the man who does the will of God lives forever" (I Jn. 2:17);

- "But these are written that you may believe that Jesus is the Christ, the Son of God, and that by believing you may have life in His Name" (Jn. 20:31).

"Revelation of God leads to worship, the warning of God to repentance, the promises of God to faith, the commands of God to obedience and the truth of God to witness. It is no exaggeration to say that without Scripture a Christian life is impossible."

John Stott

Quotations for Further Reflection

- *If I disbelieve, or believe only part of what God's Word says about Jesus, then He will be correspondingly less to me personally. I will experience Jesus only to the level my faith allows, and by my attitude I will lack in His blessings and His fellowship. Let us not be dissuaded from the position that Jesus is the Messiah, the Son of God, the Savior, even if we are accused of using an obsolete and unsatisfactory philosophy because we, in the view of some, accept mere words as facts (p. 100).*[48]

- *It is pernicious to handle Scripture, as some do, with the assumption that what is plainly says should be laid aside in favor of some novel theory giving a new and different sense to the words. When I approach God's Word with this attitude, I am already off course...I have placed my trust in my intellect...The appropriate attitude would be: "Father, I thank You for Your Word. It is true from start to finish. Still, I have problems...Please, set me straight, and show me through the Holy Spirit from Your Word how things are." (p. 128)*

- *God's Word itself clearly declares God's Holy Spirit to be the originator of the Scriptures. The inspiration of the Scripture is asserted by Scripture itself...Nothing is excluded; there is not one word in all of Scripture to which inspiration does not apply...God's Word is enough; it is completely and entirely sufficient for every person, for every age, for every situation...We can never exhaust God's Word. (p. 155)*

- *As we approach the Bible with the thought of discovering all the truth God intends for us to understand, we should determine our expectations and attitudes...theological study must not be a barren academic search for ultimate truth.* **God is not nearly so interested in what I know as He is in what I am and how I behave.** *As Andrew Murray once put it, "Scripture was not given to increase our knowledge but to change our conduct."...All of our rigorous Bible study must be or the purpose of*

---

[48] Eta Linnemann, *Historical Criticism of the Bible: Methodology or Ideology?*, Grand Rapids, Michigan: Baker Book House, 1990.

making the application to life, transferring the truth into day-by-day living...we are responsible in a special way to live out what we know (Luke 12:47-48). The quest for theological truth, then, should never be an end in itself, but a means for knowing and obeying God more perfectly.[49]

---

[49] J. Robertson McQuilkin, *Understanding and Applying the Bible*, Chicago: Moody Press, 1983, pp. 185-187.

PROOFS FOR THE WORD

This section will have to do with Christian *apologetics*. Unfortunately that is a word that is greatly misunderstood today in regard to the faith. The word apologetic has come to mean something like *"make excuses for"*. However, that's not the correct definition of the word. It actually comes from the Greek word apologia which means, ***"defense"***.

Now I hope that this section does not get too technical or academic for you. If you are not interested in the subject of apologetics (every Christian should be though!), then skip this section and continue reading and studying at the next section. I include this section because I am sick and tired of seeing our young people getting "shot down" in the classroom by highly biased, dishonest or uninformed professors! Too many of your young people have had their faith in the Bible either subtly undermined or ripped from them altogether. In the often-hostile environment of the college classroom a defense of the faith can and needs to be made. To the young person who is struggling for valid answers and proofs for his faith instead of empty platitudes, this section is dedicated. I have drawn heavily from the research and writing of Josh McDowell and his team. I heartily recommend his books! They are a *must* for every serious Bible student's library!

The word *apologia* is a good Biblical term which is used eight times in the New Testament (Acts 22:1; I Cor. 9:3; II Tim. 4:16; Phil.1:7; 1:16; II Cor. 7:11 and I Pet. 3:15). I would like to quote Peter's use of the word as a text for this section: "**...Always be prepared to give an answer**[50] **to everyone who asks you to give the reason for the hope that you have**" (I Pet. 3:15).

I included this section to help you to be able to defend your faith, especially in the Bible. Now there are many levels of apologetics. One needs to spend many months studying the subject to begin to get a grasp of its scope. *I will at best only be giving some preliminary basics on Biblical apologetics.* But as brief as it will be in regard to the existing body of information on the subject, I still hope and pray that it will do two things for you. First, **shore up your own faith with accurate knowledge**; and secondly, **give you some basic tools** to do as Peter said: "**...give an answer to everyone who asks you to give the reason for the hope that you have.**"

When we come to the subject of Biblical apologetics, we need to realize that we really do not have to defend the Bible per se. You see, *the Bible is its own greatest defense!* Most people who attack it have never really objectively studied it. If they would just take the time to do some study, more of them would become believers! J.B. Phillips said this kind of intended neglect and oversight simply means, "*...that the most important event in human history is politely and quietly bypassed. For it is not as though the evidence had been examined and found unconvincing: it had simply never been examined.*"[51] Someone else put it this way: "*The Bible is like a lion in a cage. It doesn't need to be defended or protected – just turned loose!*" So when we really "turn it loose" in our lives we find that it totally verifies itself! However, it is still helpful to understand some basic Biblical apologetics in order to **alleviate our own uncertainties and to be able to answer the honest doubter.**

---

50 *Ajpologiva*, transliterated *Apologia*, meaning verbal defense, speech in defense, or a reasoned statement or argument
51 "A New Third World", *Time*, Oct. 18, 1976, p. 16.

Often when we Christians begin to present our case for our belief in the Bible we are quickly accused of "circular reasoning". This criticism goes something like this: "You say the Bible is inspired because Jesus said so – and then you say that Jesus is divine because the Bible says so. You are reasoning in a circle!" Their illustration of the Christian argument could be illustrated like this:

Circular Reasoning

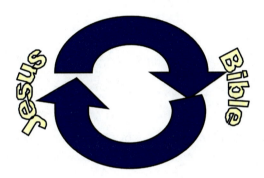

Now I'll readily admit that some Christians do engage in circular reasoning. However, it is not because that is the only way to present and defend our case – but, rather because of a lack of study and preparation on their part. A true defense of the Bible is not circular but rather linear. The linear defense is illustrated as follows:

Linear Reasoning

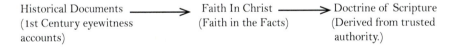

Historical Documents → Faith In Christ → Doctrine of Scripture
(1st Century eyewitness accounts) (Faith in the Facts) (Derived from trusted authority.)

FACT ⎯⎯⎯⎯⎯⎯→FAITH ⎯⎯⎯⎯⎯⎯⎯⎯→ FORMULATION

Do you see the difference? The two methods of argument are worlds apart! In the first one, the Bible is used to prove the Bible. In the second, we approach the Bible with no basic presuppositions and study it with the objectivity we would have for any other secular historical documents. As we study those documents and realize that all were written by people who actually witnessed the events they wrote about or totally verified by people who did, then the accuracy and historicity of these accounts drive us to the conclusions that this One they are writing about – Jesus Christ – was and is who He claimed to be.

At that point we are confronted with a moral choice: *believe or disbelieve...accept the evidence or reject it!* The intelligent moral decision is to make a commitment of faith in Christ! *Then, believing in Him, we begin to formulate our doctrine of Scripture from Him because, it is folly or presumptive arrogance for a believer to hold a view of Scripture lower than that of his Lord! You see, the argument does not run blind faith – blind faith – blind faith! But rather, fact – faith – formulation!*

I approach the facts first...
> study them with historic and moral objectivity...
>> then draw my conclusions...
>>> and make my moral choice!

When people continue in their disbelief in the face of the overwhelming evidence it is always on moral and not intellectual grounds! Then it is a clear case of *"I don't want to believe because I don't want to change my prejudices and lifestyle"* – rather than "I can't believe because of insufficient evidence." As C.S. Lewis shrewdly observed: *"Man is not only a sinner who needs forgiveness – he is a rebel that needs to lay down his arms!"* Nowhere is this moral rebellion against God more clearly demonstrated than in the case of continued disbelief *in spite of* the overwhelming evidence for the truth of the claims of the Bible and Jesus Christ!

Now, since the New Testament documents are our chief source of information about Jesus, *we must be convinced that they are accurate* before we will accept them and Him. You see, **the Bible says that we are to pattern our lives after Christ's** (I Pet. 2:21; II Cor. 3:18; I Jn. 2:6; Heb. 12:2; Gal. 3:19; etc.). The big question then is: *"What kind of life did He live?"* Scripture is the only place where we find the character of Christ clearly revealed. It is of *eternal significance* whether or not the character revealed there is accurate and reliable! *How can I confidently pattern my life after His unless I am sure that I have an accurate account of how He lived?*

Can you see the importance of this study? *I will not believe in Christ if I am persuaded that the Biblical accounts of His life, death, resurrection and ascension are historically inaccurate! And, I will not pattern my life after His if I am likewise uncertain as to what His character really was.* **The trustworthiness of Scripture is of utmost importance for faith!** Regardless of how they might try to rationalize or justify their continued unbelief – the skeptic must face the facts! The *"quest for the historical Jesus"* – as some theologians have put it – does not become shrouded or lost in *"tradition"*. As John Stuart Mill said:

> *"It is of no use to say that Christ, as exhibited in the Gospels, is not historical, and that we know not how much of what is admirable has been superceded by the tradition of His followers. Who among His disciples or among their proselytes was capable of inventing the sayings of Jesus or of imagining the life and character revealed in the Gospel? Certainly not the fishermen of Galilee; as certainly not St. Paul, whose character idiosyncrasies were of a totally different sort; still less the early Christian writers, in whom nothing is more evident than that the good which was in them was all derived, as they always professed that it was derived, from the higher source."* [52]

Therefore, brethren, when it comes to the matter of trustworthiness and historical verification – I want you to realize that **the Bible is the most thoroughly substantiated book of history**! Any basic study of Biblical apologetics will quickly verify this fact. Let me share just one quotation

---

52 John Stuart Mill, *"Three Essays on Religion."* Quoted in J.N.D. Anderson, *Christianity: The Witness of History*, London: The Tyndale Press, 1969, p. 34.

from A.T. Robertson. He is the author of the most comprehensive grammar of New Testament Greek, and an internationally recognized scholar in the area:

> "There are some 8,000 manuscripts of the Latin Vulgate and at least 1,000 manuscripts for the other early versions. Add over 4,000 Greek manuscripts and we have 13,000 manuscript copies of portions of the New Testament. Besides all this, much of the New Testament can be reproduced from the quotations of the early Christian writers."[53]

The Christian apologist, John Montgomery, similarly says: *"To be skeptical of the resultant text of the New Testament books is to allow all of classical antiquity to slip into obscurity, for no documents of the ancient period are as well attested bibliographically as the New Testament."*[54]

Let's look further at the matter of the New Testament documents.

ESTABLISHING THE CANON

The *number of manuscripts of the New Testament* are far more numerous than any other document of history. Perhaps that raises in your mind the very logical questions: *"What was the reason for such a large number of Scripture copies?"* and, *"How did the early church decide what was truly Scripture and what wasn't?"* Let's begin with a definition.

The word **canon** comes from the root word "reed". The "reed" was used as a measuring rod and eventually came to mean "standard". In reference to the Bible it means the **officially accepted list of books**.

---

[53] John Warwick Montgomery, *History and Christianity*, Downers Grove, IL: InterVarsity Press, 1971, p. 16.
[54] John Warwick Montgomery, "History and Christianity," His, Jan. 1965, p. 15.

Things that Prompted the Formation of an Official Canon

Church historians generally agree that there were several factors that caused the early church to establish a formal "official" list of canonical books.

1. **Apostolic martyrdom**: Because of the deaths of the original 12 Apostles and Paul (it is estimated that Paul and Peter were martyred c. 67-70 A.D.), the church realized an immediate need to **guard and pass on their doctrine**. Since they were the working companions of Christ Himself – whom He had chosen to continue His work – their writings must be preserved.

2. **Heresy**: There was an increasing amount of religious writing floating around – much of which was professing to be apostolic and therefore authoritative. These apocryphal writings as they are called were rejected by the church as a whole.

    Closely related to this was the **Marcionian heresy**. Marcion made a distinction between the inferior Creator God of the Old Testament and the God and Father who was revealed in Christ. He therefore believed the church should throw out all Biblical references to this Old Testament God – and he personally set the pace! He threw out all of the Old Testament and much of the New that to him referred to this "Semitic God".

    > "It is important to note that the church did not create the canon…a book is not the Word of God because it is accepted by the people of God. Rather, it was accepted by the people of God because it is the Word of God. That is, God gives the book its divine authority, not the people of God. They merely recognize the divine authority which God gives to it"
    > (Josh McDowell, *The New Evidence that Demands a Verdict*, p. 21).

    The result was that in the process **he tossed out about everything but Luke and 10 of Paul's letters**. Those types of heretical opinions and writings made it necessary to separate the true from the false – the orthodox from the spurious.

3. **Missionary Expansion**: The church was also rapidly growing, and expanding into other countries with different languages that needed the Scriptures in their own tongue. The Word began to be translated into other languages as the church expanded. These translations have also become a great resource and treasure for Biblical criticism and textual analysis and comparison. Some of these major early translations were:

   A. The ***Syriac Version*** (150-250 A.D.) which was for the Syrians. It used the Aramaic alphabet.

   B. The ***Latin Versions*** (300-400 A.D.) which was obviously written in Latin – the Vulgate (meaning "common" or "popular") by St. Jerome being the most famous.

   C. The ***Coptic Versions*** (300-400 A.D.) were in the language of the Egyptians.

   D. The ***Armenian Version*** (c. 400 A.D.) was for the Armenian speaking people.

   Today we have more than 9,000 copies of these early translations! They eloquently and prolifically testify that from the very beginning **Christianity was a missionary faith!** The early Christians were indeed going out into all of their then known world in obedience to the Great Commission of Christ! *We find no other ancient literature that was so widely translated into other languages.* This process is still going on today because the Bible is still the most widely translated book of history! All or part of it has been translated into over 2,500 languages today.[55]

---

55 http://www.gospelcom.net/ibs/aboutibs/translation.php [Nov. 2, 2003]

4. **Political persecution**: The emperor Diocletian bitterly persecuted Christians (c. 302-305 A.D.) One of his edicts called for the burning of all Scriptures. So ***Christians literally had to decide which books they would die for!*** That makes you choose very carefully! You don't die for something you're unsure of!

How Did They Decide?

There were many factors that precipitated the need for an official canon. But, how did the early church Fathers choose? What was their criteria for determining which books were to be included in the canon and which ones were to be rejected? Geisler and Nix list the following criteria that writing had to meet[56]:

1. Is it *authoritative* – i.e., does it claim to be the Word of God?

2. Is it *Apostolic* – i.e., was it either written or approved by the Apostles?

3. Is it *prophetic* – i.e., was it written by a servant of God?

4. Is it *authentic* – i.e., does it tell the truth about God, man, sin, etc.?

5. Is it *dynamic* – i.e., does it possess the life transforming power of God?

6. Was it *received* – i.e., did the people of God for whom it was written receive it as such?

Witness of the Post-Apostolic Fathers

In the writings of these post-Apostolic church fathers we find many references to the various books that were accepted:

---

56 Adapted from *A General Introduction to the Bible*, Norman L. Geisler and William E. Nix, Moody Press, 1968, p. 141.

1. As early as 95 A.D. we have references by Clement, bishop of Rome, referring to Books like *Matthew, Luke, Romans, 1 Corinthians and Hebrews.*

2. Irenaeus (A.D. 180), who became Bishop of Lyons in Gual witnessed to the canonical recognition of:

Matthew	I and II Corinthians	I and II Timothy
Mark	Galatians	Titus
Luke	Ephesians	I Peter
John	Philippians	I John
Acts	Colossians	Revelation
Romans	I and II Thessalonians	(c. 70-155/160 A.D.)

This is especially significant when we realize that Irenaeus was brought up at the feet of Polycarp (A.D. 115) *who was a disciple of John.*

John ⟶ Polycarp ⟶ Irenaeus

3. By the end of the 2nd Century, the 27 books of the N.T. were basically agreed upon by the church:

   A. C. 200 A.D. Tertullian, bishop of Carthage, an important defender or apologist of the faith, used the expression *"New Testament"* – thereby formally recognizing it with equal authority with the Old Testament.

   B. Athanasius of Alexandria, published a list of divine books in c. 367 A.D. It contained the Old Testament and the exact 27 books we have in the New Testament. *Historians say it is the first list that matches perfectly the list we have today.*

   C. Jerome agreed and used the same 27 books when he translated the Latin Vulgate abut 385 A.D.

At this point you might want to turn to the Appendix on Manuscript Evidence and see the chart of "Quotations of the New Testament by

Early Church Fathers". By their vast number of quotations you can easily see that the church had a widely accepted list of canonical books.

Church Councils

There were two church councils in North Africa – *Hippo in 393 and Carthage in 397 A.D.* – that officially rendered the 27 books of the New Testament as the only ones that could be read in the churches.

Principle
A book's acceptance into the canon did not elevate it to "Scripture". Its inclusion was recognition by the church fathers that it was already Scripture!

As one writer put it: **"*The Bible is not an authorized collection of books, but a collection of authorized books.*"**

Principle
If God cared enough to give us His Word – He likewise cared enough to guard it from loss or corruption!

I think the following quotation is an excellent summary of both the process and result of the church's choice of the canon:

> "*The churches were providentially kept from accepting any illegitimate books...they examined freely and unhurriedly the books presented to them. At times certain ones hesitated for a while before coming to complete agreement. But never did the believers as a whole make a definite choice which they later had to repent of...the church definitively and firmly accepted as divine some books unfavorable to its own inclinations, and everywhere it rejected as merely human others which*

would favor its inclinations the most. There is only one explanation for this fact: God Himself watched over the canon."

The Apocryphal Writings

These books or writings that were not included in the official church canon are referred to as ***apocryphal writings***. The word apocrypha comes from the Greek work apokruphos meaning hidden or concealed. St. Jerome in the 4th century was the first to use the term in reference to these non-canonical writings. Their number truly abounds! There are many books on the market you can buy for a more detailed discussion of them if you are interested. However, unless you are particularly interested in church heresy, it is not really worth your time! Apart from bits of historical and cultural information – often incorrect at that – there is really very little for the Christian.

For the sake of division we can divide the apocryphal writing into Old Testament related ones and New Testament related ones.

Old Testament Apocryphal Writings:

I Esdras	*Bel and the Dragon*
II Esdras	*The Song of the Three Hebrew Children*
Tobit	*The Prayer of Manasseh*
Judith	*I Maccabees*
Additions to Esther	*II Maccabees*
The Wisdom of Solomon	*Baruch*
Ecclesiasticus	

The Biblical scholars Geisler and Nix give a number of reasons why they were rejected: [57]

---

57 Adapted from *A General Introduction to the Bible,* Norman L. Geisler and William E. Nix. Moody Press, 1968, p. 173.

1. *Philo*, the Jewish philosopher (20 B.C. - 40 A.D.) quoted the Old Testament pontifically but never recognized the Apocrypha as inspired.

2. The Jewish historian, Josephus (30 - 100 A.D.) explicitly excludes the Apocrypha in his listing of scripture.

3. ***Jesus and the New Testament writers never once quoted an apocryphal writing*** – even though there are hundreds of other O.T. quotations in their teachings and writings. For the Christian, this fact alone is conclusive.

4. The Jewish scholars of *Jamnia* (A.D. 90) did not recognize the Apocrypha.

5. No canon or council of the Christian church for the first four centuries recognized the Apocrypha as inspired.

6. Many of the great church Fathers spoke out against the Apocrypha. Irenaeus refers to *"an unspeakable number of apocryphal and spurious writings, which they themselves* (i.e. the heretics) *had forged, to bewilder the minds of the foolish."* Origen said: *"The Church possesses four Gospels, heresy a great many."*[58]

7. Many Roman Catholic scholars through the Reformation period rejected the Apocrypha.

8. *Martin Luther* and the other Reformers rejected the authority and canonicity of the Apocrypha.

It was not until 1546 at the Counter Reformation Council of Trent that the Apocryphal books received full canonical status by the Roman Catholic Church.

New Testament Apocryphal Writings:

Epistle of Barnabas   *The Gospel of Thomas*

---

[58] Edwin Yamauchi, "The Word from Nag Hammadi," *Christianity Today*, Jan. 13, 1978, p. 19.

Epistle to the Corinthians	*The Protevangelium of James*
Epistle of Clement	*The Assumption of Mary*
Shepherd of Hermas	*The Gospel of Philip*
Didache or Teaching of the Twelve	*The Gospel of Truth*
Apocalypse of Peter	*The Gospel of the Nazarenes*
The Acts of Paul and Thecla	*Epistle of Polycarp to the Philippians*
Epistle to the Laodiceans	*The Seven Epistles of Ignatius*
The Gospel According to the Hebrews	*(and many more)*

The above lists of books were rejected by the church for the following reasons:

1. *"They abound in historical and geographical inaccuracies and anachronisms."*

2. *"They teach doctrines which are false and foster practices which are at variance with inspired Scripture."*

3. *"They resort to literary types and display an artificiality of subject matter and styling out of keeping with inspired Scripture."*

4. *"They lack the distinctive elements which give genuine Scripture its divine character, such as prophetic power and poetic and religious feeling."*[59]

The apocryphal book The Gospel of Thomas was a rather recent discovery of the Gnostic library at Nag Hammadi, Egypt. There are altogether 50+ of these apocryphal gospels – many of which are known simply by title only, or by a few scattered quotations and allusions by the early church Fathers. Edwin M. Yamauchi refers to them as "...non-canonical writings of a motley variety about the purported deeds and revelations of Jesus Christ."[60] As previously stated, the early church Fathers generally rejected these writings. Eusebius describes such apocryphal gospels as follows:

---

59 Merrill F. Unger, *Unger's Bible Dictionary*, Chicago: Moody Press, 1971, p. 70.
60 Edwin Yamauchi, "The Word from Nag Hammadi," *Christianity Today*, Jan. 13, 1978, p. 19.

> "*Again, nothing could be farther from apostolic usage than the type of phraseology employed, while the ideas and implications of their contents are so irreconcilable with true orthodoxy that they stand revealed as the forgeries of heretics.*" [61]

These apocryphal gospels arose because the straightforward accounts of the birth and childhood of Jesus, recorded in the Gospels of Matthew and Luke, do not totally satisfy the fallen human curiosity of many people. They began to add their fanciful embellishments – fill in those "hidden years of Christ" with their own ideas of what He was doing!

Examples from the Infancy Gospel of Thomas will suffice to demonstrate the difference between the fancifulness of man's imagination and the truth of God's revelation. According to that writing, when Jesus was five years old, He made 12 sparrows from clay and "zapped them" with life and they all flew away! On another occasion, Jesus purportedly cursed a child who had bothered Him with the words: "*You insolent, godless dunderhead...See, now you also shall wither like a tree.*"[62] Another lad who accidentally bumped into Jesus was smitten dead. Others who accused Him were blinded. An assistant in His father's carpenter shop, Jesus was able to stretch beams of wood to the proper size! There is a great gulf between these fantasies and the stark realism of God's Word! How different is Jesus Christ from these projections!

The conclusions are rather obvious: "*The apocryphal gospels, even the earliest and soberest among them, can hardly be compared with the canonical gospels. The former are all patently secondary and legendary or obviously slanted.*"[63] After one has spent a little time reading them, he comes back to God's Word with renewed conviction and enthusiasm!

Morton Enslin said: "*Their total effect is to send us back to the canonical gospels with fresh approval of their chaste restraint in failing to fill in the intriguing hidden years.*" [64] A. Roberts and J. Donaldson, scholars on the early church fathers, said: "*...the predominant impression which they leave on*

---

61 Ibid.
62 Ibid.

our minds is a profound sense of the immeasurable superiority, the unapproachable simplicity and majesty, of the Canonical Writings."[65]

Joachim Jeremias, one of the most outstanding scholars on the Apocrypha, wrote *Unknown Sayings of Jesus. In it he concluded: "...the extra-canonical literature, taken as a whole, manifests a surprising poverty. The bulk of it is legendary, and bears the clear mark of forgery. Only here and there, amid a mass of worthless rubbish, do we come across a priceless jewel."*[66]

All of these apocryphal writings make us profoundly thankful for the Bible as we have it! *The contrast between them and true scriptures is too great to be overlooked by any eye trained to perceive truth. Yamauchi concludes: "The study of the Agrapha, particularly in the apocryphal gospels, reveals the relative poverty and inferiority of the mass of the extra-canonical literature, and by contrast highlights the precious value of the sayings of Jesus preserved in the New Testament."*[67]

PROPHECY

"And we have the word of the prophets made more certain, and you will do well to pay attention to it, as to a light shining in a dark place, until the day dawns and the morning star rises in your hearts. Above all, you must understand that no prophecy of Scripture came about by the prophet's own interpretation. For prophecy never had its origin in the will of man, but men spoke from God as they were carried along by the Holy Spirit" (II Pet. 1:19-21).

---

63 Edwin Yamauchi, "The Word from Nag Hammadi," *Christianity Today*, Jan. 13, 1978, p. 22.
64 Ibid.
65 Ibid.
66 Ibid.
67 Ibid.

PROPHETIC EVIDENCE

"There existed long before this time certain men more ancient than all those who are esteemed philosophers, both righteous and beloved by God, who spoke by the divine Spirit, and foretold events which would take place, and which are now taking place. They are called prophets. These alone both saw and announced the truth to men, neither reverencing nor fearing any man, not influenced by a desire for glory, but speaking those things alone which they saw and heard, being filled with the Holy Spirit."[68]

When we come to the subject of prophecy, we come to one of the most exciting and yet most greatly misunderstood and abused areas of Biblical studies. But just what is prophecy? Let's begin with a definition.

In the Bible, prophecy is understood in two ways. In the Old Testament, prophecy primarily has to do with "**foretelling future events**." This is what we might call ***predictive prophecy***. In the New Testament, prophecy is primarily not *foretelling but forth-telling*. It means to "**stand up and tell forth God's word**" – so this is what we could call preaching today. Now there was some foretelling in the New Testament – but the overwhelming majority was forth-telling. (For a more detailed discussion of this see the section on "Gifts of the Spirit" in my book **Ministry of the Holy Spirit** on line at: www.jlwilliams.org). In our discussion here, we will be dealing with predictive prophecy of the "foretelling of future events" long before they occurred. If it can be demonstrated that prophets and men of God in the Old Testament period prophesied things hundreds of years beforehand that were accurately fulfilled – then that is yet another cogent argument in support of the belief that the Bible is more than a human book!

---

68 "Justin Martyr, Dialogue with Trypho 7." Quoted in William Barclay, *The Making of the Bible*, New York: Abingdon Press, 1965, p. 41.

Now, ***predictive prophecy can only be validated by their fulfillment.*** We have a rather easy means for checking them out! As you well know, the world today is filled with people who claim to have the powers to foretell future events. Some profess to be able to do it by the aid of astrology, others by tarot cards, yet others by tea leaves! Every year around December or January the newsstands are filled with magazines and newspapers in which astrologers are giving their predictions for the coming year. If one were to take the time to read these (don't waste your time) and list these prophecies and then check them out during the coming year against current events – you would find great discrepancies! Their rate of accuracy of prediction is indeed very small – and even many of the ones that do come true have human explanations. That's where Biblical prophecy parts company with these false human "prophets". False prophets have been with us since the earliest days of history. For the people of God then there was a very real problem of knowing the true from the false. God of course anticipated that problem and set forth a test that would divide the pseudo from the true prophet.

Here is His standard of judgment for a prophet: "…**a prophet who presumes to speak in My Name anything I have not commanded him to say, or a prophet who speaks in the name of other gods, must be put to death. You may say to yourselves, 'How can we know when a message has not been spoken by the Lord?' If what a prophet proclaims in the name of the Lord does not take place or come true, that is a message the Lord has not spoken. That prophet has spoken presumptuously. Do not be afraid of him**" (Deut. 18:20-22).

So there's the test – 100% accuracy of fulfillment! No other religion in the world has such a wealth of fulfilled prophecy as Christianity! No other world religious leader's coming was foretold hundred of years in advance by such minute detail as was Christ's! The Old Testament was written over an approximate 1,500 year period and contains several hundred prophecies and references to the coming of Christ the Messiah. These prophecies can be conveniently divided into two types: Prophecies of a Kingly Messiah and prophecies of a Suffering Messiah.

Jesus Christ fulfilled both! The accurate fulfillment of those hundreds of prophecies is explicable only in terms of the fact that Jesus was indeed the Messiah of God – and the Bible indeed His revelation of those prophecies and their fulfillment!

Obviously, we do not have the time or space in one chapter to list and expound all of these prophecies and their fulfillment. However, I will list some of the major ones for you. I hope that you will take time to look up and study them in detail in your Bible.

Prophecies Concerning the Birth of Christ

		Prophecies	Fulfillment
1	Born of the Seed of Woman	Gen. 3:15	Gal. 4:4 Matt. 1:20
2	Born of a Virgin	Isaiah 7:14	Matt. 1:18, 24-25 Luke 1:26-35
3	That He would be the Son of God	Ps. 2:7 I Chron. 17:11-14 II Sam. 7:12-16	Matt. 3:17; 16:16 Mark 9:7 Luke 9:35; 22:70 John 1:34, 49 Acts 13:30-33
4	He would be of the seed of Abraham (a Jew)	Gen. 22:18; 12:2-3	Matt. 1:1 Gal. 3:16
5	He would be a son of Isaac (Jewish) and not Ishmael (Arabic)	Gen. 21:12	Matt. 1:2 Luke 3:23, 34
6	He would be a son of Jacob and not Esau	Gen. 35:10-12 Num. 24:17	Matt. 1:2 Luke 1:33; 3:23, 34
7	He would be out of the tribe of Judah	Gen. 49:10 Micah 5:2	Matt. 1:2 Luke 3:23 Heb. 7:14
8	He would be of the family line of Jesse	Isa. 11:1, 10	Matt. 1:6 Luke 3:23

9	He would be of the House of David and heir to his throne	II Sam. 7:12-16 Jer. 23:5	Matt. 1:1; 9:27; 15:22 Mark 9:10 Luke 3:23; 18:38-39 Acts 13:22-23 Rev. 22:16
10	The approximate time of His birth was foretold	Dan. 9:25	Luke 2:1-2
11	He would be born at Bethlehem	Micah 5:2	Matt. 2:1, 4-8 Luke 2:4-7 John 7:42
12	He would be presented with gifts at His birth	Ps. 72:10 Isa. 60:6	Matt. 2:1, 11
13	There would be a massacre of infants	Jer. 31:15	Matt. 2:16
14	His parents would flee to Egypt with Him	Hosea 11:1	Matt. 2:14

Prophecies Concerning His Nature as Deity

		Prophecies	Fulfillment
1	He was pre-existent before His Incarnation	Ps. 102:5 Prov. 8:22-23 Isa. 9:6-7; 41:4; 44:6; 58:12 Micah 5:2	John 1:1-2; 8:58; 17:5, 24 Col. 1:17 Rev. 1:17; 2:8; 22:13
2	Some of His characteristics were foretold	Ps. 45:7 Isa. 11:2-4	Luke 2:52
3	He shall be called "Lord"	Ps. 110:1 Jer. 23:6	Luke 2:11; 20:41-44
4	He shall be called "Immanuel" or "God with us"	Isa. 7:14	Matt. 1:23 Luke 7:16

5	He shall be a Prophet	Deut. 18:18	Matt. 21:11 Luke 7:16 John 4:19; 6:14; 7:40
6	He would be also a Priest, like Melchizedek	Ps. 110:4	Heb. 3:1; 5:5-6
7	He would be a Judge	Isa. 33:22	John 5:30 II Tim. 4:1
8	He would be a King	Ps. 2:6 Jer. 23:5 Zech. 9:9	Matt. 21:5; 27:37 John 18:33-38
9	He would be specially anointed of the Holy Spirit	Ps. 45:7 Isa. 42:1; 61:1-2	Matt. 3:16-17; 12:17-21 Mark 1:10-11 Luke 4:15-21, 43 John 1:32
10	He would have a special zeal for God	Ps. 69:9	John 2:15-17

Prophecies Concerning His Ministry

		Prophecies	Fulfillment
1	He would be preceded by a messenger	Isa. 40:3 Mal. 3:1	Matt. 3:1-2 Luke 1:17 John 1:23
2	His ministry would begin in Galilee	Isa. 9:1	Matt. 4:12-13, 17
3	His ministry would be characterized by miracles	Isa. 35:5-6; 32:3-4	Matt. 9:35; 11:4-6 Mark 7:33-35 John 5:5-9; 9:6-11; 11:43-47
4	He would teach with parables	He would teach with parables	Matt. 13:34
5	He was to enter the Jewish Temple	Mal. 3:1	Matt. 21:12

6	He was to triumphantly enter Jerusalem on a donkey	Zech. 9:9	Luke 19:35-37; 21:6-11
7	He would be a "stumbling stone" to the Jews	Ps. 118:22 Isa. 8:14; 28:16	Rom. 9:32-33 I Cor. 1:23 I Pet. 2:6
8	He would be a "light" to the Gentiles	Isa. 60:3; 49:6	Acts 13:47-48; 26:23; 28:28
9	He would be rejected by His own people	Ps. 69:8; 118:22 Isa. 53:3	Matt. 21:42-43 John 7:5, 48
10	He would be hated without a cause	Ps. 69:4 Isa. 49:7	John 15:25
11	He would be betrayed by a friend	Ps. 41:9; 55:12-14	Matt. 10:4; 26:49-50 John 13:21
12	He would be sold for 30 pieces of silver	Zech. 11:12	Matt. 26:15; 27:3
13	The money would be thrown in God's House	Zech. 11:13	Matt. 27:5
14	The money would be used to buy the Potter's Field	Zech. 11:13	Matt. 27:7
15	He would be forsaken by His disciples	Zech. 13:7	Matt. 26:31 Mark 14:50
16	He would be accused by false witnesses	Ps. 35:11	Matt. 26:59-61
17	He would remain silent before His accusers	Isa. 53:7	Matt. 27:12-19
18	He would be wounded and bruised	Isa. 53:5 Zech. 13:6	Matt. 27:26
19	He would be smitten and spit upon	Isa. 50:6 Micah 5:1	Matt. 26:67 Luke 22:63
20	He would be mocked	Ps. 22:7-8	Matt. 27:31
21	He would fall beneath the weight of the cross	Ps. 109:24-25	Matt. 27:31-32 Luke 23:26 John 19:17
22	His hands and feet would be pierced	Ps. 22:16 Zech. 12:10	Luke 23:33 John 20:25

23	He would be crucified with thieves	Isa. 53:12	Matt. 27:38 Mark 15:27-28
24	He would make intercession for His persecutors	Isa. 53:12	Luke 23:34
25	His friends would stand afar off	Ps. 38:11	Matt. 27:55-56 Mark 15:40 Luke 23:49
26	The people would shake their heads at Him	Ps. 22:7; 109:25	Matt. 27:39
27	He would be stared at while on the cross	Ps. 22:17	Luke 23:35
28	His garments would be gambled for	Ps. 22:18	John 19:23-24
29	He would suffer thirst	Ps. 22:15; 69:21	John 19:28
30	Gall and vinegar would be offered Him	Ps. 69:21	Matt. 27:34 John 19:28-29
31	He would cry out a forsaken cry	Ps. 22:1	Matt. 27:46
32	He committed Himself to God	Ps. 31:5	Luke 23:46
33	Not one of His bones would be broken	Ps. 34:20	John 19:33
34	His heart would be broken	Ps. 22:14	John 19:34
35	His side would be pierced	Zech. 12:10	John 19:34
36	Darkness would cover the land	Amos 8:9	Matt. 27:45
37	He would be buried in a rich man's tomb	Isa. 53:9	Matt. 27:57-60
38	He would be resurrected from the dead	Ps. 16:10; 30:3; 41:10; 118:17 Hosea 6:2	Matt. 28:6 Mark 16:6 Luke 24:46 Acts 2:31; 13:33
39	He would ascend into heaven	Ps. 68:18	Acts 1:9

| 40 | He would be seated at the right hand of God | Ps. 110:1 | Mark 16:19
Acts 2:34-35
Heb. 1:3 |

I hope you noticed *how very specific and detailed those prophecies and their fulfillment were!* He would be a Jew, from a specific tribe of Israel; a specific family and house; He would be born in one specific town of all of the towns in the world; He would begin His ministry in another specific town; He would have a certain kind of ministry; die a specific kind of death accompanied by many specific detailed circumstances!

It is sometimes said that Jesus deliberately set out to fulfill these Old Testament prophecies and thereby try to prove His messiahship. That might sound like a good argument on the surface but it will not hold up under close examination. Why? Simply because *many of the prophecies that were fulfilled by Christ were completely beyond human contact or manipulation.* For example, there would have been no way that Jesus could have manipulated:

1. The place of His birth (Micah 5:2);
2. The time of His birth (Dan. 9:25; Gen. 49:10);
3. The manner of His birth (Isa. 7:14);
4. His betrayal (Ps. 41:9);
5. The manner of His death (Ps. 22:16);
6. People's reactions of mocking, spitting, staring, etc. (Isa. 50:6; Ps. 22:7-S'1
7. His being pierced by a sword (Zech. 12:10);
8. The circumstances of His burial (Isa. 53:9).

When you stop to recall that the Old Testament was completed by no later than 450 B.C. – a gap of 450 years between the completion of the Old Testament and the events of the New – then you realize that *there was a minimum of 450 years between the prophecies and their fulfillment in*

Christ! Once again, there is no other reasonable explanation other than that the Bible is indeed God's Word!

What About Coincidence?

There are always those who would say that it was just coincidence that Jesus fulfilled all of those prophecies. Well, it takes far more faith to believe that than it does to believe in fulfilled prophecy! True, a few of the prophecies could have been fulfilled by Christ coincidentally – but not all of them! In fact, if you can produce just one other person out of history or contemporary society other than Jesus who has fulfilled only half of the predictive prophecies concerning the Messiah, then you could have made a quick $1,000! The Christian Victory Publishing Company of Denver had this proposition standing for a number of years – with no challengers.

Dr. Peter Stoner, in his book, Science Speaks (Moody Press, 1963), conclusively shows by the mathematical principles of probability that coincidence is ruled out as a means of explaining the fulfilled prophecies. Stoner says that by using the modern science of probability in reference to just eight prophecies, *"…we find that the chance that any man might have lived down to the present time and fulfilled all eight prophecies is 1 in 10^{17}."* To break that down a little, that would be 1 in 100,000,000,000,000,000. In order to help us begin to grab a hold of a number that large, Dr. Stoner gives the following illustration. He says that suppose that,

> *"…we take 10^{17} silver dollars and lay them on the face of Texas. They would cover all of the state two feet deep. Now mark one of these silver dollars and stir the whole mass thoroughly, all over the state. Blindfold a man and tell him that he can travel as far as he wishes, but he must pick up one silver dollar and say that this is the right one. What chance would he have of getting the right one? Just the same chance that the prophets would have had of getting these eight prophecies and having them all come true in any one man, from their day to the present time, providing they wrote them in their own wisdom.*

Now these prophecies were either given by inspiration of God or the prophets just wrote them as they thought they should be. In such a case the prophets had just one chance in 10^{17} of having them come true in any man, but they all come true in Christ ...This means that the fulfillment of these eight prophecies alone proves that God inspired the writing of those prophecies to a definiteness which lacks only one chance in 10^{17} of being absolute."[69]

Dr. Stoner then ups his prophecies and their corresponding probable fulfillment from 8 to 48. He says, *"we find the chance that any one man fulfilled all 48 prophecies to be 1 in 10^{157}."* He then gives another illustration that really blows your mind with its incomprehensibility:

"This is really a large number and it represents an extremely small chance. Let us try to visualize it. The silver dollar, which we have been using is entirely too large. We must select a smaller object. The electron is about as small an object as we know of. It is so small that it will take 2.5 times 10^{15} of them laid side by side to make a line, single file, one inch long. If we were going to count the electrons in this line one inch long, and counted 250 each minute, and if we counted day and night, it would take us 19,000,000 years to count just the one-inch line of electrons. If we had a cubic inch of these electrons and we tried to count them it would take us, counting steadily 250 each minute, 19,000,000 times 19,000,000 times 19,000,000 years 6.9 times 10^{21} years.[70]

With this introduction, let us go back to our chance of 1 in 10^{157}. Let us suppose that we are taking this number of number of electrons making one, and thoroughly stirring it into the whole mass, then blindfolding a man and letting him try to find the right one. What chance has he of finding the right one? What kind of a pile will this number of electrons make? They make an inconceivably large volume."[70]

That would be the chance of one man fulfilling 48 prophecies! Now are you still interested in going for that $1,000 prize money? I hope not – because Christ has already exclusively qualified!

---

69 Peter W. Stoner, *Science Speaks*, Chicago: Moody Press, 1963, pp. 100-107.
70 Ibid., pp. 109-110.

Conclusions

Let's summarize what all of these fulfilled prophecies strongly suggest:

1. That there is indeed an active God in the Universe who is working out His plan in history.
2. That this God was guiding the production of the Old and New Testament and revealing Himself in it.
3. It evidences the inspiration of the Bible.
4. It authenticated the deity of Jesus Christ.

So when you put the cumulative witness of the 13,000 manuscripts of the New Testament, the astounding evidence of archaeology, and the accuracy of predictive prophecy fulfilled by Jesus Christ – you are driven to the unavoidable conclusions that ***the Bible is indeed God's inspired word!*** As Gene Getz said:

> *"How do we know the Scriptures were really inspired by God and are accurate in their facts? Actually the Bible itself bears witness in many ways to its accuracy and reliability. The way it is authored, its fulfilled prophecies, its verification through recent archaeological discoveries, its supernatural relevance – all these things point to supernatural guidance in its composition and preservation. When a person really becomes aware of its origin, its content, and its uniqueness, it actually takes more faith to believe this Book is purely human in its origin than to believe it is divinely inspired. In fact, many people who criticize the Bible and do not believe it is accurate have had very little exposure to its actual history and content. Many times their statements are based upon very superficial judgments. Anyone who has studied the Bible carefully cannot but recognize its supernatural dimensions, even a non-Christian."*

"I am watching over
My word to perform it"
(Jer. 1:12).

ARCHAELOGICAL EVIDENCE

When we study Biblical archaeology, we enter the realm of one of the youngest – but most exciting – sciences of Biblical studies. *The stones of the Holy Land literally cry out in defense of the trustworthiness of the Bible!* However, not nearly all of the evidence is in yet because fewer than 5% of the known Biblical sites have been excavated to date, and many of these only partially. The evidence is yet fragmentary, although still very exciting and convincing! That very fact makes it difficult to write about the subject. There are so many new discoveries in the field of archaeology that before a book on the subject is finally printed it has already been superseded and outdated by new discoveries! But as fragmentary as the evidence is, many scientists have now had their view of the Bible either completely changed or radically altered by what the archaeological evidence to date has revealed. William F. Albright is a good case in point. He is the late renowned professor emeritus of Johns Hopkins University and called the "Dean of American Biblical Archaeologists." He said the following about his pilgrimage of belief in the trustworthiness of the Biblical records:

> "*During these 15 years (between World Wars) my initially rather skeptical attitude toward the accuracy of Israelite historical tradition had suffered repeated jolts as discovery after discovery confirmed the historicity of details which might reasonably have been considered*

legendary."⁷¹ His conclusion was this: "There can be no doubt that archaeology has confirmed the substantial historicity of Old Testament tradition."⁷²

Nelson Glueck (pronounced "Glek"), former president of the Jewish Theological Seminary in the Hebrew Union College in Cincinnati – and considered one of the world's greatest Biblical archaeologists – similarly says: *"In all of my archaeological investigation I have never found one artifact of antiquity that contradicts any statement of the Word of God."*⁷³

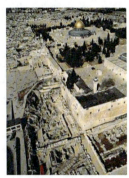

Excavations at the southwest corner of the Temple Mount (in foreground) and the Wailing Wall

Dr. Donald J. Wiseman, distinguished professor of Assyriology at the University of London and author of numerous books and articles on Biblical archaeology, says: *"I would still maintain that the historical facts of the Bible rightly understood find agreement in the facts culled from archaeology equally rightly understood. That is, the majority of errors can be ascribed to errors of interpretation by modern scholars and not to substantiated 'errors' of fact presented by the Biblical historians. This view is further strengthened when it is remembered how many theories and interpretations of Scripture have been checked or corrected by archaeological discoveries."*⁷⁴

Dr. Wiseman read, writes and speaks 14 dialects and languages of the Near East! He and his colleagues have discovered over 250,000 documents and artifacts from Old Testament times. He concludes the following about them: *"...in 30 years of both working in the field and study of finds I have never yet found that archaeology when rightly interpreted, has*

---

71 William F. Albright, *History, Archaeology, and Christian Humanism*, New York: McGraw-Hill Book Co., 1964.
72 William F. Albright, *Archaeology and the Region of Israel*, Baltimore: Johns Hopkins Press, 1942, p. 49.
73 Josh McDowell, *Evidence that Demands a Verdict*, Vol. 1, Arrowhead Springs, CA: Campus Crusade for Christ, Inc., 1972, p. 24.
74 Donald J. Wiseman, "Archaeology and Scripture," *The Westminster Theological Journal*, May, 1971.

clashed with the clear statement of Scripture...the discoveries have only confirmed that the Bible is God's Word to man in real, historical situations."⁷⁵

Miller Burrows of Yale says: *"On the whole... archaeological work has unquestionably strengthened confidence in the reliability of the scriptural record. More than one archaeologist has found his respect for the Bible increased by the experience of excavation in Palestine."*⁷⁶

The inscription reads "Pontius Pilate, Prefect of Judea".

The collective evidence of Biblical archaeology to date only increases our faith in the Bible. Sir Frederic Kenyon, director and principal librarian of the British Museum, said: *"The trend of all of this increased knowledge has been to confirm the authority of the books of the Old Testament while it illuminates their interpretation. Destructive criticism is thrown on the defensive; and the plain man may read his Bible confident that, for anything that modern research has to say, the Word of God shall stand forever."*⁷⁷

When I was in the Holy Land I had the opportunity to personally see many of these archaeological sites and the artifacts from them. One interesting one was a stone found at an amphitheater by the sea of Caesarea. There archaeologists unearthed a stone with Pontius Pilate's name on it. He had built the theater and dedicated it to his Emperor, Tiberius. That stone provides us with the only existing extra-Biblical reference to Pontius Pilate. I saw that stone and my wife took my picture standing by it. *So the stones are still crying out in support of the Bible!*

No doubt the most famous and significant archaeological find to date was made – not by a professional archaeologist – but by a Bedouin shepherd boy looking for a stray sheep. When he accidentally threw a

---

75 David Virtue, "Archaeologist Finds Bible Best Historical Source," *North Carolina Christian Advocate*, Oct. 22, 1978, p. 3.
76 Millar Burrows, What Mean These Stones? Quoted by Paul Little, *Know Why You Believe*, Chicago: InterVarsity Press, 1968, p. 49.
77 Frederic Kenyon, *Journal of Transactions of the Victoria Institute.* Quoted by Paul Little, Know Why You Believe, Chicago: InterVarsity Press, 1968, pp. 57-58.

stone into a cave and heard it break something, he climbed up to the rock cliffs to see what he had broken. What resulted was the find to the now famous "Dead Sea Scrolls" of the Qumran community. That colossal find has done much for both Old and New Testament Biblical Studies. Let me share a few significant things from that discovery.

THE DEAD SEA SCROLLS

In 1947-1948 one of the greatest archaeological discoveries relevant to the Bible was made. It occurred in some caves around a plateau located 7½ miles south of the city of Jericho. The area is exceedingly desolate and foreboding. High up on the rocky cliffs of this area there are a number of caves. Below the caves there is a rather large plateau believed to have originated in the 8th to 7th centuries B.C. The site had been occupied in the time of the kings of Judah. King Uzziah, who "**built towers in the desert and dug many cisterns**" (II Chron. 26:10), appears to have built a fortified post and dug a circular cistern there. The place is commonly identified today with the "**City of Salt**" mentioned in Joshua 15:62. However, the most important occupation of this area was between 130 B.C. and A.D. 70. [78]

It appears that during that time, the area became an important Jewish religious center (about 135 B.C.) but was abandoned temporarily after a great earthquake in 31 B.C. The Jews again occupied it until A.D. 68 when the Romans took it in conjunction with their seizure of Jerusalem – which consummated in A.D. 70 with the destruction of both the temple and the city of Jersulem. Jews again used it during the Jewish revolt under Bar Kochba (Simeon Benkosebah) from about 132-135 A.D.[79]

---

78 F. F. Bruce, *New Light from the Dead Sea Scrolls*, Holman Study Bible, Philadelphia: A.J. Holman Co., pp. 1265-1266).
79 B*ible and Spade*, Winter, 1978, Vol. 7, No. 1, pp. 5-6.

Qumran was the center of a Jewish religious community for the better part of 200 years. Some 200-400 people are thought to have lived there at one time – presumably in a celibate lifestyle. Most scholars now believe that they were a group known as the Essenes, a very strict religious group of separatists. They had opposed the influence upon them to be assimilated into the pagan culture of their day, so they withdrew to the wilderness. In this way they believed they would be a people prepared for the Lord, ready to be His chosen and fitted instruments when the time came for Him to act decisively in the world. They drew their Biblical authority for this from Isaiah 40:3: "**In the desert prepare the way for the Lord; make straight in the wilderness a highway for our God.**"

The date of the community and subsequently the date of the scrolls can be rather accurately established by five points of reference:

1. Carbon 14 tests on the linen wrappings of the scrolls (c. 327 B.C.-A.D. 73);

2. A large amount of coins found in the community (c. 135 B.C.-A.D. 68);

3. Pottery chronology for the jars in which the scrolls were found;

4. Comparative paleography (science of ancient handwriting analysis);

5. Linguistic analysis of Aramaic documents found in the caves.[80]

Content of the Caves

The various caves yielded remains of over 500 books – no doubt belonging to the library of the Qumran community. Many of these books are only small fragments and the merest scraps. Some had literally been used by the local rat population for nests! Their preservation was largely due to the hot, dry climate of that particular Dead Sea region.

---

80 (*Bible and Spade*, Winter, 1978, Vol. 7, No. 1, pp. 5-6).

Cave One was an archaeological bonanza! It yielded literally thousands of manuscript fragments as well as fragments of the jars and cloth that had wrapped and housed the scrolls. The manuscripts from Cave One differ from those found in the other caves, in that they had been placed in earthenware jars before being deposited in the caves. The residents of Qumran had no doubt hidden their Scriptural treasures in the caves for protection during a period of opposition and siege – with the hopes of later returning and claiming them.  That opportunity never came for them and so for centuries the scrolls remained hidden and unknown to the modern world. But in the providence of God, a casual toss of a stone into cave by a Bedouin lad broke a jar, and soon sent shock waves throughout the world of Biblical archaeology!

Between 1948 and 1956, archaeologists and Bedouins located some 270 caves altogether in the region. Of these, 40 yielded pottery and other objects. However, only in 11 caves were manuscripts found like those of Cave One. Altogether there have been found over 100 copies of Old Testament books in Hebrew and Aramaic. In addition to pieces of Hebrew scripture, the caves also yielded fragments of the Greek translation of the Old Testament commonly called the Septuagint. William F. Albright acclaimed this find: "The greatest manuscript discovery of modern times", and dated the great Isaiah scroll (now referred to as 1Q Isa around 100 B.C.) About its authenticity he said, *"What an absolutely incredible find! And there can happily not be the slightest doubt in the world about the genuineness of the manuscript."* Take a moment now to see the outline of the contents of Caves One through Eleven (Appendix III, p. 211.)

Significance for Biblical Studies

1. It is no longer possible to date portions of entire Old Testament books as late as some scholars used to date them. ***You cannot now date any Biblical book later than the early second century B.C.***

2. The Dead Sea Scrolls do not support the existence of a "deutero" or "trito" Isaiah – at least not during the second century B.C. The complete Isaiah scroll and the long fragment of it from Cave One both *treat the book as a unit* and not as several sections.

> "Why talk of two Isaiahs when most people don't know of one"
> (D.L. Moody)

3. They give new information on the history of the Hebrew language, trends in spelling, formation of word, and pronunciation. They also prove that **Hebrew was not a completely dead language during New Testament times** because many kinds of literature were being written in Hebrew: religious, commercial, contractural and military. We gain clearer meanings of some Hebrew words that were not previously clear in Old Testament usage. Since the Revised Standard Version of the Bible was under translation when these discoveries were made, some of them were included in that translation.

4. But the biggest issue solved by the Dead Sea Scrolls was the mater of **textual corruption**. When it comes to Old Testament studies, we do not have the abundance of manuscripts like we do of the New Testament. Until the Dead Sea Scroll discovery, the previous oldest existent Hebrew manuscript was the Masoretic text dating to about 900 A.D. The great Isaiah scroll from Qumran dates from 150-100 B.C. – so **with the discovery of that one scroll Biblical archaeology made a jump of 1,000 years**!

Now we have a real tangible way to check to see how much textual corruption has occurred by all the hand copying by the scribes for those hundreds of years! The result? *When you lay the 900 A.D. scroll side by side with the 150 B.C. scroll, there is practically no difference*! **There is absolutely no doctrinal difference and little verbal variance**! As Howard F. Vos, professor of history and archaeology at Kings' College, put it:

> *"Probably it is reasonably correct to say that there is at least 95 percent agreement between the various biblical texts found near the Dead Sea and the Old Testament we have had all along. Most of the variations are minor, and none of the doctrines have been put in jeopardy."*[81]

5. As Professor Vos says, there is some **minor textual variance**. Let me share another quotation that will demonstrate the nature of those textual variances: *"A comparison of Isaiah 53 (of the Masoretic Text and the Dead Sea Scroll of Isaiah 53) shows that only 17 letters differ from the Masoretic text. Ten of these are mere differences in spelling, like our 'honor' or 'honour', and produce no change in the meaning at all. Four more are very minor differences, such as the presence of the conjunction, which is often a matter of style. The other three letters are the Hebrew word for 'light' which is added after 'they shall see' in verse 11.* **Out of 166 words in this chapter, only this one word is really in question, and it does not at all change the sense of the passage.** *This is typical of the whole manuscript."*[82]

Roland DeVaux underscored the same thing: *"And so new material has been provided for textual criticism, but we must at once add that the differences only have a bearing on minor points: if certain restorations can now be proposed with more confidence, and some obscure passages become clear,* **the content of the Bible is not changed.**"[83]

Concerning the almost unbelievable accuracy of the copy work by the scribes for hundreds of years, F.F. Bruce said: *"A few scribal errors, indeed, found their way into the text in the course of the thousand years separating the Qumran manuscripts from the Masoretic*

---

[81] "Archaeology and the Text of the Old Testament", *Bible and Spade*, Winter, 1978, Vol. 7, No. 1, p. 14.
[82] R. Laird Harris, "How Reliable is the Old Testament Text?" *Can I Trust My Bible.* Quoted by Paul Little, *Know Why You Believe*, Chicago: InterVarsity Press, 1968, p. 41.
[83] Roland DeVaux, "The Bible and the Ancient Near East." Quoted by Howard Vos, "Archaeology and the Text of the Old Testament," *Bible and Spade*, Winter, 1978, p. 14.

manuscripts; the impressive feature was that these were so few and relatively unimportant."[84]

The Bible scholar, R. Laird Harris concludes: *"We can now be sure that copyists worked with great care and accuracy on the Old Testament, even back to 225 B.C. At that time there were two or three types of text available for copying. These types differed among themselves so little, however, that we can infer that still earlier copyists had also faithfully and carefully transmitted the Old Testament text. Indeed it would be rash skepticism that would now deny that we have our Old Testament in a form very close to that used by Ezra when he taught the law to those who had returned from the Babylonian captivity."*[85]

Gleason Archer summarizes the Dead Sea Scroll discoveries as follows: *"Nothing in the new discoveries from the Qumran caves endangers the essential reliability and authority of our standard Hebrew Bible text."*[86]

The big question that arises in one's mind as he compares these two texts – separated by 1,000 years, and yet essentially the same – is *"How?* Please explain how people without the aid of a modern printing press could hand copy portions of scripture for hundreds of years with as few textual variations as the Dead Sea Scrolls have from the much later Masoretic text." The answer lies in the work of the scribes.

Thank God for the Scribes!

"There was already good reason to believe that the Jewish scribes of the first thousand years A.D. carried out their work of copying and

---

84 F. F. Bruce, *The Books and the Parchments,* Westwood: Fleming H. Revell Co., 1963, p. 1269.
85 R. Laird Harris, "How Reliable is the Old Testament Text?" *Can I Trust My Bible.* Quoted by Paul Little, *Know Why You Believe,* Chicago: InterVarsity Press, 1968, p. 42.
86 Gleason Archer, *A Survey of the Old Testament,* Chicago: Moody Press, 1964, p. 25.

recopying the Hebrew Scriptures with the utmost fidelity. The new discoveries bore impressive testimony to this fidelity."[87]

The Bible is unlike any other book of antiquity in its transmission. **No other book had such a dedicated group of scribes – generation after generation who existed solely to copy the Scriptures**! Today with all the modern conveniences – computers, scanners, copiers, printing presses, etc. – we just cannot fully appreciate the dedication of these men! What an exhausting procedure they went through day after day, week after week, month after month, year after year – just to ensure the accurate transmission of Scriptures. How would you like to have the job of hand copying the entire Old Testament?

Their procedure was as follows: they would copy a line from Scripture, letter after letter after letter until they had finished it. They would then go back and count the letters in the line and put the number at the end of it. They began to copy the next line following the same procedure. When they had finished a page or column using this procedure, they would then go back and count the letters all over again – and if the two sets of figures did not perfectly match up – *that page would be destroyed!* It was just that kind of fanatical dedication to the accuracy of the Scriptures by the scribes that made it possible for two texts a thousand years apart to be essentially the same almost down to the letter! We will never know their names – but we eternally owe them a debt of thanksgiving!

Conclusion

The Dead Sea Scrolls demonstrate the accuracy and trustworthiness of the Bible. Every one who struggles with honest doubts should take heart! Remember that the evidence is on the side of faith and not on the side of doubt – and archaeology constantly demonstrates it! F.F. Bruce said that the witness of the Dead Sea Scrolls is that "The general Bible

---

[87] F. F. Bruce, *The Books and the Parchments*, Westwood: Fleming H. Revell Co., 1963, p. 1269.

reader... *could go on using the familiar text with increased confidence in its essential accuracy.*"[88]

There has not been an argument brought up against the Bible that does not have an answer. If you think that you have found one, you would do well to place your confidence in the trustworthiness of the Scriptures – which have proven themselves accurate time and time again in the face of doubt, opposition and skepticism. Archaeology is increasingly demonstrating that we would do better to place our faith more and more in the Bible – and less and less in our limited knowledge, the latest theological opinions, or "scholarly research"! *Many are the hammers of doubt and skepticism that have beaten upon the anvil of God's Word – but the hammers all lie broken on the ground and the anvil stands firm!*

An article in Time magazine speaks rather cogently to this issue: "*In 100 licensed sites in Israel, archaeological digging continues to turn up new evidence that the Bible is often surprisingly accurate in historical particulars, more so than earlier generations of scholars ever suspected...After more than two centuries of facing the heaviest scientific guns that could be brought to bear, the Bible has survived – and is perhaps the better for the siege. Even on the critics' own terms – historical fact – the Scriptures seem more acceptable now than they did when the regionalists began the attack...The miraculous can be demythologized, the marvel explained, but the persistent message of the Bible will not go away. Both in the Jewish and Christian Bibles it is irreducible; some time, somewhere, God intervened in history to help man...ordinary human history was interrupted and has never since been the same.*"[89]

Human history has indeed been redemptively interrupted by God Himself! The Bible records it – and archaeology is testifying to it! In the words of Sir Frederick Kenyon: "*The Christian can take the whole Bible in his hand and say without fear or hesitation that he holds in it the true Word of God, handed down without extensible loss from generation to generation throughout the centuries.*"

---

88   Ibid.
89

Let's turn from the Dead Sea Scrolls to perhaps the most archaeologically earth-shaking discovery – the civilization of Ebla.

THE CIVILIZATION OF EBLA

After 10 years of work, two Italian scientists, Paolo Matthiae and Giovanni Pettinato, from the University of Rome have made one of the greatest archaeological discoveries of modern times. Many archaeologists and scientists place it on the level of the Dead Sea Scroll find of 1947. The discoveries there were not of biblical texts like at Qumran – but of a hitherto practically unknown civilization which casts some very important light on the *pre-patriarchal background of the Old Testament*.

A Word About Ancient History

Since the discoveries at Ebla have to do with ancient history and early language, let's look at the historical context in which to place Ebla. The first civilized inhabitants of ancient Babylonia (modern Iraq) were the *Sumerians* – perhaps as early as 5,000 B.C. They founded the first cities, and they also developed an elaborate pictographic system of writing with some two thousand signs. These signs are preserved for us on *cuneiform* (clay tablets) documents, and are considered to be the forerunner of the alphabet. Signs and sounds were put together, and writing as we know it was born. The Sumerians and their script – *Sumerian* – dominated the area for more than a thousand years. Finally they succumbed to the great Sargon – a western Semite – who built his *Akkadian* empire upon the conquered Sumerian one. He and his successors retained the Sumerian writing. In the Ebla tablets studied thus far, much of the language is Sumerian. The remainder has now been dubbed *Eblaite*.

ANCIENT EBLA

There is a 50 foot high mound covering 140 acres (40 miles from the

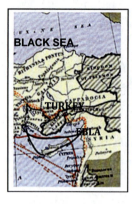

modern city of Aleppo, in Northern Syria). It is now referred to as *"Tell Mardikh"*. In 1968, the two Italian scientists discovered an inscribed statue there which confirmed the Tell as the location of ancient Ebla. Our only previous knowledge of the existence of Ebla was found in ancient Sumerian and Akkadian texts, and on the world's oldest known map, dating from c. 2360-2180 B.C. (known as the old Akkadian period), the name on the map clearly reads: *"Settlement of the fortress of Ebla"*. However, no scientist, historian or archaeologist ever could have guessed at the importance of Ebla before its discovery. Their excavations reveal the existence of a very powerful civilization which literally reached from the Red Sea to Turkey and east to Mesopotamia. Previous to this discovery, scholars considered Mesopotamia – first dominated by the Sumerians and then the Akkadians – and Egypt to be the major civilizations in the area. The area of Ebla was thought to be only a buffer between them and a cultural wasteland of insignificant villages inhabited only by nomads.

Dr. Ignace J. Gelb of the University of Chicago Oriental Institute said: *"This find struck the scholarly world like a thunderbolt… These discoveries reveal a new culture, a new language, a new history. Ebla was a mighty kingdom on an equal footing with the most powerful states of the time."* [90]

Indeed, so powerful did Ebla's kings become that they apparently contended with Sargon of Akkad, founder of the world's first empire, for domination of the Euphrates River. The struggle ended when Sargon defeated the Eblaites sometime before 2300 B.C. Sargon's victory inscription read: *"He worshiped the god Dagan, who gave him from that time onwards the upper Country, Mari, Yarmuti, and Ebla, as far as the Forest of Cedars and the Mountain of Silver."* [91]

---

90 Howard LaFay, "Ebla: Splendor of an Unknown Empire," *National Geographic*, Dec. 1978.
91 Ibid.

However, this conquest was probably more of an economic exaction rather than an actual conquest. For less than a century later, Sargon's grandson, Naram-Sin captured Ebla and burned it – probably about 2250 B.C. When he defeated Ebla, Naram-Sin likewise erected a monument to himself which read: *"Naram-Sin, the strong, the conqueror of...Ebla, never before subdued in history."*[92]

But Ebla again rose from this defeat – finally to be defeated about 2,000 B.C., never to rise again. From that time until the 1960's, Ebla was lost in antiquity and obscurity. This archaeological discovery, however, eloquently proves that the area of Ebla was not a "cultural backwater" as was previously believed – but an advanced culture with a sophisticated system of keeping records, thus all of the tablets. It was a kingdom second to none in importance of its day in the Near East. At its zenith of power, Ebla had a population of a quarter of a million. The bureaucracy of the city was much like our bureaucracy today! It consisted of 4,700 officials, run by 103 leaders who had 210 aides – sounds just like the U.S. government doesn't it?

This discovery also shows that Ebla was a polytheistic religious people, much like the other nations of that day – with an army of scribes who were the official record keepers.

Historical Significance of Ebla

The Ebla discovery clearly represents the largest 3rd millennium find of ancient clay tablets ever. They come from that ancient city's Royal Archives – reputedly now **the oldest governmental archives ever discovered**. They include the oldest *bilingual texts* ever found. These texts contain thousands of Sumerian words with their equivalent in Eblaite. There are also scores of economic texts that reveal a flourishing economy; *legal documents* – hence the earliest law code (one of these stated the death penalty for raping a virgin); *mythological texts, treaties,* and many others.

---

92 Ibid.

Some of these tablets were "supertablets" over a foot square which contained up to 6,000 lines of inscription!

Because of the discovery of the statue in 1968 confirming the location of ancient Ebla, a renewed effort went into the dig. As a result, in 1974 the first 42 clay tablets were found. Then by 1976 over 17,000! Dr. Pittinato said: "*All the other texts of this period recovered to date do not total a fourth of these from Ebla.*"[93]

All of the evidence is not nearly in yet. Because of the large volume of tablets found, it will take many years to fully assess all of the evidence. Also, the scientists are slow to release it because of possible political conflicts with the Syrian government who just might stop the dig. So predictably, the emphasis is on the *cultural and historical* rather than the Biblical aspects of the discovery. Archaeological discoveries that have a strong emphasis on Jewish history are not popular in Arab lands!

But even the historical and cultural implications are literally earth-shaking: "*Ebla reveals an ancient empire that alters forever our perception of ancient history...these documents...have scholars rethinking civilzation's formative years.*"[94] Historians are already saying that this discovery "*...will rewrite the history of the ancient Middle East...The ultimate impact on the recent construction of history in civilization is incalculable.*"[95] David Noel Freedman, noted University of Michigan archaeologist who is working with the Italians on the discovery, said: "*It is as if we were suddenly to find out about Rome and the Roman Empire.*"[96]

Biblical Significance of Ebla

Time magazine said: "*It provides the best evidence to date that some of*

---

93 Howard LaFay, "Ebla: Splendor of an Unknown Empire," *National Geographic*, Dec. 1978.
94 Ibid.
95 Lowell Cauffiel, "Archaeological Find Lends Credibility to Bible History," *National Courier*, Nov. 26, 1976, p. 6.
96 "A New Third World," *Time*, Oct. 18, 1976, p. 63.

the people described in the Old Testament actually existed." [97] Let me briefly summarize some of the Biblical implications:

1. The tablets contain **accounts of a creation and a flood** which are strikingly similar to those found in the Old Testament and ancient Babylonian literature.

2. There are over 5,000 geographic names appearing on the tablets – and some have Biblical importance. They refer to a place called *"Urusalima"* – clearly Ebla's name for Jerusalem – making it unquestionably the **oldest reference to the Holy City** by hundreds of years. Other Biblical cities like Hazor are also mentioned. Some of the tablets document trade with a number of Old Testament cities and places – including *Sodom* and *Gomorrah*, before their destruction. It is also very interesting that these five cities of the plain, southeast of the Dead Sea, are listed in the same order on the Ebla tablets as in the Biblical list: Sodom, Gomorrah, Admah, Zeboiim, Bela (Gen. 14:2). So this is yet another **confirmation of Biblical geography.** As the archaeologist Freeman said: "Behind the tradition in the Bible about these cities there is now established fact."[98]

3. The Ebla tablets also make frequent mention of "Ebrium" or "Eber", identified in Genesis as the great-great-great grandson of Noah and the great-great-great-great grandfather of Abraham (Gen. 10:24; 11:14-16). Many other personal names similar to those in the Bible are also mentioned[99]:

---

97 "A New Third World," *Time*, Oct. 18, 1976, p. 63.
98 Edwin Yamauchi, "Ebla: A Spectacular Discovery," *Evangelical Newsletter*, De. 1, 1978, p. 4.
99 LaSor, William S, (Professor of Old Testament, Fuller Seminary) "Major Archaeological Discoveries at Tell Mardikh", *Christianity Today*, Sept. 24, 1976.

Personal Names found in the Ebla Tablets

ab-ra-mu	Abram
is-ra-ilu	Israel
e-sa-um	Esau?
sa-u-lum	Saul
Mi-ka-ilu	Michael
mi-ka-ya	Micah
da-u-dum	David? (found in no other ancient text other than the Bible)

Concerning the **appearance of such Old Testament names** as *Eber,* archaeologist Freeman says: *"We always thought of ancestors like Eber as symbolic. Nobody ever regarded them as historic – at least not until these tablets were found. Fundamentalists could have a field day with this one, and rightly so."*[100] Freeman continues: *"For years, there has been unwarranted skepticism by scholars, and that includes myself, that many of these Old Testament places and personalities actually existed. Most of us regarded the Biblical information as pretty legendary."*[101]

Speaking further of the implications of the Ebla find for Biblical understanding, Freeman concludes: *"The little dessert that goes with it is that we can get insight into the background of the Bible. If any scholar would have asked these questions 10 years ago, he would have been laughed at."*[102]

Concerning the potential importance of this discovery for Biblical studies, Dr. LaSor said: *"We know that these were various peoples in the region of Syria and Palestine prior to the arrival of Abraham and the Patriarchs, and that these peoples played a significant part in molding the events recorded in the Bible. No longer is it possible to think of Abraham as the creation of post-exilic writers. The Tell Mardikh discoveries, to be sure, do not 'prove the Bible.' Nor can any archaeological discovery. The only way to prove the Bible is to take it on faith and apply it to life. It will prove itself to be true. But Tell Mardikh will probably throw a great amount of light on some of the background of the book of Genesis and the events it records."*[103]

4. It is also interesting to note that a line on one tablet says: *"The kings came anointed with oil"* indicating that the Eblaite kings were

---

100 " A New Third World," *Time,* Oct. 18, 1976, p. 63.
101 Lowell Cauffiel, "Archaeological Find Lends Credibility to Bible History," *National Courier,* Nov. 26, 1976, p. 6.
102 "A New Third World," *Time,* Oct. 18, 1976, p. 63.
103 William S. LaSor, "Major Archaeological Discoveries at Tell Mardikh," *Christianity Today,* Sept. 24, 1976, p. 49.

anointed with oil much like Old Testament kings like Saul and David were (I Sam. 10:1; II Sam. 2:4).

5. The Ebla tablets also have a wealth of listing of gods, in fact over 500! Many of their names for pagan deities are also found in the Old Testament:

Ebla Tablets	Old Testament
Il	El
Dagan	Dagon
Kamish	Chemosh
Ashtar	Astarte
Adad	Hadad
Rasap	Resheph
Spish	Shemesh

Highly significant is the fact that possible references to the Hebrew name for God – Yahweh – have been found. One scholar concludes: *"So Ya or Yahweh was known at Ebla sometime in the 3rd millennium – although of course he was not the same all powerful, transcendent and monotheistic God later worshipped by the Israelites."* [104]

6. Perhaps the greatest impact that the Ebla find will have on Old Testament studies is linguistic. The tablets are in Sumerian and a previously unknown Canaanite dialect now dubbed "Eblaite" – now the oldest known Semitic language in writing. Eblaite is very similar to Hebrew and Phoenician – but predating them by at least 1400 years. Our previous oldest written discoveries from the ancient Near East are cuneiform documents in:

    Sumerian
    Old Akkadian
    Egyptian Hieroglyphics

---

104 Adam Mikaya, "The Politics of Ebla," *Biblical Archaeology Review*, Sept./Oct. 1978, p. 6.

However, linguistically speaking, these are quite remote from Biblical Hebrew or Aramaic. The closest thing we have to Biblical writings are *Ugaritic tablets from Ras Shamara*. However, this Ugaritic is written in alphabetic cuneiform, which provides *consonants only*. Biblical Hebrew was written with the consonants only – leaving the vowels to be supplied by the reader. However, the vowels were added by the Masoretes[105] somewhere between the 6th and 10th centuries A.D. These vowel points indicated the proper vocalization.

So because of the Masoretes we know how Hebrew in their day was pronounced. But, we have very little certain evidence of how Hebrew was vocalized in the time of the prophets. Here is where the Ebla tablets may help – because this discovery provides vowels as well as the consonants.

William LaSor said: "If the language (of Ebla) indeed proves to be Northwest Semitic, it will antedate by hundreds of years all remains that we have of these languages. The impetus that this will give to Semitic studies goes beyond our imagination."[106] One of the Italian archaeological discoverers of Ebla said: "On the basis of vocabulary, grammatical signals, and sentence structure, this heretofore unknown language was more closely related to Hebrew than any of the other principal Semitic languages."[107] Archaeologist Freeman concludes: *"The Ebla tablets are more significant for elucidating the Hebrew Bible than any other archaeological discovery ever unearthed."*[108]

---

[105] Masoretes: Jewish scholars, resident chiefly at Tiberias in Palestine. The word comes from masorah meaning tradition – so they were adding the traditional pronunciation. The text is known as the *Masoretic Text*.
[106] William LaSor, "Major Archaeological Discoveries at Tell Mardikh," *Christianity Today*, Sept. 24, 1976, p. 49.
[107] Paul G. Maloney, "Assessing Ebla," *Biblical Archaeology Review*, March, 1978, p. 7.
[108] Adam Mikaya, "The Politics of Ebla," *Biblical Archaeology Review*, Sept./Oct., 1978, p. 6.

Conclusion

Once again the *"stones are crying out"* in defense of the historic trustworthiness of the Bible. Like the Dead Sea Scroll find, this discovery will likewise take years to fully decipher. We only hope and pray that the delicate and tense situation of the Middle East will not prohibit full excavation and disclosure of the Ebla civilization. I believe that there is much more Biblical confirmation buried there!

The basalt torso of Ibbit-Lim, King of Ebla. The discovery of this fragment of a statue at Tell Mardikh in 1968 identified the site for the first time as ancient Ebla.

"The Bible has withstood many attacks through the centuries from enemies of all sorts, but in the last century it has been called upon to withstand repeated attacks in the house of its friends. The Bible is now freely doubted by the preachers in the pulpits and the teachers in the seminary classrooms of our land" (R. Laird Harris).

Quotations for Further Reflection

- *Let faith support us where reason fails, and we shall think because we believe, not in order that we may believe.* [109]

- *A substantial proof for the accuracy of the Old Testament text has come from archaeology. Numerous discoveries have confirmed the historical accuracy of the biblical documents, even down to the occasional use of obsolete names of foreign kings....Archaeologist Nelson Glueck asserts, "It may be stated categorically that no archaeological discovery has ever*

---

109   A. W. Tozer, *The Knowledge of the Holy*, New York, NY: HarperCollins, 1961, p. 6.

controverted a biblical reference. Scores of archaeological findings have been made which confirm in clear outline or exact detail historical statements in the Bible."[110]

- *While many have doubted the accuracy of the Bible, time and continued research have consistently demonstrated that the Word of God is better informed than its critics. In fact, while thousands of finds from the ancient world support in broad outline and often in detail the biblical pictures, not one incontrovertible find has ever contradicted the Bible.*[111]

---

110 Josh McDowell, *The New Evidence that Demands a Verdict*, Nashville: Thomas NelsonPublishers, 1999, p. 89.
111 Ibid., p. 98.

Part 2
How

PREREQUISITES FOR STUDYING THE WORD

"Oh, how I love Your law! I meditate on it all day long. Your commands make me wiser than my enemies, for they are ever with me. I have more insight than all my teachers, for I meditate on Your statutes. I have more understanding than the elders, for I obey Your precepts. I have kept my feet from every evil path so that I might obey Your word. I have not departed from Your laws, for You Yourself have taught me. How sweet are Your words to my taste, sweeter than honey to my mouth! I gain understanding from Your precepts; therefore I hate every wrong path" (Ps. 119:97-104).

From the above verses we see a ***heart attitude*** in David that was the necessary prerequisite for understanding God's Word. The world is sadly lacking in wisdom and understanding today! Our world is filled with colleges, universities and community colleges. Because of humanistic philosophy we have practically made a god out of education. For years, we have operated under the false belief that man could basically solve all of his ills through education. Given the proper time and education – we could educate man from ignorance, darkness

and superstition to enlightenment. We would go from "protoplasm to paradise" – all through our own educational systems, we would truly be "man come of age!" However, we never seem to be able to quite get there! Paul said to Timothy that one of the signs of the last days of civilization would be that man would be "**always learning but never able to acknowledge the truth**" (II Tim. 3:7).

If we are going to be able to really learn and come to truth – and experience what David said about having "**more insight than all my teachers**" – then we are going to have to meet God's conditions for receiving true knowledge. What are those conditions or prerequisites for properly studying God's Word?

1. First, *we must be spiritually alive*. Jesus said: "**The Spirit gives life; the flesh counts for nothing. The words I have spoken to you are spirit and they are life**" (John 6:63). Paul said: "**The man without the Spirit does not accept the things that come from the Spirit of God, for they are foolishness to him, and he cannot understand them, because they are spiritually discerned**" (I Cor. 2:14). Several other times in his writings Paul reminds his hearers of when they were dead to the things of God, and that it was the disobedience of man that led to their hardness of heart. "**For although they knew God, they neither glorified Him as God nor gave thanks to Him, but their thinking became futile and their foolish hearts were darkened**" (Rom. 1:21). In Ephesians he calls this "*Gentile living*," and says:

    "**So I tell you this…you must no longer live as the Gentiles do, in the futility of their thinking. They are darkened in their understanding, and separated from the life of God because of the ignorance that is in them due to the hardening of their hearts**" (Eph. 4:17-18).

Likewise, Paul reminds the Corinthians that disobedience leads to spiritual blindness by the "prince of this world." He says: "**The god of this age has blinded the minds of unbelievers, so that they cannot** see the light of the gospel of the glory of Christ, who is the image of God" (II Cor. 4:4).

So until a person is *regenerated by the Holy Spirit of God* he is incapable of perceiving spiritual truth! He no more has the capacity of understanding God's Word than a blind man does of perceiving color or a deaf person does of perceiving sound!

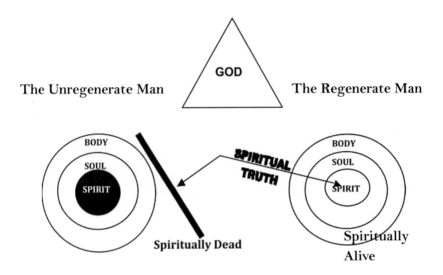

2. Secondly, **we must be spiritual and not carnal.** Tragically many Christians – even though they are truly regenerate – still walk more by the *flesh* or the old nature than *by the Spirit* and their new nature. Therefore, spiritual immaturity characterizes their life more than maturity in Christ. Paul discussed this warfare that goes on between the "**flesh**" and the "**Spirit**" in Romans 8:

> "Those who live according to the sinful nature have their minds set on what that nature desires; but those who live in accordance with the Spirit have their minds set on what the Spirit desires. The mind of sinful man is death, but the mind controlled by the Spirit is life and peace; the sinful mind is hostile to God. It does not submit to God's law, nor can it

do so. Those controlled by the sinful nature cannot please God" (Rom. 8:5-8).

This was the very problem that Paul had with those carnal Christians at Corinth! Therefore, he wrote to them and said: **"Brothers, I could not address you as spiritual but as worldly – mere infants in Christ. I gave you milk, not solid food, for you were not yet ready for it. Indeed, you are still not ready. You are still worldly..."** (I Cor. 3:1-3).

Earlier in that same Epistle, Paul further contrasted the light that may be received by the spiritually mature with that which the "babes in Christ" or Christians can receive: **"For I resolved to know nothing while I was with you except Jesus Christ and Him crucified...We do, however, speak a message of wisdom among the mature...God's secret wisdom..."** (I Cor. 2:2, 6-7).

Characteristics of the Spiritual Christian

Perhaps it would be helpful to look at some of the characteristics of the Spiritual Christian.

(1) The first and most obvious fact about the spiritual Christian is that he or she is seeking to **"walk by the Spirit"** (Gal. 5:16) as opposed to the flesh. It is not just a periodic or sporadic thing – but a lifestyle, as Paul said. The first characteristic – and the one from which the following ones are all derived – is that he is spiritual and not carnal. ***He walks by the Spirit.*** God's Holy Spirit becomes the very atmosphere of his life!

(2) The second thing that makes the difference between the carnal and spiritual Christian is this: *the carnal Christian still loves the things of this world more than the things of God.* Jesus clearly said that the heart attitude that finds favor with God is the one that has a ***spiritual hunger and thirst*** rather than a worldly one:

- "**Blessed are those who hunger and thirst for righteousness, for they will be filled** (satisfied)" (Matt. 5:6);

- "**...Jesus stood and said in a loud voice, 'If anyone is thirsty, let him come to Me and drink. Whoever believes in Me, as the Scripture has said, streams of living water will flow from within him'**" (Jn. 7:37-38).

The Bible makes it clear that God refuses to reveal Himself to just any casual passer-by! Jesus indicated this in His Sermon on the Mount when He said: "**Do not give dogs what is sacred; do not throw your pearls to pigs...**" (Matt. 7:6).

(3) A third important characteristic of the spiritual Christian is that he is *humble*. Christ said that the Holy Spirit would "**guide you into all truth**" (Jn. 16:13). It is a basic principle that the Spirit only leads the humble – never the proud!

James admonishes his hearers to "**...humbly accept the word planted in you, which can save you**" (James 1:21). Jesus said: "**I praise You, Father, Lord of heaven and earth, because You have hidden these things from the wise and learned, and revealed them to little children**" (Matt. 11:25).

The Apostle Paul reminded the Corinthian Christians how "**Not many of you were wise by human standards; not many were influential; not many were of noble birth**" but that "**God chose the foolish things of the world to shame the wise; God chose the weak things of the world to shame the strong**" (I Cor. 1:26-27).

If we expect the Holy Spirit to guide us into truth, we must have a humble, teachable spirit. As Roy Putnam said: *"I don't stand 'on the Word'; I rather stand 'under the Word' to be judged, chastened, corrected, quickened, and corrected by it."* The late Dr. Donald G. Barnhouse put it similarly when he said: *"Before I thunder in the court I try to stand barefoot before the Burning Bush."*

(4) Fourthly, the spiritual Christian is **obedient**. Jesus clearly said

that when our will was predisposed to obedience we would know the Father's will: "**If anyone chooses to do God's will, he will find out whether My teaching comes from God...**" (Jn. 7:17). Likewise, Jesus says: "**Whoever has My commands and obeys them, he is the one who loves Me. He who loves Me will be loved by My Father, and I too will love Him and show Myself to him**" (Jn. 14:21).

It is a spiritual principle that light begets light – "**in Your light we see light**" (Ps. 36:9). Therefore, we apply what we have learned – then and only then does God give us *more understanding*. Jesus said that light is not given to be hidden – but rather put on a lampstand so all could see (Mk. 4:21-25). Application is the proof of obedience! It is a law of life that "that which is not expressed dies." Jesus said the same thing in what I call the <u>***secret of spiritual growth***</u>: "**Whoever has will be given more, and he will have an abundance. Whoever does not have, even what he has will be taken from him**" (Matt. 13:12).

Here we see the most basic principle of life applied to spiritual truth: "either use it or lose it!" It is not *what I do to the Word – but what I allow the Word to do to me that's important!* "*Master the Book and then let it master you!*"

3. Thirdly, **we must be under doctrinal teaching**. Today millions of people – and sadly many Christians – are being *spiritually, emotionally and intellectually* "ripped off" by false prophets. These prophets often come under the guise of religious leaders, theologians, philosophers, and educators.

Consequently, because many Christians are not under sound doctrinal teaching they are being "**...tossed back and forth by the waves, and blown here and there by every wind of teaching and by the cunning and craftiness of men in their deceitful scheming**" (Eph. 4:14). St. Paul warned that this would happen – and that many would even prefer false teachers to true ones: "**For the time will come when men will not put up with sound doctrine. Instead, to suit their own desires, they will** gather around them a great number of teachers to say what their itching ears want to hear. They will turn their ears away from the truth and turn aside to myths" (II Tim. 4:3-4).

This turning aside from reality or truth to fantasy and mythology is certainly increasingly characteristic of the day and age in which we are living! Therefore more than ever Christians must "**Let the word of Christ dwell in you richly**" (Col. 3:16) – and this can only happen by being under sound Apostolic/Biblical teaching! There are a number of important passages that speak to this.

A. We note that this was one of the chief marks of the early church after Pentecost. They did not assume that just because they had received God's Holy Spirit that they could go out on their own. No! Luke records that "**they devoted themselves to the apostles' teaching…**" (Acts 2:42).

B. Another good example for the absolute need for doctrinal teaching is found in the account of *Philip's encounter with the Ethiopian eunuch.* This man was riding home from worshipping in Jerusalem, and while he was riding in his chariot he was reading from the Isaiah scroll. Philip came alongside him and asked if he understood what he was reading. The Ethiopian replied with great honesty: "**How can I, unless someone explains it to me?**" (Acts 8:31). This clearly teaches us that *much of the Bible cannot be understood without some guidance.*

This principle is also born out by the fact that Paul said that elders in the church must be "**able to teach**" (I Tim. 3:2), so that they "**…can encourage others by sound doctrine and refute those who oppose** (contradict) it" (Titus 1:9). Paul was vitally interested that "sound doctrine" be taught (Titus 2:1), and that it be entrusted into the hands of faithful men who would likewise instruct others: "**And the things you have heard me say in the presence of many witnesses entrust to reliable men who will also be qualified to teach others**" (II Tim. 2:2).

C. It is the role of the doctrinal teacher to *instruct the Believers in the faith* – as well as stir them to *stand for it and defend it before an unbelieving world*: "**...I felt I had to write and urge you to contend for the faith that was once for all entrusted to the saints**" (Jude 1:3).

D. Paul calls the church the "**...pillar and foundation of the truth**" (I Tim. 3:15). He then breaks forth in praise over the glory of the faith: "**Beyond all question, the mystery of godliness is great: He appeared in a body, was vindicated by the Spirit, was seen by angels, was preached among the nations, was believed on in the world, was taken up in glory**" (I Tim. 3:16)

Since the church is the "**pillar and foundation of the truth**" – it is absolutely necessary that *every believer be an active part of a church that faithfully teaches and applies the Word* – committed to proclaiming the Gospel!

4. Fourthly, ***we must be a diligent and disciplined student***. Many people today say they would like to be able to understand the Bible better – but *few are willing* to pay *the price of commitment to study*! Many ministers would like to be great expositors of the Word – but few will correct and rearrange their priorities and commit themselves to first things. It is not that the things they give themselves to are not important – but it is usually a matter of *the good being an enemy of the best*!

It is similar to what Jesus said to the Pharisees in another context, about their meticulous tithing: "**...You should have practiced the latter without leaving the former undone**" (Lk. 11:42). As the great Biblical expositor, John Stott, said: "The systematic *preaching* of the Word is impossible without a systematic *study* of the Word."

Under another heading we have already looked at the emphasis Paul placed on study where he said to Timothy: "**Do your best (be diligent) to present yourself to God as one approved,** a workman who does not need to be ashamed and who correctly handles the word of truth" (II Tim. 2:15).

Paul himself was a living testimony of this principle. We can see the quality of his study constantly coming through in his writings. *He never lost his commitment to reading and studying* – even in old age. When he writes Timothy to hurry to visit him, he says something that is very instructive for us concerning his study and devotional habits. He asks Timothy to bring "**my scrolls, especially the parchments**" (II Tim. 4:13). We do not know what the books were for sure – but no doubt the "**parchments**" referred to the Scriptures! Even as an old man in prison he never lost his desire to read, study and learn!

When it comes to the study of the Word – ***give God your best time***! I don't know what your best, most alert, wide-awake time of the day is – but whenever it is, *give it to God in prayer and the study of His Word*. Don't give Him your tired, worn-out, anemic leftovers! For most people that is the first thing in the morning after a good night's sleep. However, there are some people – and I am one of them – that are "night people" and find later hours good for reading, study and meditation. Please remember also that ***hurry is the death of prayer and study***! So the wise student will find his best hours – and prayerfully give them to God for the study of His Word!

SUMMARY OF PREREQUISITES FOR STUDYING THE WORD

1. We must be **spiritually alive**.

2. We must be **spiritual and not carnal**.

<u>Characteristics of a Spiritual Christian</u>:

A.   Walks by the Spirit
B.   Has a spiritual hunger and thirst;
C.   Has a humble, teachable spirit;
D.   He is obedient;

3. We must be **under doctrinal teaching**.

4. We must be **a diligent and disciplined student**.

Quotations for Further Reflection

- *How is it possible to say we believe in Jesus and yet see it make so little difference in how we live? Cathy [a carnal Christian] is a classic example of what we see all too often in the "modern" believer. Her faith operated exclusively in the realm of her personal, subjective, private experience...she made her decisions essentially as a moral relativist – what was right was dictated by the situation she was in, not from any consideration of whether her behavior violated any absolute truths...we try to control Jesus by limited Him to our terms. Jesus will accept our faith, but He will never accept our controls...He can only begin to be the Lord of your life today – not next Monday or next month but now. And the great and joyful paradox is that while He totally transforms us, He makes us more ourselves than ever before.*[112]

- *...O Christ...make us strong to overcome the desire to be wise and to be reputed wise by others as ignorant as ourselves.*[113]

---

112 Rebecca Manley Pippert, *Out of the Salt Shaker and Into the World*, Downers Grove, IL: Intervarsity Press, 1999, pp. 49-50, 54.
113 A. W. Tozer, *The Knowledge of the Holy*, New York, NY: HarperCollins, 1961, p. 59.

PRINCIPLES OF INTERPRETING THE WORD

"...the holy Scriptures...are able to make you wise for salvation through faith in Christ Jesus. All Scripture is God-breathed and is useful for teaching, rebuking, correcting and training in righteousness" (II Tim. 3:15-16).

This section really gets down to the meat of this entire study! All of the things thus far have helped us *intelligently approach and appreciate* the Word. Now we must apply it all – and correct application can only come from correct *interpretation*. Here is where the Word really becomes flesh to us personally! I cannot say too much about the importance of correctly interpreting God's Word. I believe that it grieves God far more to see His children abusing His Word than it does for Him to see His enemies attack it! Jesus said that the "**Scriptures could not be broken**" (Jn. 10:35), but the Holy Spirit through Peter, declared that they could be twisted to one's own destruction (II Pet. 3:16)! You need to make sure that your interpretation is correct. If your interpretation is wrong then your application will also be wrong! On one occasion Jesus corrected the Sadducees over their incorrect understanding of the resurrection, and said: "**You are in error because you do not know the Scriptures or the power of God**" (Matt. 22:29).

Their theology of the resurrection was completely wrong because of their wrong interpretation of the Scriptures. Remember: Twisted

Scripture can never result in straight theology! Since this is God's Word we need to make every effort to correctly understand it. John Stott said: *"If the Bible is indeed God's Word written, we should spare no pains and grudge no effort to discover what He has said (and says) in Scripture."*[114]

Let me introduce you to two words: *"hermeneutics"* and *"homiletics."* Those are two words that seminarians, preachers and theologians throw around a great deal – and they are of great importance for the serious Bible student. **Hermeneutics** is the science of interpreting scripture. **Homiletics**, on the other hand, is the art of preaching, teaching or communicating scripture. Good *homiletics* are derived from good *hermeneutics*. When preaching is poor, dull, uninteresting, irrelevant, etc., it is because of inadequate preparation in the area of hermeneutics.

Christ's homiletics (to put His preaching and teaching into our theological terms) were always captivating, relevant and life-changing. The officers who were sent to arrest Jesus on one occasion returned saying: "**No one ever spoke the way this man does**" (Jn. 7:46). After His great Sermon on the Mount, the Scripture says: "**...the crowds were amazed at His teaching, because He taught as one who had authority, and not as their teachers of the law**" (Matt. 7:28-29). Because His teachings (homiletics) were so very relevant to their lives, the people ... **listened to Him with delight**" (Mk. 12:37). They rejected and rebelled against the homiletics of the Scribes and Pharisees because they were burdensome, cumbersome, legalistic and irrelevant – but they flocked to Christ because His teaching was truth...reality!

Because the religious leaders of Christ's day did not correctly know God, they constantly abused His Scriptures. They were perhaps sincere and dedicated – but that is not enough. Jesus clearly taught that true worship must spring out of truth: "**...true worshipers will worship the Father in spirit and truth, for they are the kind of worshipers the Father seeks. God is spirit, and His worshipers must worship in spirit and in truth**" (Jn. 4:23-24). Truth, or "ultimate reality" as Webster

---

114 John Stott, *Understanding the Bible*, Glendale, CA: Regal Books, 1972, p. 206.

defines it, is something as *it really* is as opposed to what we might think or wish it to be. When we know God through His Holy Spirit – who witnesses to our spirit (Rom. 8:16) – then we can begin to worship Him according to truth. We worship God for Who He really is as opposed to how we previously conceived Him to be. Then and only then will our worship be pleasing to Him and fulfilling to us – and it all began with a correct understanding of His Word. The best interpreter of any book is its author, so the better we know the author the *better we understand the book*! Therefore, the better we know God through His Incarnate Word – as revealed in His Written Word – the better we will know and worship Him. *Knowledge of God and knowledge of His Word* are inseparably connected!

What are some of the basic principles of hermeneutics or interpreting God's Word?

1. **The Principle of Natural Interpretation**

    This has sometimes been called the "**principle of simplicity.**" That means that the Bible itself has no difficulty. If there is any problem, it is due to *our misunderstanding* and not with God's Word itself. **God has spoken to be understood!** He intended that Scripture be plain to its readers. We must approach the Bible with that basic presupposition in mind. When you or I speak, we speak to communicate...to be understood...to transmit truth. Now, that's the way it should be – but many people do not speak the truth and are thus liars! The Bible clearly says that man and God are different at this point. Whereas it is common or "natural" for man in his fallen condition to lie – the Bible clearly says that God cannot, and therefore does not, lie (Num. 23:19; Titus 1:12). He speaks to be understood – and all He speaks is truth for He is Truth!

    It is natural for us to expect that God has spoken to be clearly understood. It was the Gnostics who approached God and Scripture with the presupposition that in it were hidden all kinds of "secret" information that could only be known by themselves. They therefore stressed salvation through a secret gnosis or "knowledge". This movement was clearly rejected by the church, and rightly so! This same esoteric approach is often true of many of the contemporary cults today (see my book on: *Identifying And Dealing With The Cults*). God has not cloaked His will in secrecy so only a few may attain it. He has spoken to be *clearly understood and therefore obeyed*. This is the only natural way to approach God!

2. **The Principle of Comparative Interpretation**

This might also be called the "***principle of harmony***." This principle reminds us that **the Bible must be seen as a whole** - and every individual part must be interpreted within the context of the whole. When done so, one part will never contradict another! Since God has spoken to be understood, we can only expect to fully understand Him when we have studied and compared all He has said to us on a particular subject. Error always results when we isolate what He has said at one point, from everything else He has spoken on that matter. As F.F. Bruce said:

"Any part of the human body can only be properly explained in reference to the whole body. And any part of the Bible can only be properly explained in reference to the whole Bible."

Article XX of the Church of England says that no passage of Scripture may be so expounded "...that it be repugnant to another." So we must seek the "**whole will of God**" (Acts 20:27) on each issue as opposed to snatches! We must stress the principle of comparison: **compare Scripture with Scripture**! That means that the Bible is its own best commentary and therefore explains itself. Concerning this matter, Dr. Donald G. Barnhouse said:

"For any given doctrinal subject, read the entire volume, selecting every verse that bears on the truth under study. Put all of these passages together, and the **synthesis of the result is the true Bible doctrine on the question with which you are concerned**. *A verse from Moses, and one from Ezekiel, and one from Paul, put side by side, each illuminating*

the others, fit into the perfect pattern of the whole design and give the whole light which God has been pleased to reveal on that particular theme...Many heresies arise from a false interpretation of a single verse of Scripture, and the matter is even sadder when we realize that the interpretation would have been corrected if the heretic had taken time to collate all of the passages covering the subject on which he erred. The one sure method of continuing in the path of truth is to have before you all that the Bible reveals on any possible point of discussion." [115]

Barnhouse underscores the importance of the comparative method of interpretation by the following statement and example:

"The fathers and reformers never found it strange to take a verse out of Genesis and fit it to a verse in John, and to bring a verse from Job alongside to cast yet more light on a doctrine. Such a method, which would be outrageous in any other work, is a necessity in the study of the Bible...It would be impossible to know the Biblical doctrine that surrounds the familiar symbol of the Lamb without taking the account in the sacrifice of Abel, that of Abraham offering up Isaac, that of Moses and the Passover, and putting them together with the order of the day of atonement, to form the Foundation of the doctrine of the Lamb, as the atoning sacrifice of sin. Only then we can understand the continuing development of the doctrine throughout the rest of the Scriptures. In Isaiah, we discovered the first hint that the Lamb is to be a man (53:5-6). In the fourth Gospel, we see John the Baptist pointing to Jesus as the One who is God's Lamb, come to bear away the sin of the world (1:29). In the Epistles, we discover that Christ, our Passover, has been sacrificed for us (I Cor. 5:7); and by the time we reach the Revelation we are ready to join with the myriad's to sing: **"Worthy is the Lamb that was slain to receive power, and riches, and wisdom, and strength, and honor and glory, and blessing"** *(Rev. 5:12)...We must follow the method of bringing texts from all parts of Scripture and putting them together to form one coherent entity of doctrine."* [116]

When we learn to study and interpret the Bible comparatively we

---

115 Donald Grey Barnhouse, *The Invisible War*, Grand Rapids: Zondervan Publishing House, 1965, p. 12.
116 Donald Grey Barnhouse, *The Invisible War*, Grand Rapids: Zondervan Publishing House, 1965, pp. 14-15.

will have many of our surface difficulties solved – and will also begin to arrive at a more systematic theology.

There is one other matter along this line I would point out. Not every part of the Bible is equally clear. There are areas of ambiguity and obscurity. The Bible is silent on some issues. When you come to one of these areas remember the following:

A. *There are many clear passages on every major doctrine in the Bible.* On any area that is essential for our salvation and general well-being – the Bible is crystal clear!

B. When you come to a verse or subject that is not completely clear, *always interpret the obscure by the obvious.* God has clearly spoken on every area that we need revelation concerning – so interpret the cloudy by the clear. Don't get hung up or side-tracked on a verse that is hard to understand. Interpret it through other clear passages that speak to the issue at hand.

C. Finally, when you come to a point of doctrine where Christians of equal commitment, dedication and scholarship disagree – be careful! All Christians agree on 98% of doctrine – and that is the basis of their fellowship. The Bible does seem to allow some latitude of interpretation on some things (Sabbath observance, dietary habits, etc.), and we should do the same. So *never make a secondary doctrine a point of fellowship.* Don't make secondary issues the primary planks in your theological platform. Remember, someone has defined a fanatic as one who majors on the minors as though they were the majors!

Study scripture comparatively. Speak clearly where God has...be silent where He is silent...and never equate your opinions with *His Will* or your doctrine with *His*!

3. **The Principle of Literal Interpretation**

This is a principle that many people either radically misunderstand

– or vehemently rebel against. The moment you mention "literal interpretation" people begin to say: *"Surely you don't think that the Bible is to be taken literally, do you?!"* You see, there is a common fallacy that says: *"Well, there are many interpretations of the Bible, and mine is as good as yours!"* That may sound good to us – but it is just not true! Not all interpretations of the Bible are equally valid; many are absolutely heretical! Many of the interpretations of the religious leaders of Christ's day were false. The same was true of the false prophets in the Old Testament, and it is true of the cults today. All interpretations of Scripture are not equally valid. Again we remind you of Peter's warning about people who "**distort...Scriptures, to their own destruction**" (II Pet. 3:16).

The problem over literal interpretation, I believe, comes over our understanding of what is really meant – and conversely not meant – by the phrase "literal interpretation." Bernard Ramm defined it this way: *"To interpret literally is nothing more or less than interpreting words and sentences in their normal, usual, customary proper designation."*

When you or I speak, we expect to be taken literally! For example, suppose I say to my children: "Please go to your rooms and clean them up." Now suppose they begin to interpret *my words to them as many try to interpret God's Word.* They might begin to say among themselves: *"Well, you know that Daddy did not <u>literally</u> mean for us to go to our rooms and clean them...after all, there are many ways of interpreting what he has said!"* Far from it! I expect to be interpreted literally – and you do too. If that were not the case communication would not be possible! We would always be wondering: *"Do they mean that literally, figuratively, allegorically, or spiritually?"* We all expect to be taken literally – even though we may have communicated what we have said  figuratively or through some other form of speech. The Bible does the very same thing. Consistency requires that the same principle of communication and interpretation be applied both to what God has said and to what we say!

The Bible is full of various *literary forms and figures of speech* – but behind them all *a literal truth is being communicated*. When the Bible uses phrases like: "shrewd as snakes and innocent as doves" (Matt. 10:16)…"**Look, the Lamb of God, who takes away the sin of the world!**" (Jn. 1:29)…"**...Go tell (Herod) that fox...**" (Lk. 13:32)…"**...streams of living water...**" (Jn. 7:38), etc., we all should know what they mean. All of our speech is likewise filled with figures of speech seeking to communicate a literal truth:

Examples

…"He's a couch potato!" (meaning lazy person)

…"Let's go pig out!" (meaning eat a lot), etc.

Can you imagine trying to explain some of our colloquial figures of speech to someone from another country and culture?! They are very explicit and graphic to us because we clearly understand the **literal truth being communicated by the figure of speech**. We must seek the same thing when we interpret the Bible. If we wrongly interpret these literary forms it will be just as disastrous to our Bible study as it will to our every day conversation! A good case in point is the Mormon cult. They have taken various *anthropomorphic* expressions in the Bible that are related to God – and come up with a completely false doctrine of God. To try to prove their doctrine of the non-spirituality of God they will often point to such verses as follows where God is spoken of with human physical attributes:

- "**Apple of the eye...**" (Ps. 17:8);
- "**... the eye of the Lord...**" (Ps. 33:18);
- "**the arm of the Lord...**" (Ps. 98:1);
- "**My hand...**" (Isa. 50:2);
- "**My face...**" (Isa. 54:7);
- "**My arm...**" (Isa. 59:1-2); etc.

To clearly refute the heretical Mormon doctrine of the non-spirituality of God, all you have to do is quote a couple other similar verses such as:

"**He will cover you with His feathers...**" (Ps. 91:4)
"**Hide me in the shadow of Your wings...**" (Ps. 17:8).

If you consistently use their false principle of interpretation you not only get a non-spiritual god – but also one who has wings and feathers! How absurd and blasphemous! Everyone clearly understands that **God was communicating literal truths to us in figures of speech we could clearly understand**! Jesus constantly did the same thing by encapsulating **spiritual truths in natural parables** that brought them down to our level of understanding. You see, we do not think or learn basically by the theoretical, or abstract – but by the concrete. God never communicates to us in general, nebulous terms – but rather in vivid ones out of the world of our experience. Then we can more easily grasp the literal truth that He is trying to communicate to us.

The principle is this: *"Every part of the Bible is to be taken literally."* That is the only natural, logical, normal way to interpret it!

Another principle closely akin to the above one is as follows: Even though there is only one correct *literal interpretation* of any given scripture, there may be a number of possible *correct applications*. It is only logical that if our interpretation is incorrect – then our application will also be incorrect. **Correct application cannot come from incorrect interpretation!** This is where the rubber hits the road!

4. The Principle of Grammatical Interpretation

As we have seen from the above discussion, language is important. God chose human language (as opposed to spiritual or angelic) as the vehicle to reveal Himself to man. So it is both the "Word of God" and the "Word of man." Because He has chosen to use our language, we must read it like we must any other book in regard to the rules of vocabulary, grammar, syntax; (order of words in a sentence) etc. – and not do violence to them. There are many great Biblical doctrines that are determined by grammar. The following are a couple of examples in point:

A. **The crucifixion of the believer with Christ** (Romans 6). Because of the *tense of the verb* here we know that our crucifixion with Christ is a *past experience* and not a *future* one. Christ's death on the cross also included us. When we understand this we will no longer hopefully and wishfully look forward to some future time when we might really get spiritual and crucify self! You can't crucify yourself. That's why Paul said that by faith you must "**count yourselves dead…**" – think of yourselves as dead, as far as sin is concerned (Rom. 6:11). So here *the proper interpretation is based on the tense of the verb!*

B. **The blessings of Abraham** (Gal. 3:15-16). Here the argument rests on one letter making the difference between *singular and plural*. "**The promises were spoken to Abraham and to his seed. The Scripture does not say 'and to seeds,' meaning many people, but 'and to your seed,' meaning one person, who is Christ**" (Gal. 3:16).

So here one letter makes an eternity of difference! It is the difference between the blessing promised coming exclusively through Christ - or through many! How exact God's Word is!

C. **The filling of the Spirit** (Eph. 5:18ff). Here again we see the very great importance of the *tense of a verb*. Paul says: "**…be filled with the Spirit**" (Eph. 5:18). The verb is in the *present tense.* That denotes *continuous present action.* Whereas our crucifixion with Christ was a past experience never to be repeated, our filling with the Spirit is a *dynamic continuing experience.* It is best translated: "be continuously being filled with the Spirit." A proper understanding of that verse will clear up a great deal of misunderstanding, fear and confusion concerning the filling of the Holy Spirit!

Also, we need to remember that *words do not have the same meaning in one culture that they have in another.* In addition, *words often go through an evolution in their meaning* so that what they once meant they no longer mean. A good example is the word "**meek**." Today, we mean something by it that the Biblical writers did not mean. For example, the dictionary defines meek as: *"patient and mild; easily imposed on."* That's not the Biblical meaning at all! It means a well harnessed power; power under control. Therefore to call Christ meek by Webster's definition is quite wrong!

We can never neglect grammar! I am especially thankful that God had the New Testament written in Greek, because it is generally a far more exact and precise language than either English or most of our other contemporary languages spoken today.

5. **The Principle of Historical Interpretation**

   A. One of the first things we should expect to find revealed in this method of interpretation is historical progression, or historical movement. Therefore, what God does and requires at one historical point in time may change at another because the former was a prelude for the latter. Again we can see the matter of ***progressive revelation revealed and worked out in historical interpretation***. A good example of this would be the sacrifices of the Old Testament. In that historical period, God was setting the stage and preparing His people for what He was going to do in a later period of history – the perfect sacrifice of Jesus Christ for sin. Therefore, when the fulfillment has come historically, the former things no longer hold. Indeed, they become idolatrous and *sin* when clung to and perpetrated at the expense of the fulfillment!

   It would be sin for us – as Christians who are living in the full light of the Gospel of Christ – to continue much of the Old Testament observances. Paul underscores this principle of interpretation and understanding of the workings of God in his Epistle to the Galatians. There he points out that Christ is the fulfillment of the law: "**Before this faith came, we were held prisoners by** the law, locked up until faith should be revealed. (There is the historical progression) **So the law was put in charge to lead us to Christ that we might be justified by faith. Now that faith has come, we are no longer under the supervision of the law** (There is the fulfillment)" (Gal. 3:23-25).

In Colossians he reiterates the same principle and says: "**See to it that no one takes you captive through hollow and deceptive philosophy, which depends on human tradition and the basic principles of this world rather than on Christ...Therefore do not let anyone judge you by what you eat or drink, or with regard to a religious festival, a New Moon celebration or a Sabbath day. These are a** *shadow of the things that were to come*; **the** *reality***, however,** *is found in Christ*" (Col. 2:8, 16-17). Because of a misunderstanding of this principle of interpretation, many people get caught up in and worship the shadow rather than the substance - Christ!

The writer of Hebrews also demonstrates this historical, progressive interpretation. In Hebrews Chapters 6 through 10 he contrasts the ministry of the priests of the past with our new High Priest, Jesus Christ: "**We have this hope as an anchor for the soul, firm and secure. It enters the inner sanctuary behind the curtain, where Jesus, who went before us, has entered on our behalf. He has become a high priest forever, in the order of Melchizedek...If perfection could have been attained through the Levitical priesthood (for on the basis of it the law was given to the people), why was there still need for another priest to come – one in the order of Melchizedek... He of whom these things are said belonged to a different tribe, and no one from that tribe has ever served at the altar. For it is clear that our Lord descended from Judah, and in regard to that tribe Moses said nothing about priests. And what we have said is even more clear if another priest like Melchizedek appears, one who has become a priest not on the basis of a regulation as to his ancestry but on the basis of the power of an indestructible life...The former regulation** is set aside because it was weak and useless (for the law made nothing perfect), and a better hope is introduced, by which we draw near to God...Because of this oath, Jesus has become the guarantee of a better covenant. Now there have been many of those priests, since death prevented them from continuing in office; but because Jesus lives forever, He has a permanent priesthood. Therefore He is able to save completely those who come to God through Him, because He always lives to intercede for them...The point of what we are saying is this...(human priests) serve at a sanctuary that is a copy and shadow of what is in heaven...But the ministry Jesus has received is as superior to theirs as the covenant of which He is mediator is superior to the old one, and it is founded on better promises. For if there had been nothing wrong with that first covenant, no place would have been sought for another...By calling this covenant 'new,' He has made the first one obsolete; and what is obsolete and aging will soon disappear...For this reason Christ is the mediator of a new covenant...The law is only a shadow of the good things that are coming – not the realities themselves. For this reason it can never, by the same sacrifices repeated endlessly year after year, make perfect those who draw...**we have been made holy through the sacrifice of the body of Jesus Christ once for all**" (selected verses from Hebrews 6:19-10:10). In these verses we can graphically see the principle of ***historical interpretation and historical progression and revelation*** worked out!

B. Secondly, this principle teaches us to look for the **original meaning of a passage**. Our problem is that we have a great tendency to project our 21st century ideas, definitions, concepts, world view, interpretations, etc., back onto the Bible. ***We must learn not to read back into Scripture ideas of today***. In other words, don't try to squeeze 1st century happenings into 21st century baggage! The key to helping us find the original historical meaning is to ask questions like these:

- *"What did the author intend to convey to his original hearers or readers?"*

- *"What would his original hearers have understood him to have meant by what he said?"*

So we must learn to transport ourselves back in time and imagine ourselves as one of the original hearers. We must be somewhat like the prophet Ezekiel when God told him to go be with the house of Israel. The word says: **"The Spirit then lifted me up and took me away...I came to the exiles...And there, where they were living, I sat among them..."** (Ezek. 3:14-15).

I believe something of the same experience can be ours through the help of the same Holy Spirit that transported Ezekiel. When we sit where they sat, and experience what they were experiencing and then **listen to God's Word from their perspective**, I believe we can begin to get something of the **correct historical interpretation**.

When we gain this original sense we will not misinterpret, misappropriate, or misapply God's Word. Let's look at one historical example that is often *misinterpreted* and therefore *misappropriated* by some people today. It is found in Matthew 10. Here we find Jesus giving His original disciples a specific commissioning:

"He called His twelve disciples to Him and gave them authority to drive out evil spirits and to heal every disease and sickness...These twelve Jesus sent out with the following instructions: 'Do not go among the Gentiles or enter any town of the Samaritans. Go rather to the lost sheep of Israel. As you go, preach this message: 'The kingdom of heaven is near.' Heal the sick, raise the dead, cleanse those who have leprosy, drive out demons. Freely you have received, freely give'" (Matt. 10:1-8).

Now, this was a *specific commissioning to a very specific group* of 12 men. I do not believe that we can appropriate it today! However, I have often heard well-meaning and sincere (but wrong!) preachers and people claiming these verses as a justification for their various ministries. They will say that we are to go out and "**Heal the sick, raise the dead, cleanse those who have leprosy, drive out demons...**" and claim the first part of verse 8 as their justification. However, I never hear them also appropriate and apply the second part of verse 8 – that says: "*You received without pay, give without pay!*" (They always ask for money and take up offerings!)

Do you see the point?! You really cannot appropriate and apply one part without the other! The point again is this: This was a specific commissioning given by Jesus to His original 12 disciples – we can learn from it but we cannot appropriate it as our commissioning today. Let's further analyze the historical context here for a moment. Look at how specific and limiting the scope and application of this passage is:

1. A specific group of men: "**...His twelve disciples...The names of the twelve Apostles are these...These twelve Jesus sent out...**"

2. A specific scope of ministry: "**Do not go among the Gentiles or enter any town of the Samaritans. Go rather to the lost sheep of Israel.**" (i.e., the 75 x 125 miles that composed Palestine).

3. A specific method of presentation: "**As you go, preach...**" (no teaching)

4. A specific message: "**The kingdom of heaven is near.**"

5. A specific procedure: "**Heal the sick, raise the dead, cleanse those who have leprosy, drive out demons. Freely you have received, freely give. Do not take along any gold or silver or copper in your belts; take no bag for the journey, or extra tunic, or sandals or a staff...search for some worthy person... stay at his house...If the home is deserving, let your peace rest on it; if it is not, let your peace return to you. If anyone will not welcome you...shake the dust off your feet when you leave that home or town**" (Matt. 1:8-14).

So whereas this was a specific, limited commissioning by Jesus to His original 12 disciples - The Great Commission (Mtt. 28:19-20) is for all of His disciples! Let's contrast the two for a moment:

"Therefore go and make disciples of all nations (an impossible task for only 12 men – as opposed to the limited scope of the commissioning of Matthew 10, of Palestine), **baptizing them** (again an impossible task for only 12 men!) **in the name of the Father and of the Son and of the Holy Spirit, and teaching them** (as opposed to only preaching in Matthew 10) **to obey everything I have commanded you. And surely I am with you always, to the very end of the age"** (Here we conclusively see that the time context is of such a length that it would be impossible for those 12 alone to fulfill!). So we *can* and *must* appropriate this Great Commission! It is for every Christian in every age until the "**end of the age!**"

Note: Since they were only going to Jews, they would be totally familiar with the concept of the "**Kingdom of God**" from the Old Testament. That alone was their message and not *what we understand as the Gospel*, because it had not been fully historically enacted yet – Christ had not yet been crucified and raised. The problem that the hearers would have had was in knowing whether or not this announcement of the Kingdom was really true. After all, Alfred Edersheim says that there were more than 64 people in the time of Christ who also claimed to be the Messiah (*The Life and Times of Jesus The Messiah*). Jesus therefore gave them the power to perform miraculous signs to authenticate their message.

6. **The Principle of Cultural Interpretation**

Great confusion is caused within the Body of Christ today by a neglect or abuse of this crucial principle of Biblical interpretation! Before we further define this principle, we need first to look at the matter of culture itself: *"Behavior typical of a group or class."* Culture is relative! Since culture is relative by nature, ***there are some things in***

the Word of God that are relative. When we do not know the difference between what is cultural or relative in the Word and what is absolute – we will live in great spiritual confusion.

The history of Christianity clearly demonstrates that we Christians have always had a struggle at this point. The church has often encultured the Gospel – always resulting in great shame to the cause of Christ! The missionary advance of the church has often been greatly slowed and retarded because well-meaning missionaries have gone out with a Gospel that has become so encultured by their particular culture (Americanism, Anglicanism, etc.) – that the nationals often ended up rejecting the Gospel. Not because the Gospel was irrelevant or had no appeal, but because it was so enculturated in what was to them an alien culture. We Christians constantly *relativize the absolutes* and *absolutize the relative*! It is absolutely crucial that we correctly study God's Word and **know the difference between God's absolutes that are transcultural and man's culture that is relative and limited!** Our principle is this:

Principle #1: **God's laws are absolute and transcultural – but man's culture is limited and relative**.

That means that *"God designed Scripture to give orientation in any culture, in any age and in any moral climate."* Therefore, we must be alert in our Bible study to the things revealed there that were cultural and therefore not relevant to our culture today. However, we must also apply this principle:

> God designed Scripture to give orientation in any culture, in any age, and in any moral climate.

Principle #2: **Even though certain cultural practices in the Bible are relative, there are still principles behind those practices that are absolute**.

Illustration

Spiritual Principle ⟶ Cultural Practice
(Absolute)   (Relative)

(The Spiritual Principle is behind or illustrated in the Cultural Practice)

Now let's go to God's Word for a couple of examples that will underscore these principles. First I want us to look at a very misunderstood passage and principle from Paul – the principle of Headship. Paul discusses this principle in I Corinthians 11:2-3: "**I praise you for remembering me in everything and for holding to the teachings, just as I passed them on to you. Now I want you to realize that the head of every man is Christ, and the head of the woman is man, and the head of Christ is God.**"

Paul begins here by reminding them of the traditions that he taught them. Then in verse 3 he sets forth the spiritual principle. That principle says that in God's economy He has set up certain lines of authority. That line of authority could be demonstrated as follows:

Now, this principle is greatly misunderstood by many today. Many people are rebelling at this principle – primarily because they do not understand it. Their problem is that they are seeing and interpreting this principle in terms of *superiority* and *inferiority*. Obviously this is not what Paul is saying by the inspiration of the Holy Spirit. It would be blasphemy and heresy if he was! Why? Because Christ is not inferior to God nor God superior to Christ! They are coequal Members of the Godhead along with the Holy Spirit.

A few moments ago I used a phrase that may have slipped by you, as far as understanding goes. I mentioned "God's economy." I said that "***in God's economy He has set up certain lines of authority***." Now to understand what Paul is saying here, you must understand the principle of economy in the Godhead. Please stay with me here, because this is very important! All cultic groups go astray at this point. Because they do not properly understand the Biblical principle of economy they always end up making *Christ and the Holy Spirit inferior to God*. The moment you say that you have to also be consistent and make woman inferior to man! But that is not the principle here at all! If you will look up the word "economy" in a dictionary you will find that the older definition of it is: "*The management of household or private affairs; the system or arrangement or mode of operation or functioning of something.*" That's exactly what the Biblical meaning is. The word literally means "**One who rules or governs a household**" (Gal. 4:2).

The **economic principle of the Godhead** is as follows: "*The various activities of the three Persons of the Trinity are not separate activities since God is One. So in relationship to Themselves, everything the Father, Son, and Holy Spirit do is one, because They are one. However in relationship to this world and to man, Their activities are different. Internally They are One – but the external activities in relationship to us are different.*" It is evident that a distinction must be made between the One who sends, the Father – and the One who is sent, Jesus (Jn. 8:42).

The key is this: ***The change is not in the Person but in the economic relation***. The Bible teaches us that the Father is specially related to God's work in *creation*; the Son by Incarnation is specially related to God's work in redemption; and the Holy Spirit by His indwelling is specially related to God's work in *sanctification*. The entire Trinity of Persons of course comes to the world – but their various acts and relationships to the world are different, and these different acts are attributed to the various members of the Godhead.

In their economic relationship to us: **the Father is God above us; the Son is God with us; and, the Holy Spirit is God in us**. Theologically, this is called the "Economic Trinity" whereby God has progressively revealed Himself as *Father*, then as *Son* and finally as *Holy Spirit*. They are *one in essence or nature*, i.e., they are all God – but in relationship to us they are different *functionally*. Now, I hope I did not lose you on that! But we can't understand the very important and greatly misunderstood principle that Paul is giving us here unless we grasp it! So let's summarize again our principle through several interrelated statements:

1. Woman is not inferior to man because Christ is not inferior to God.

2. Man and woman are both equal before God – but different functionally.

3. This different functioning and relationship to each other and the world is God's established economy or order for them.

4. God's economy for man and woman is that in this world the woman is to be under the man's authority as the man is under Christ's authority. But this no more means that man is superior to woman than God is superior to Christ.

How is that absolute Biblical principle *culturally* worked out? In Paul's day a woman demonstrated that she was under authority by wearing a veil over her head, and a man by not wearing a veil. After setting forth the **absolute Biblical principle**, Paul goes on to explain how it was to be *demonstrated in his culture*:

"Every man who prays or prophesies with his head covered dishonors his head. And every woman who prays or prophesies with her head uncovered dishonors her head – it is just as though

her head were shaved. If a woman does not cover her head, she should have her hair cut off; and if it is a disgrace for a woman to have her hair cut or shaved off, she should cover her head. A man ought not to cover his head, since he is the image and glory of God; but the woman is the glory of man...the woman ought to have a sign of authority on her head. In the Lord, however, woman is not independent of man, nor is man independent of woman. For as woman came from man, so also man is born of woman. But everything comes from God. Judge for yourselves: Is it proper for a woman to pray to God with her head uncovered?" (I Cor. 11:4-13).

In the culture of Paul's day a woman externally demonstrated an internal commitment or truth (economy) in a highly visible way. *She demonstrated that she was under authority by wearing a covering or a veil.* To her and to the world that veil meant that she was under a particular man's covering or authority. The woman who did not wear a veil was in essence saying: *"I am under no man's authority...I'm available!"* She was a prostitute. One way that culture sometimes dealt with a prostitute was to shave her head and thereby bring public shame upon her and force her to veil herself! A man, on the other hand, was to put nothing on his head as he prayed or prophesied. A covering on his head would have meant something between himself and his spiritual head, Christ. He demonstrated that he was under God's authority by not putting a covering on – and a woman did the reverse.

The spiritual principle that is absolute is perfectly clear: In this economy we are all to be living under authority: Man under God's and woman under man's. In Paul's day they had a very visual way of demonstrating this principle – but it was cultural and therefore relative. ***The Biblical principle is absolute but the cultural practice demonstrating it is relative.***

Let's look at another good example of this principle of Biblical interpretation. Again it is a highly misunderstood one. It concerns the matter of long hair on men. Paul says: *"**Does not the very nature of things teach you that if a man has long hair, it is a disgrace to him, but that if a woman has long hair, it is her glory? For long hair is given to her as a covering**"* (I Cor. 11:14-15).

Here we see Paul again using another example to emphasize the same *principle.* It too is a cultural example from his day – that a man should not wear long hair. He says: **"Does not the very nature of things teach you that if a man has long hair, it is a disgrace to him..."** The key word here is the word "nature." What does it mean? It cannot mean "nature by creation" because man's hair naturally will grow as long as a woman's. Paul uses here the word phusis. It means "nature by custom" and not "nature by creation."

What he is saying is this: *"**As a Christian, we should be sensitive to the culture around us...we should do the natural thing in that culture... the customary thing**."* The natural, customary thing for a man of that day to do was to wear his hair shorter than a woman's – a short cropped hair style and a beard. A woman's long hair was both her glory and covering or sign of authority (verse 15). For a man to wear exceptionally long hair – the length of a woman's of that day – was an outward sign that he was rebelling against God's authority and order. So Paul said to demonstrate *this principle* by the customary practice of the day in regard to length of hair. The principle then is this: ***A Christian should be sensitive to his culture***. He should not be either the first to leave the old or the first to try the new!

There are many other places in the New Testament where we see this principle being worked out. Paul says that we should be sensitive to a brother's culture so as not to be a stumbling block to him: **"... make up your mind not to put any stumbling block or obstacle in your brother's way...If your brother is distressed because of what you eat, you are no longer acting in love. Do not by your eating destroy your brother for whom Christ died. Do not allow what you consider good to be spoken of as evil...Let us therefore make every effort to do what leads to peace and to mutual** edification...It is better not to eat meat or drink wine or to do anything else that will cause your brother to fall" (Rom. 14:13-21).

The issue was a Christian eating *meat that had been offered to idols.* Paul knew that it was okay in and of itself to eat it because there are no other gods but God, so the meat was really not offered to anyone real! The T-Bone steak had just been deliciously charcoaled in a rather unusual context! However, the man of that culture might really have a problem with seeing a freer brother doing that and therefore stumble. Paul says to **be sensitive to anything in another culture that might become a stumbling block if ignored or gone against**.

The attitude of the Christian relative to cultural issues should be as Paul expressed in I Corinthians 9: "**Though I am free and belong to no man, I make myself a slave to everyone, to win as many as possible. To the Jews I became like a Jew, to win the Jews. To those under the law I became like one under the law (though I myself am not under the law), so as to win those under the law. To those not having the law I became like one not having the law (though I am not free from God's law but am under Christ's law), so as to win those not having the law. To the weak I became weak, to win the weak. I have become all things to all men so that by all possible means I might save some. I do all this for the sake of the Gospel..."** (I Cor. 9:19-23).

The principle here is: "**I do all this for the sake of the Gospel...**" When that is your motivation, you will be sensitive to whatever culture you are in – so that there you might better communicate the Gospel. You will try not to violate any cultural practices that would cause either a nonbeliever or new believer to misunderstand or reject an absolute principle.

We must understand the principle of cultural interpretation so we will be able to distinguish **the absolute principles from God's Word** from the cultural practices of man. Then we will not *relativize the absolutes* or *absolutize the relatives!* And, we will not be guilty of so enculturating the Gospel that people will not be able to distinguish between God's absolute principles and our particular cultural practices of those principles.

7. The Principle of Contextual Interpretation

In coming to this principle we come to the one that in many ways is the most important one of all. This is the most immediate of all principles to apply in discussing or studying a portion of scripture. My first and foremost question in trying to understand and properly interpret a verse of scripture should be: "What is the context of this verse?" It is the most immediate principle to apply, but for the sake of emphasis I have chosen to discuss it last in the hopes that it will have a more lasting impact on your mind!

What is the principle of contextual interpretation? *"Every text has a context – and a text taken out of context becomes a pretext!"* That simply means that **if you wrench a text out of its context you can make it mean and say what you want rather than what God meant!** This happens all of the time. You can therefore take the Bible out of context and make it say anything you want. You can justify almost any practice or prejudice by taking verses out of their context. Every ancient and contemporary heresy has used scripture to justify its position! But these unorthodox and sometimes wild interpretations have come about by someone taking verses out of context. They went to the Bible to try to prove or substantiate their theology or beliefs. Remember: we never go to the Bible to try to *prove our beliefs – we go to the Bible to test our beliefs!* Again, our principle says this:

Principle
Every word of the Bible is true in its context.
Isolated from its proper context, it may be very untrue!

Let me give you a good example of this: the story of Job. For about 37 long chapters Job has to contend with the opinions of his so-called "comforters." Their opinions were wrong! Therefore, if you tried to develop a *theology of suffering* from the first 37 chapters – it would be wrong! Their opinions were recorded in the Bible – not that we should follow them, but that they might be contradicted. This becomes clear when you read the last chapter. There Job even admits that his opinions were incomplete and sometimes wrong: "**Surely I spoke of things I did not understand, things too wonderful for me to know**" (Job 42:3). Then God clearly indicts and condemns all of the counsel that Job had received from his friends, and says to them: "**I am angry with you...because you have not spoken of Me what is right, as My servant Job has**" (Job 42:7). If you tried to form a theology of suffering from what is recorded in the Bible, based on the opinions of Job's friends – *it would be entirely wrong*! To take the first 37 chapters of Job away from the context of chapter 42 would lead to theological disasters.

Too many people use the Bible like a kind of "spiritual ouiji board." They go to it without any real spiritual preparation or contextual study, and take a spiritual plunge. That's what I call the "*'Lucky dip' method!*" I have people coming up to me all of the time saying that they needed some guidance from the Lord so they went to their Bible and took a plunge. It works like this. You stand your Bible up on its binding, allow it to randomly fall open and let your finger come down on the page. Whatever verse your finger comes to is your "verse for the day" or God's guidance for that particular question or problem! Now, I know that God may have given some people guidance on occasion through that method – BUT THAT IS NEITHER HIS NORMAL NOR DESIRED WAY OF GUIDING YOU!

The guidance you receive may be like that received by one unfortunate chap who used this method. He was struggling for some guidance on a particular subject so he decided to use this method. After all, some of his Christian friends said that it had worked for them! He placed his Bible closed standing on its binding, allowed it to fall open and let his finger fall on a verse. The verse was this: **"And Judas went out and hanged himself."** Well he certainly did not want to appropriate that verse – so he tried again. This time his finger fell on another verse that said: **"Go thou and do likewise."** Well, he really didn't like that one – so he thought, "Just once more and I am sure I will get the guidance I need." So this third time his finger came to the verse: "**...and whatsoever thou doest, do quickly.**" Now, all of those are verses out of the Bible – but taken out of their context they could lead to disaster if applied! I'm sure you get the point!

Every verse in the Bible is true – but only in context. Taken out of its context it may be quite untrue. When you take a verse out of its context you make a two-fold error. ***You not only make it say something that it does not say; you also miss what is really says!*** There is a double error and danger involved in taking verses out of context.

You might be asking yourself about right now: "*What is the context? How can I find it?*" It is really quite simple: Let me outline it:

A. The most **immediate context** is found in the verses immediately *preceding* and *following* the particular verse in question. Here a Bible translation that has paragraph divisions is very helpful. The paragraph separates the thought units – so they will help us decide the immediate context.

B. The **larger context** is the book the passage is found in. *What was the writer's purpose?...What is his theme?* etc.

C. The **theological context** is the study of that theme or subject *in the light of everything else the Bible says about it.*

Tragically most people ignore these steps, take verses from their context – and end in confusion, and even heresy! There are myriads of examples of such verses that are misinterpreted today because they are taken out of their context.

Benediction or Malediction?

At the end of many church services I have heard the following verse quoted or prayed as a benediction: "**May the Lord keep watch between you and me when we are away from each other**" (Gen. 31:49). As good as that might sound as a benediction – it is not! You remember the story. Jacob had worked 14 years for Laban for the hand of his daughters in marriage. He had worked seven years for Leah and seven more for Rachel. You will recall how he had only wanted to marry Rachel and thought he was working for her – but was deceived at the wedding and married Leah instead. He had to work another seven years for Rachel. Their father, Laban, constantly changed his working agreements with Jacob – and Jacob did a little deceiving himself! Finally, Jacob fled with his wives, children and flocks in the night – and Laban pursued. When Laban caught up with Jacob they argued over their grievances and finally made a covenant between themselves.

To tangibly demonstrate this covenant they built a pillar of stones, and said: "**This heap is a witness between you and me today… May the Lord keep watch between you and me when we are away from each other. If you mistreat my daughters or if you take any wives besides my daughters, even though no one is with us, remember that God is a witness between you an me…This heap is a witness, and this pillar is a witness, that I will not go past this heap to your side to harm you and that you will not go past this heap and pillar to my side to harm me. May the God of Abraham…judge between us**" (Gen. 31:48-53).

The context of that verse gives it its correct interpretation. It becomes clear that this is not a benediction or promise of blessing – but a malediction. These two men were cheats! They had been doing con jobs on each other for a long time. Each knew that he could not trust the other with his back turned! They were saying that even though they could not keep their eyes on each other all the time while they were separated, God would watch between them – and curse or punish the one who broke this covenant. This is indeed a malediction based on the mistrust of two people who were enemies and mutual deceivers! Therefore, I don't think that is a very appropriate benediction at the conclusion of a worship service! Out of context it might sound like a very nice benediction – but *in context it is quite the opposite*!

"A Little Child Will Lead Them..."

Often times a group of people will be talking about some issue when a nearby child interjects his or her opinion. It may sound very profound and relevant to the point under discussion. Upon hearing this bit of "childish wisdom" someone patronizingly exclaims: "*Well, you know what the Bible* says: '*A little child will lead them...*'"

Well, let's take a look at the context of that verse. It is taken out of the 11th chapter of Isaiah. That chapter has to do with the Millennial reign of Christ at His Second Coming. Isaiah begins by describing the greatest political revolution the world will ever experience. All governments will be subjected to Christ's rule and man will live under a theocracy, rather than under democracy, socialism, communism or dictatorships. As Isaiah says: "**A shoot will come up from the stump of Jesse; from his roots a Branch will bear fruit. The Spirit of the Lord will rest on Him – the Spirit of wisdom and of understanding...with righteousness He will judge the needy, with justice He will give decisions for the poor of the earth. He will strike the earth with the rod of His mouth; with the breath of His lips He will slay the wicked**" (Isa. 11:1-5).

The writer now moves from the judgment work of Christ at His Second Coming to the fruit of it. Since injustice, wickedness, and evil have been destroyed from the earth, true peace reigns. During this millennial reign of Christ, nature will also be changed. It will undergo the greatest ecological revolution ever! *The curse that was placed on the natural realm due to the fall of man is removed* (Gen. 9:2). No longer will there be a carnivorous animal or poisonous insect or reptile.

Isaiah describes the peace and harmony of that period as follows: "The wolf will live with the lamb, the leopard will lie down with the goat, the calf and the lion and the yearling together; and *a little child will lead them*. The cow will feed with the bear, their young will lie down together, and the lion will eat straw like the ox. The infant will play near the hole of the cobra, and the young child put his hand into the viper's nest. They will neither harm nor destroy on all My holy mountain, for the earth will be full of the knowledge of the Lord as the waters cover the sea" (Isa. 11:6-9).

Those certainly are glorious verses! What a day that will be! Utopia will truly be a universal reality – and man will be taken by God back to the original created state of peace and harmony of Eden! *Hallelujah!* That's the same thing that Paul wrote about in Romans, when he said: "**The creation waits in eager expectation for the sons of God to be revealed. For the creation was subjected to frustration, not by its own choice, but by the will of the One who subjected it, in hope that the creation itself will be liberated from its bondage to decay and brought into the glorious freedom of the children of God. We know that the whole creation has been groaning as in the pains of childbirth right up to the present time**" (Rom. 8:19-22).

Again, you can see that the context gives us the correct interpretation of that verse in Isaiah. It is true that God does sometimes speak through children – although that is not His normal method. Their simplicity of faith and honesty will sometimes cause them to see the truth and speak it when adults will not! But this verse in Isaiah is not a "proof text" for that kind of thing.

A Verse For Dying – Or Living?

I have often heard someone quote the following verse at the death of a loved one. I have also heard it used often as a funeral text: "**No eye has seen, no ear has heard, no mind has conceived what God has prepared for those who love Him" (I Cor. 2:9).

Concerning the death of someone, this verse is used to say that *"What our eyes have not seen nor our ears ever heard, nor what we have never even conceived or in our hearts and minds – this dearly departed one is now knowing and experiencing!"* Well, there is certainly an element of truth in that, because when a believer dies, his walk of faith becomes one of sight; and that knowledge which has been incomplete is now full (I Cor. 13:12). *But this particular verse does not speak to that.* **It is not primarily a verse for dying – but a verse for living!**

Let's put it into its context: Here Paul is writing the Corinthians and reminding them of the message he had preached among them: **"When I came to you, brothers, I did not come with eloquence or superior wisdom as I proclaimed to you the testimony about God. For I resolved to know nothing while I was with you except Jesus Christ and Him crucified…My message and my preaching were not with wise and persuasive words, but with a demonstration of the Spirit's power…We do, however, speak a message of wisdom among the mature, and not the wisdom of this age or of the rulers of this age, who are coming to nothing. No, we speak of God's secret wisdom, a wisdom that has been hidden and that God destined for our glory before time began. None of the rulers of this age understood it, for if they had, they would not have crucified the Lord of glory. However, as it is written: 'No eye has seen, no ear has heard, no mind has conceived what God has prepared for those who love Him' but God has revealed it to us by His Spirit. The Spirit searches all things, even the deep things of God…We have not received the spirit of the world but the Spirit who is from God, that we may understand what God has freely given us. This is what we speak, not in words taught us by human wisdom but in words taught by the Spirit, expressing spiritual truths in spiritual words"** (I Cor. 2:1-13).

What Paul then is saying is that since we have the Spirit of God we can know and experience what the unregenerate man cannot because he is dead to these realities. As Paul says: **"The man without the Spirit does not accept the things that come from the Spirit of God, for they are foolishness to him, and he cannot understand them, because they are spiritually discerned"** (I Cor. 2:14).

Paul says that there is a whole dimension of reality that we can know that the unregenerate never can. And, we do not have to die to know it. God reveals it to us now through His Spirit and His Word! Again, this is a verse for living and not for dying! It has to do with *the revelation we have now through God's Holy Spirit working through His Holy Word.*

"When Two Or Three Get Together..."

Probably this last verse that we are going to look at together gets the award for being the most currently abused verse in the New Testament! We hear it constantly used in church meetings and prayer meetings. I hear radio and TV preachers, "healers" and evangelists quote it often. I am referring to the verse where Jesus said: **"For where two or three come together in My Name, there am I with them"** (Matt. 18:20). That verse is probably used most within the context of prayer. A minister or teacher might begin by saying: *"Well, our numbers are few – but remember that Jesus said: 'For **where two or three have gathered together in My name, there I am in the midst**' – so let's pray!"*

Well now, the sincerity and faith of the people involved cannot be questioned. I have been guilty of wrongly using that verse myself in my earlier ministry. But a careful study of the context reveals that *this verse primarily has to do with church discipline.* Of course discipline within the church should only be carried out within the context of prayer, so prayer is related – but this is not primarily a teaching by the Lord on prayer.

A good study Bible that has paragraph divisions and titles will indicate this. This section is variously titled: *"Discipline in the Church," "When A Brother Sins," "Church Discipline,* and *"Discipline and Prayer."* Now let's look at the entire section and then place verse 20 within its proper context. To make sure we understand it, I will give a very brief verse-by-verse exposition as we go along:

- **"If your brother sins against you, go and show him his fault, just between the two of you. If he listens to you, you have won your brother over"** (Matt. 18:15). This verse hardly sounds like it is giving us instructions on the proper preparation for prayer! No! Here ***Jesus lays on each member of the Body the responsibility to "reprove" any known sin in a brother who is a part of our fellowship***. But it must be done <u>privately</u>.

We all have a great tendency to shrink from the responsibility of this – but we can't escape the clear word of Christ on this matter! As one Christian psychiatrist said concerning this *"Our discomfort springs from a 'kindness' fostered by culture rather than from a true mercy and love found in the Scriptures. We hate to have the boat rocked."*[117]

We do not go to our brother to condemn or judge him. *"The exercise described in Matthew 18 is a **rescue operation** from start to finish. It is designed not to condemn but to reconcile."*[118] There are many benefits in this procedure established by Christ. One of the most important is that it avoids unnecessary gossip. You take the matter right to its source. But suppose that he will not listen to you when you confront him. Suppose he says to you: *"Mind your own business!"* You do not let that stop you - love will not let you give up on a brother that easily! You move to the next step.

- **"But if he will not listen, take one or two others along, so that 'every matter may be established by the testimony of two or three witnesses'"** (Matt. 18:16).

---

117 John White, *Eros Defiled*, Downers Grove, IL: InterVarsity Press, 1977, p. 162.
118 Ibid.

If the sinning brother refused your love and reproof, Christ says that you are to take one or two others and approach him again. This helps you remain objective and gives balance to the judgment. Of course, it goes without saying that the choice of brothers to accompany you on this redemptive mission is very crucial. You want mature men who are motivated by love. *Never take young, or carnal, Christians on this type of mission* – because they would have a great tendency to be either *condemnatory* or *vindictive*. They would also probably not have the honesty and emotional maturity to deal with such an encounter. This is a function for a mature, loving elder!

- **"If he refuses to listen to them, tell it to the church; and if he refuses to listen even to the church, treat him as you would a pagan or a tax collector"** (Matt. 18:17).

Hopefully, this stage will not have to be reached because the brother will have repented in the earlier two steps. However, it was reached at the church at Corinth, as we read in I Corinthians 1:1-7. I want to emphasize in passing here that *Christ is assuming that every believer will be actively a part of the fellowship of some local church*. This presupposes that **we have placed ourselves in submission to the authority of the church for our teaching and discipline!** If we fall into sin and then refuse the church's discipline, we are to be excommunicated or ex-fellowshipped. Why? Because our lack of submission to the church's discipline says that we have broken fellowship with both Christ and His Body. The Body testifies to this by its disciplinary excommunication. **The church only ratifies what we have already decided by our sin, disobedience and lack of submission!**

Unfortunately, church discipline can become very messy! Not because the procedure outlined here by Christ is bad – but because of the hang-ups we bring to such a session. As the psychiatrist, John White said:

"Group meetings that deal with a sinner are ugly because of the anxiety and guilt we all bring to them. Instead of our being free to love and to plead, to warn and to rebuke, we are hung up with our own inner

problems. We are inhibited. We are ourselves guilt-ridden. ("What will she think of me if I say that?") We are not prepared to lay cards on tables, or to call spades, spades. Consider Jesus at the well with the adulterer woman...love can be every bit as blunt as hostility. <u>*We beat around the bush, not because we're tactful, but because we're cowards.*</u> *Jesus was blunt because He cared for the woman...We approach group discipline with all the hypocrisy with which we conduct our social lives. And because we are not accustomed to being simple, real, loving and direct, we are ill-equipped to deal with real and deadly issues. So we botch it..."*

Once again it must be emphasized that the purpose of such disciplinary church meetings is only to restore a brother to fellowship with the Lord and with the Body. The restoration of fellowship is the goal, because that is what has been broken. Remember, "*Sin destroys fellowship. It is only if we walk in light that we have fellowship one with another. To win a brother is to restore godly fellowship with him.*"[119] Also, when Christ says that the excommunicated person is to be to you as "**a pagan or a tax collector**," He is not telling us to treat him like dirt! As Christians, how are we to treat the lost?

We are to love them and do everything we can to win them! That's exactly the way we are to treat this rebellious brother. This is exactly where the Corinthian Church fell down. They had disciplined and excommunicated a sinning brother (I Cor. 5:1-6). The procedure Christ had outlined worked in this incident and the man repented of his sin. However, the church would not accept him back – so Paul had to write and chastise them for this, and ask them to restore fellowship with him. "**The punishment inflicted on him by the majority is sufficient for him. Now instead, you ought to forgive and comfort him, so that he will not be overwhelmed by excessive sorrow. I urge you, therefore, to reaffirm your love for him**" (II Cor. 2:6-7).

---

119 John White, *Eros Defiled*, Downers Grove, IL: InterVarsity Press, 1977, p. 162.

How tragic it is that the church is so quick on condemnation and so slow on forgiveness! We will forgive a sinner of anything – but let one of our brethren fall into sin, and we hold it against him and remind him of it for life! God does not treat our sin that way – and we must not treat a brother's sin differently!

- **"I tell you the truth, whatever you bind on earth will be bound in heaven, and whatever you loose on earth will be loosed in heaven"** (Matt. 18:18).

  *Here is another verse with which I have heard many radio and T.V. preachers do havoc! They usually apply it to some physical sickness, family or financial trouble, etc. They will say something like "we bind that sickness" or "we loose you from the bonds of this habit" etc. However, within the context of what Christ is saying here, "to bind means to withhold fellowship; to loose, to forgive. But there is a secondary meaning...To bind was to forbid or to command – to declare what was or was not permitted. To loose was to allow, to leave free to choose."[120] We can clearly see that this verse has to do with **binding from fellowship (excommunication)** and **loosing from the sin that barred them from fellowship** (restoration) so that the fellowship with our brother can be re-established.*

- **"Again, I tell you that if two of you on earth agree about anything you ask for, it will be done for you by My Father in heaven"** (Matt. 18:19).

  This verse is very closely associated with the preceding one since it begins with "**Again, I tell you...**" Christ is saying that if two of you agree about the binding or loosing of a brother on earth, it will be done by the Father in heaven. In other words, *the Body of Christ is only acting out on earth what the Father has already done in heaven.*

  I hope that you can see that you cannot pull the last part of that verse out of its context and use it as some type of blanket

---

120 Ibid., p. 159.

guarantee for prayer. I hear it quoted constantly that way – as though the Father is obligated to answer our every prayer as long as "*...two of you on earth agree about anything...*" That of course is making the verse mean something Christ never said! He is saying that *He will grant anything we shall ask concerning discipline!*

- "**For where two or three come together in My Name, there am I with them**" (Matt. 18:20).

Now I hope that you understand the context of verse 20 by all that has preceded it. If this is a prayer passage, then we really have some problems to deal with! If there must be "*...two or three gathered in His Name*" – what is the isolated missionary or Christian worker to do? Can he not adequately draw upon the resources of God through prayer because he is alone? Must there be "two or more" so you can control God with a numerical power play? Obviously not! *Every individual believer can call upon the complete resources of God.* He does not have to have "two or three" to get God into action or get prayer answered!

What Christ was saying is that when His Body is gathered together here on earth to carry out the disciplinary procedure that He has just listed, that *He will be in their midst concerning and giving the power and authority for this action.* He is saying "*It is as though I Myself am there physically in your midst carrying out this discipline action.*"

That this is the only correct interpretation of these verses is clearly pointed out by the following verses. There we find Peter's reactions to Christ's teaching. His immediate reactions to what Christ had said were: "***Lord, how many times shall I forgive my brother when he sins against me? Up to seven times?***" (Matt. 18:21). It is very clear that Peter and the rest of the disciples understood that Jesus was speaking here about *discipline* and not about prayer!

I do not think that it is accidental that the institutional church in America is in the sad, anemic state that we often find it today! Could it be because we have misinterpreted this teaching of Christ?! I think so! One of the greatest problems in the church today is the *lack of discipline* on the one hand and the *lack of prayer* on the other. I believe that we can trace much of the problem to the abuse of these verses. We have taken the only teaching from the lips of Christ on church discipline and turned it into our chief prayer text! In the process **we have abandoned discipline and misunderstood the nature of prayer!** The result has been disastrous for the internal health and external witness of the church. As John White said: *"The church is a glorious oak, beautiful to behold, but rotten at the core. It cannot be reformed. It must be renewed. It cannot by renewed by structures but by men and women."*[121] He then concludes by quoting John Howard Yoder: *"If (real church discipline is) practiced, it would change the life of churches more fundamentally than has yet been suggested by the currently popular discussion of changing church structures."*[122]

Now, none of us like to do this type of thing! It is very much like spanking your child. It is very unpleasant – so we avoid the emotional conflict and cop-out on our responsibility as parents. In the church we do the same thing! Rather than approach a disobedient brother through the procedure that Christ so clearly outlined – we prefer to deal with it within the church as the world does. We turn a blind eye – *"you ignore my sin and I will ignore yours!"* Our clear choice is to either **be obedient to the words of Christ here and be the true church <u>discipline and all</u>** – or be another social club!

As John White so aptly put it, our choice is: *"Club versus church. Human society versus fellowship in Christ. In the one you can afford to live and let live. Sin is an embarrassment that you cope with expediently. It is not a moral issue but a social inconvenience. But in God's view it is deadly and destroys fellowship. Take your pick. Do you choose to be a 'Christian' club member or members of the body of Christ? You cannot have it both*

---

121 John White, *Eros Defiled*, Downers Grove, IL: InterVarsity Press, 1977, p. 169.
122 Ibid.

ways. It you are a member of Christ's body, you go to your brother and seek reconciliation. To say you are not bothered by his sin is to say you have betrayed God's standards and adopted the club's. It is far cozier to be a club member than a member of the body."[123]

God grant us the courage to fully be the church!

SUMMARY

I hope that you can see the importance of these principles of Biblical interpretation. When we read God's Word with an understanding of them, then we will be able to "**correctly handle the Word of Truth**" (II Tim. 2:15). If we ignore and abuse these principles then we will be in grave danger of "**...twisting the scriptures to our own destruction**" (II Pet. 3:16 NASB)! Let's take a moment to list and review the principles discussed in this chapter:

1. The principle of NATURAL interpretation;
2. The principle of COMPARATIVE interpretation;
3. The principle of LITERAL interpretation;
4. The principle of GRAMMATICAL interpretation;
5. The principle of HISTORICAL interpretation;
6. The principle of CULTURAL interpretation;
7. The principle of CONTEXTUAL interpretation.

All 7 principles are very important and need to be remembered. However, Principle 7 or "**Contextual interpretation**" is by far the most important and most immediate principle to apply in Bible Study. It is the one that we should apply first – but it is the one that we abuse the most!

---

[123] Ibid., p. 160.

Always look at the immediate context of any verse the very first thing, and in most cases you will gain the proper interpretation. If you are still confused, then proceed to apply the other principles. If you have gone through all seven and still are confused – write me!

Perhaps about right now you might be thinking: *"Well, what's the use of even reading and studying the Bible?!* I can't possibly remember all of those principles and when to apply which one!" That may sound like a very good excuse on the surface – but it is really a lame one! Let me give you an analogy. Suppose someone handed you a very complicated legal document. At the top it said that it was the "Last Will and Testament" of some unknown or far distant rich relative. The document says that you are a beneficiary of $1,000,000. However, there are stipulations, requirements, conditions – and a lot of "ifs, ands, buts, and wherefores". The more you read the will, the more you get confused by all of the legal terminology. You say: *"I'm no lawyer – I can't understand all of this stuff!"* So you tear the will up and toss the pieces in the fire! Is that what you would do? I certainly doubt it! You would hire a team of "Philadelphia lawyers" or go to law school if necessary and take courses – you would stop at nothing to meet the requirements so you could get your hands on that money! You would find someway to properly understand that will and meet its requirements so that you could get your inheritance!

And yet, the King of Kings and Lord of Lords has given you in the Bible His "Last Will and Testament" – making you an heir to riches you never dreamed of! Yet, you casually shrug it off with *"I don't understand the Bible!"* How very inconsistent we are! We will do anything for material blessings which are temporal – and do almost nothing for spiritual blessings which are eternal!

Let's realize that all of our excuses concerning Bible study are just that – EXCUSES! We need to repent to God and recommit ourselves to a lifetime of serious study of His Word. And it is with prayer that I commit this book to you to that exciting end!

> "We do not adjust the Scriptures to fit the times – but rather expound the Scriptures to change the times."
> (Stephen Olford)

Quotations for Further Reflection

- *Many Christians who are faithful in reading the Bible devotionally feel "blessed" only when they find a surprising thought suggested to them by the text, a thought that bears no direct relationship to the intent of the author. To them, seeking to know God's will through careful study to understand the intended meaning of the author seems dry and boring. In the same way, many Christians use Scripture in a "magical" way to give specific direction to decisions they must make. Where to go, what to buy, what employment to accept – all of those are discovered through Scripture passages that, by marvelous coincidence, have a double meaning. First, there is the message intended by the author, and then the unrelated coincidental parallel to their own current experience...* **The Bible should not be used as a normal source of miraculous revelation of God's will in matters not intended by the author.** [124]

---

[124] J. Robertson McQuilkin, *Understanding and Applying the Bible,* Chicago: Moody Press, 1983, pp. 27-28.

PRACTICAL STEPS IN STUDYING THE WORD

In this section of the book I would like to make some practical suggestions to help you get started in applying these principles of Biblical interpretation. I hope that this section will really give you some handles so you can grab hold of God's Word and get going for yourself!

1. First, take time to *prepare yourself spiritually for your Bible study time*. Remember this very simple principle: Before going to God's Word – go to God first and ask that His Holy Spirit "**guide you into all truth**" by illuminating your heart and mind (Jn. 16:13; Ps. 119-18; Eph. 1:17-19; 3:14-19; Phil. 1:9-14, etc.).

Principle
Before going to God's Word – *go to God first*
and ask that His Holy Spirit "guide you into all truth" by illuminating your heart and mind!

Remember that the author of any book is always its best interpreter! Spend some time talking to the Author of Scripture in prayer before beginning your study. Prayer is the greatest preparation for Bible Study, because God has promised to guide the prayerful, humble spirit. God leads the sincere and humble – never the proud and haughty! *A prayerful, alert and obedient spirit* is the one that will receive great light from a study of God's Word.

2. Secondly, have some ***good Biblical tools and aids*** on hand. When it comes to Biblical resources one can spend a small fortune! However, that does not have to be the case. A pastor or Christian teacher would naturally have a much larger and more extensive library of Biblical resources than the average Christian. However, there are many commentaries available that are literally a compacted treasure of finger-tip Biblical information! There are many free aids available on the Internet, such as www.crosswalk.com or www.christianitytoday.com, "Bible Study Tools" – and there are programs like "Quick Verse" available within any budget range.

The following are some suggested tools to have as companion tools for Bible study. I will also try to give a word or two of explanation under each.

    A. **Several good translations of the Bible**: A *translation* as opposed to a *paraphrase* seeks to give as exact as possible *word-for-word rendering from the Hebrew or Greek into English* without being "wooden" and unreadable. Scholars generally seek to capture what is often called the *"dynamic equivalent"* of a sentence – *meaning-for-meaning* – rather than the exact word-for-word rendering, which can be very hard to read and understand from one language to another. The problems along this line for translators are graphically pointed out by the following quotation. It was made about two thousand years ago by Cicero when he was confronted with the prospects of translating Plato's *Protagoras* into Latin.

> *"It is hard to preserve in a translation the charm of expressions which in another language are most felicitous...If I render word for word, the result will sound uncouth and if compelled by necessity I alter anything in the order of wording, I shall seem to have departed from the function of a translator."*[125]

That then is the dilemma of the Bible translator – to remain faithful to the original text, and yet make it readable. As one Bible translator put it: "...*faithfulness in translation means being faithful not only to the original language but also to the 'target' or 'receptor' language.*" A few of the more popular translations used among Christians today are as follows:

> New Revised Standard Version (NRSV)
> New American Standard Bible (NASB)
> Today's English Version (TEV) or "Good News Bible"
> New International Version (NIV)
> New Living Translation (NLT)

Why So Many Translations?

The Christian bookshelf is almost crowded with translations today! Since World War II there have been more than 30 new translations produced – in addition to at least 18 earlier versions that were already in print. Many of these are very excellent. However, it should be remembered that there is no such thing as a perfect translation! Since we do not have the original autographs, all of our Bibles today are translations – and none are inspired by God and therefore perfect as were the originals! That fact should always be remembered lest we think that our particular "pet" translation is perfect!

---

[125] Kenneth L. Barker, "An Insider Talks About the NIV", *Kindred Spirit*, Fall 1978, p. 7.

Every translation was obviously produced by humans so they reflect somebody's theological bias. That is the very fact that causes other translations to be produced! People are always dissatisfied with translations which reflect theological views that differ from their own. For example, both the Revised Standard Version (RSV) and the New English Bible (NEB) were translated by scholars who generally held to a more liberal theological view point and higher criticism. *"They did not believe the bible was verbally inspired, to them it was basically a human book."*[126] That theological persuasion can be seen in those translations at several points. Therefore, they have tended not to be as widely used among conservative Christians as for instance the KJV.

The King James Translation

For most people, the KJV will never be surpassed in grandeur and poetic beauty! However, it should be remembered that the KJV was translated several hundred years ago. It was based on the best scholarship of the early 1600's and was an attempt to put the Bible into the language of the people of the 17th century[127]. However, there have been many archaeological discoveries that have improved our understanding of much of Biblical history, geography, culture and language since 1611. Indeed, archaeology had not even been born as a science when the KJV was translated. Also, it was translated from only 8 basic manuscripts. Today we have over 13,000 manuscripts in whole or in part. Even though there is real beauty in much of the KJV rendering – most of us today do not speak Shakespearean English! Words change over a period of years and therefore do not carry the same meaning. *There are over 300 words used in the KJV that have gone through a*

---

126 Stanley N. Gundry, "Which Version is Best?" *Moody Monthly*, Jan. 1979, p. 41.
127 It is very interesting to note that the KJV was initially opposed by the Puritans. They preferred the Geneva Bible of 1560, and would not even allow a copy of the KJV on the Mayflower! So even though the KJV is the Bible of many conservatives and fundamentalists today – it was originally opposed by the conservatives of that day!

word evolution to the extent that they do not mean today what they meant then. That can be confusing for the 21st century Bible reader. Just as the KJV was an attempt to put the Bible into the language of the day – so are the more recent translations of our day. (Please see Appendix IV for further discussion on the "King James Only" controversy)

Which Translation is Best?

A. That is a very common question among Christians today! Different scholars have different views, because they also have different tastes and different theological persuasions. There was a survey made in 1972 of 46 well-known Bible scholars, clergymen and theologians. Generally, the RSV was chosen the most and got first place in *"scholarship"* and *"best whole Bible."* The ASV took first place in *"most accurate"* (29, p. 44). The KJV came in last in 9 out of the 10 categories, including accuracy and scholarship. But there are still thousands who feel that the KJV is the "real Bible" and that it came down on Mt. Sinai from the very finger of God! I do not believe that the KJV will lead a person astray at any point concerning major points of doctrine or cause them to lose their salvation – but it will certainly keep one clouded in confusion at many points! While it is a good translation in many ways – we now have better ones available to the English reader.

Evangelical scholars tend to prefer the RSV, the NASB or the NIV. The NIV has many commendable features. It is called the "international" version because it was translated by scholars from across the English speaking world: The United States, Great Britain, Canada, Australia, and New Zealand. That diversity helped to guard it from denominationalism, parochialism and general sectarian bias. Dr. Donald W. Burdick, one of the translators of the NIV, gives this summary of its distinctives:

1. It is the work of over 100 scholars.
2. It is a faithful rendering of the Greek text.
3. It is done in currently idiomatic English that all can understand.
4. It is neither woodenly literal nor loosely paraphrastic.
5. Its translators all hold to the inerrancy of Scripture.
6. It is marked by an easy dignity that well becomes the lofty character of the Word of God.[128]

Obviously number 5 is very important to the conservative Bible student. We prefer someone translating the text who holds to the inerrancy of the Scriptures. The scholars who translated the NIV also demonstrated their high view of Scripture and reverence for God by beginning all work sessions with prayer. That certainly ranks in importance as a necessary prerequisite for translating God's Word!

Let me conclude this section on translations with the following quotation by a Bible teacher who expressed his preference as follows: *"I prefer a version that is literal enough to be concerned about word-for-word equivalency where reasonably possible, but flexible enough to read as good English. Two recent versions stand at the top of my list: the New American Standard Bible and the New International Version."*[129]

Many translations can be obtained within a Parallel Bible. As many as eight translations can be compared and contrasted, and any number of variations are available – for instance, NIV/NASB/KJV/NLT.

Here is an example of how considering the subtle variances in each may enrich your understanding of a single verse:

---

[128] Kenneth L. Barker, "An Insider Talks About the NIV," *Kindred Spirit*, Fall 1978, p. 9.
[129] Stanley N. Gundry, "Which Version is Best?" *Moody Monthly*, Jan. 1979, p. 42.

- "Let no corrupt communication proceed out of your mouth, but that which is good to the use of edifying, that it may minister grace unto the hearers" (Eph. 4:29 KJV).

- "Do not let any unwholesome talk come out of your mouths, but only what is helpful for building others up according to their needs, that it may benefit those who listen" (Eph. 4:29 NIV).

- "Don't use foul or abusive language. Let everything you say be good and helpful, so that your words will be an encouragement to those who hear them" (Eph. 4:29 NLT).

- "Let no unwholesome word proceed from your mouth, but only such a word as is good for edification according to the need of the moment, so that it will give grace to those who hear" (Eph. 4:29 NASB).

B. Have a **good paraphrase or two for reference**. Whereas a translation seeks to give a word-for-word rendering, or *"dynamic equivalent"* from the original Biblical language; a paraphrase seeks only to give a thought or concept rendering. A paraphrase would take the basic thought that the writer was seeking to get across and then translate that as a whole. A couple of the more popular examples of this are the *J. B. Philips Translation* and *The Living Bible*.

C. **A good study Bible**: Many Christians find one of these very helpful. Generally these types of Bibles have good concordances, explanatory notes, geography, etc. in them. The NIV Study Bible is the best available, but some other popular ones are:

>   *NASB Open Bible*
>   *The Harper Study Bible*
>   *The Ryrie Study Bible*
>   *Nelson KJV Study Bible*

D. **A good recent concordance**: A concordance will give you all of the words used in the Bible, so it is a quick handy reference tool when you want to look up a particular verse or subject. For instance, if you wanted to do a word study on "love or "faith" you would go to your concordance and quickly find every verse listed in the Bible where those words are found – and in certain ones the Hebrew or Greek word it comes from. A good concordance is essential for the serious student, along with a working knowledge of how to use it.

Also, you should have a ***personal study Bible*** (the one you use the most and carry with you) that has a ***basic concordance*** in it. Several I would suggest are as follows:

NIV Exhaustive Concordance

The New Combined Bible Dictionary and Concordance, Baker Books

Naves Topical Bible

The New Topical Textbook, Billy Graham Crusade Edition

The New Compact Topical Bible, Zondervan

Harper's Topical Concordance, Harper and Row

E. **Word Studies**: For the more serious Bible student, it is a must that you have a couple of good Word Studies. These list every word in the Old and New Testament and the Hebrew or Greek word they came from. This will really enrich your study of the Word – and often clear up some misunderstandings. This becomes especially important when you realize that there are around 6,000 English words that were used to translate over 20,000 Hebrew or Greek words! Several that I use regularly are:

Word Studies in the New Testament, M.R. Vincent

Word Studies in the Greek New Testament, Kenneth S. Wuest

NIV Theological Dictionary of New Testament Words, ed. Verlyn Vergrugge, Zondervan

Mounce's Complete Expository Dictionary

F. **A good Bible Dictionary**: There are many of these on the market today that are both good and affordable. Here are a couple you might consider:

Davis Dictionary of the Bible, John D. Davis

The New Compact Bible Dictionary, Billy Graham Crusade Edition

Halley's Bible Handbook

G. **Commentaries**: As I have previously stated, one can quickly spend a small fortune on Bible commentaries! There are several points I would make concerning commentaries.

(1) First, it is good to study what the Holy Spirit has taught godly men in the past. However, we should not slavishly follow a human teacher. This can easily lead to a cultic type of bondage to one man's interpretation (see: Matt. 23:8-10).

Jesus promised that His Spirit would teach us and guide us into truth (Jn. 16:13; I Jn. 2:27). If we are prepared, open and obedient, we can expect to be taught by God (Jn. 6:54; 1 Thess. 1:9; Ps. 119:99-100).

(2) Secondly, be careful in your choice of commentary! All men have basic presuppositions – and there are many commentaries on the market today that were written from a basic anti-supernatural, low-view-of-inspiration point of view.

These more liberal commentaries can undermine one's faith very subtly. This is because most young Christians and new Bible students do not have the "theological grid" to sift those opinions through. My advice is to ***choose books written by good conservative scholars***. I recommend books by men like Dr. Gleason L. Archer, Jr., Edward J. Young, W. F. Arndt, F. W. Gingrich, John R. W. Stott, Lordine Boettner, Francis Schaeffer, Donald G. Barnhouse, Charles Spurgeon, J. I. Packer, A. W. Tozer, F. F. Bruce, G. Campbell Morgan, etc.

(3) Lastly, ***go to a Bible commentary last rather than first so God can have a chance to speak a fresh word to you.*** It is very easy to let another man's thoughts influence, dictate, and circumscribe your own. Once we have read another man's interpretation, it is often very hard to then approach a text objectively – you have a tendency to read through the tinted glasses of his interpretation! His interpretation may be right, but at least allow God to teach you the same truth directly without going through someone else's interpretation. Then if you are still stuck in confusion, consult a commentary for some light! Here are a few I would recommend:

>*The New Testament and Wycliffe Bible Commentary (Moody Press)*
>
>*The New Bible Commentary, Revised, IVP*
>
>*The Life and Times of Jesus The Messiah, Alfred Edersheim (2 Vol.)*
>
>*Studies In the Four Gospels, G. Campbell Morgan*
>
>*Notes On The Miracles and The Parables of Our Lord, Richard Trench*
>
>*Clarke's Commentary (Older but still good)*
>
>*Matthew Henry's Commentary*
>
>*The Daily Study Bible, William Barclay, (good but liberal at points)*
>
>*Evangelical Commentary on the Bible, ed. Walter Elwell, Baker*

H. **Other Helpful Tools**:

(1) Bible Atlas

(2) Online: www.crosswalk.com

www.crossSearch.com/Reference

www.biblegateway.com

www.christianitytoday.com

Vary Your Approach to Bible Study: The Bible can and should be studied from many different angles. Each one will yield a rich treasure of knowledge. Several suggestions are as follows:

A. **Thematic or Doctrinal Study**: Study the great doctrines of the Bible from Genesis to Revelation: God, Man, Sin, Salvation, etc. Before you can arrive at a systematic theology on any point you must study it throughout the entire Bible. This type of study really begins to give one a grasp of "**...the faith that was once for all entrusted to the saints**" (Jude 3).

B. **Word Study**: Here, instead of studying the doctrines of the Bible you study the words that teach us the great truths of God's Word: love, guidance, faith, repentance, witness, etc. This will begin to shed much more light on a great deal of God's Word. The Greek language was a much more precise language than English – so a study of the exact words will help us have a more accurate understanding and therefore application of God's Word at many points.

C. **Character Study**: Go through the Bible and study the great heroes and patriarchs of the faith: Abraham, Moses, Joshua, David, Paul, etc. It is also good to do more specialized studies: Women of the Bible, Women in the life of Christ, the 12 Disciples, Young people in the Bible used by God, Faithful in the Bible, etc.

D. **Study by Outline**: To really begin to grasp and digest a portion of the Word or an entire book, it is very helpful to outline it. This becomes sort of a blueprint of that section. Here are some suggestions in building an outline:

(1) First, ***read the passage or section through several times slowly and reflectively to get it well into your mind***. This helps you to get an overview of the entire section as

well as its *continuity*. As you read, ask yourself these questions:

> *"What is there <u>generally</u>?"*
> *"What is there <u>specifically</u>?"*
> *"What is there <u>personally</u>?"*

To help you even further, as you read it again, ask yourself:

> *"Is there any promise here for me to claim?"*
> *"Is there any thought of illumination to further pursue?"*
> *"Is there any command here for me to obey?"*
> *"Is there any sin pointed out here for me to avoid?"*
> *"Is there any new insight into God, Jesus Christ, or the Holy Spirit?"*
> *"What is God trying to say to me in this passage?"*

So **always seek to make God's Word *personal to you as you read and study***. Only then will it have relevance to your life and bring joy and excitement to your living!

(2) Next, read it again and **write down thoughts, interpretations, and observations as you read.** There is just no substitute for writing! REMEMBER, *light is illumination* – and *illumination is transient by nature!* It is illusive and fleeting and ***if you do not capture it when you receive it you will probably lose it.*** When you lose light given you – you usually cannot recall and recapture it. Writing helps us *crystallize, localize* and *focalize God's word* to us – so "WRITE, WRITE, WRITE." A pulsating pen is essential for a pursuing mind! Therefore, you must study God's Word with

an open, disciplined mind, a prayerful heart, an obedient will – and a pulsating pen!

(3) Then, **think of a title for the particular passage, chapter or book under study**. To do this, be sure to analyze it by thought units – i.e., paragraphs and not chapter divisions or verses (see section on "chapters"). Try to determine what the particular writer's purpose was: historical, theological, narrative, praise, etc. Ask yourself:

"WHY?"	*(Did he write it?)*
"WHAT?"	*(Was he trying to get across?)*
"WHERE?"	*(Was it written from?)*
"WHO?"	*(Was it written to?)*, etc.

For example, Romans through Galatians has to do principally with *Salvation* – so they could be subtitled *"The Cross"*. Ephesians through Philippians has to do with the Body of Christ and could be subtitled "The Church". I & II Thessalonians are principally about the end times and could be subtitled *"The Coming,"* etc.

(4) Try to **reduce the key passages to Biblical Principles**. *A Biblical Principle might be defined as succinct, terse, polished statement of a universal truth boiled down to its irreducible minimum! These will stay with you for life and give you the practical handles you need to apply God's Word to your everyday living.*

Memorize and Meditate on God's Word

There are great spiritual rewards that come only as a result of meditating on God's Word (Ps. 1; Josh. 1:8; Eph. 5:18-19, etc.). Generally speaking, Christian meditation is a lost discipline within the church today. New Age Zen meditation and other Eastern meditation movements are arising and growing in this Christian void.

Let me also say a word about **memorizing God's Word**. This is also a lost discipline in Christianity today. I believe that is because meditation and memorization are inseparably connected. Let me explain. Most people memorize by just learning the rote sequences of words. After a portion is learned by this method, one may know the sequence of words that compose the particular verse or portion of scripture – and yet not understand the meaning. The best way to memorize with real meaning and understanding is to **meditate on a portion of Scripture until you fully grasp its meaning**. In the process of doing this you will also likely memorize it. Then to maintain your fresh grasp of that scripture, use it often. Quote it, share it, and speak it! It is a basic law of life that you either use it or lose it! Memorize by meditation – and maintain your grasp of it by using it often. The reward of this will be freedom (Jn. 8:31-32). You will enjoy that glorious liberty of a child of God (Rom. 8:21). As King David said so many years ago: "**I will always obey Your law, for ever and ever. I will walk about in freedom, for I have sought out Your precepts**" (Ps. 119:44-45).

I would like to close by sharing with you one of the most challenging – and convicting – quotations concerning memorizing God's Word I have come across. It is from Watchman Nee.

"The young people in particular ought to...engage in memory work. During the first few years after being saved great effort should be made to memorize Scripture. Lots of passages need to be recited, such as Psalm 23, Psalm 91, Matthew 5, 6 and 7, John 15.9 1 Corinthians 13, Romans 2 and 3, Revelation 2 and 3, and so forth. Those with good memory can perhaps memorize ten or so odd verses a day, while people with a weak memory can at least remember one verse. If a person spends five to ten minutes each day reading a verse, searching and memorizing it, he will be able to finish such books like Galatians or Ephesians in approximately six months, Philippians in about four months, Hebrews in around ten months, and the Gospels such as John in nearly eighteen months. Should young brothers and sisters commence to read the Bible carefully at the start and recite at least one verse each day, they can without doubt memorize nearly all the main parts of the New Testament within four years. Such progress as outlined here has reference to

people with weak memory. Those with a strong memory do not need so much time as this for achieving such a goal."[130]

Does that convict you?! When I first started to read Watchman Nee I was amazed at his spiritual understanding and overall grasp of the Bible – especially when some of his major works were written when he was in his 20's! When I came across this book, I understood the secret of his insight! He supposedly read the Bible through 105 times before he wrote his first book! Throughout his life he averaged reading the Bible through about once a month – no wonder God blessed him so much! You may not become a writer, like Nee - but if you take God's Word as seriously as he did, it will eternally enrich your life!

Quotations for Further Reflection

- [Fanny Crosby wrote about 9,000 hymns – more than anyone in recorded Christian history. She was an accomplished harpist and organist, and she was blind.] *When Fanny was eight or nine, Mercy (her mother) moved again...and Fanny was left during the day in the care of the landlady, a Mrs. Hawley...Mrs. Hawley set Fanny to the task of memorizing the entire Bible, giving the child a number of chapters to learn each week – often as many as five. There were repeated line by line, drilled into the little girl's head "precept upon precept." Being young and gifted with a phenomenal memory, Fanny had no trouble mastering Genesis, Exodus, Leviticus, and Numbers, as well as the four Gospels, by the end of the first year. At the end of two years, Fanny could repeat by rote not only the entire Pentateuch and all four Gospels but also many of the Psalms, all of the Proverbs, all of Ruth, and "that greatest of all prose poems, the Song of Solomon." This training sufficed Fanny for a lifetime. From then on she needed no one to read the Bible to her. Whenever she wanted to "read" a portion of Scripture, she turned a little button in her mind, and the appropriate*

---

[130] Watchman Nee, *Ye Search the Scriptures*, New York: Christian Fellowship Publishers, Inc., 1974, p. 98.

passage would flow through her brain like a tape recording...People marveled at her wonderful memory. They were dumbfounded at her ability to commit a seemingly endless number of hymns to memory and dictate them without apparent difficulty, one after the other. But whenever they made a great deal of this "talent," Fanny would give them a lecture, maintaining she simply was using a gift – memory – which God gives to everyone, but which most people with sight lose through laziness. She criticized "memorandum tablets and carefully kept journals and ledgers" as destructive to "the books of the mind."[131]

- The Pharisees studied God. They memorized the Scriptures and knew every word...They felt that through study they could find God and that knowledge was the avenue to transformation. Jesus Himself commented to the Pharisees, **"You search the Scriptures, because you think that in them you have eternal life"** (Jn. 5:39). To know the Scriptures is to know God, they thought...The Pharisees considered themselves supremely righteous because of their vast knowledge. But they misunderstood a vital point. **Mere information makes no one righteous; it only makes us responsible for what we know.** It is impotent to effect real and lasting change within us. One may be overeducated and untransformed...the degree to which we know something is the degree to which we have integrated it into our everyday life.[132]

- "Let me seek Thee in longing," pleaded Anselm, "let me long for Thee in seeking; let me find Thee in love, and love Thee in finding."... Knowledge of such a Being cannot be gained by study alone...To know God is at once the easiest and the most difficult thing in the world... First, we must forsake our sins... **"Blessed are the pure in heart: for they shall see God."** Second, there must be an utter committal of the whole life to Christ in faith...a volitional and emotional attachment to Him accompanied by a firm purpose to obey Him in all things... Third, there must be a reckoning of ourselves to have died unto sin and

---

[131] Bernard Ruffin, *Fanny Crosby, The Hymn Writer*, Uhrichsville, OH: Barbour Publishing, 1995, pp. 23-24, 129.

[132] Rebecca Manley Pippert, Out of the *Salt Shaker and Into the World*, Downers Grove, IL: InterVarsity Press, 1999, pp. 84-85.

to be alive unto God in Christ Jesus, followed by a throwing open of the entire personality to the inflow of the Holy Spirit. Then we must practice whatever self-discipline is required to walk in the Spirit, and trample under our feet the lusts of the flesh. Fourth, we must boldly repudiate the cheap values of the fallen world...Fifth, we must practice the art of long and loving meditation upon the majesty of God...by a deliberate act of the will and kept so by a patient effort of the mind... **There is a glorified Man on the right hand of the Majesty in heaven faithfully representing us there. We are left for a season among men; let us faithfully represent Him here.** [133]

- Summary of Principles for Understanding Apparent Discrepancies in the Bible

    1. The unexplained is not necessarily unexplainable.
    2. Fallible interpretations do not mean fallible revelation.
    3. Understand the context of the passage.
    4. Interpret difficult passages in the light of clear ones.
    5. Don't base teaching on obscure passages.
    6. The Bible is a human book with human characteristics.
    7. Just because a report is incomplete does not mean it is false.
    8. New Testament citations of the Old Testament need not always be exact.
    9. The Bible does not necessarily approve of all it records.
    10. The Bible uses non-technical, everyday language.
    11. The Bible may use round numbers as well as exact numbers.
    12. Note when the Bible uses different literary devices.
    13. An error in a copy does not equate to an error in the original.
    14. General statements don't necessarily mean universal promises.
    15. Later revelation supercedes previous revelation.

We should not build a doctrine on an obscure passage. The rule of thumb in Bible interpretation is "the main things are the plain things, and the plain things are the main things." This is called the perspicuity

---

[133] A. W. Tozer, *The Knowledge of the Holy,* New York, NY: HarperCollins, 1961, pp. 20, 115-117.

(clearness) of Scripture. If something is important, it will be clearly taught in Scripture, and probably in more than one place.[134]

---

[134] Josh McDowell, *The New Evidence that Demands a Verdict*, Nashville: Thomas Nelson Publishers, 1999, pp. 47, 49.

Appendix I

IMPORTANT NEW TESTAMENT RELATED DATES

37 B.C. – 4 A.D.	Reign of King Herod ("The Great"). King Herod died at age 70 in the 750th year of Rome, 4 B.C., according to Josephus.
	(Note: The Western tradition of the observance of December 25th did not arise until the 4th century, so has no authority; the Eastern church still observes January 6th as Christ's birthday.)
5 or 4 B.C.	Birth of Christ [135]

---

[135] Jesus Christ was not born in the year 1 A.D. as you might suppose. An error occurred in the preparation of our calendar that accounts for this. The Romans were the dominating world power when Christ was born. *They generally dated all events from the foundation of Rome in approximately 753 B.C.* Therefore, all Roman dates were followed by the letters A.U.C., which was the abbreviation *for anno urbis conditae* meaning *"in the year of the founding of the city"*. Dating all events by a calendar invented by the pagan Romans was not satisfactory with Christians for long. So in the 6th century the Pope wanted to have a calendar which would date all events form the birth of Christ rather than from the founding of Rome. He commissioned a monk named *Dionysius* to do the work. This calendar when finished was gradually adopted by all of Christendom. Modern scholars though have found that some dates of Roman history near the beginning of the Christian era cannot be reconciled with the calendar of Dionysius. For example, Roman annals say that Herod the Great, who ruled Judea when Jesus was born, died in the Roman year of 750 *anno urbis*. Dionysius placed the birth of Jesus in the year of 754 *anno urbis*, in contradiction to well established Roman records. So Jesus was most probably born in 749 or 750 *anno urbis* or 5 or 4 B.C.

28 A.D.	Beginning of John the Baptist's ministry
c. 27 or 28 A.D.	Baptism of Christ/Earthly ministry begins
30 A.D.	Crucifixion of Christ (Resurrection and Ascension)
c. 33 – 35 A.D.	Conversion of Paul
46 – 48 A.D.	Paul's First Missionary Journey
50 A.D.	Jerusalem Council
51 – 53 A.D.	Paul's Second Missionary Journey – I and II Thessalonians
54 – 58 A.D.	Third Missionary Journey – Galatians, I and II Corinthians, Romans } Doctoral Epistles
58 A.D.	Paul's Arrest
58 – 60 A.D.	Imprisonment in Caesarea
60 – 61 A.D.	Sent to Rome – Colossians, Philemon, Ephesians, Philippians
63 – 65 A.D.	Release and Rearrest – I and II Timothy, Titus } Pastoral Epistles
67 A.D.	Paul's Death

Summary

4 B.C. – 30 A.D.   Life of Christ

30 A.D. – 62 A.D.   Apostolic Age

62 A.D. – 96 A.D.   Post-Apostolic Age
    (70 A.D. – Destruction of Jerusalem and Temple by Romans)

Appendix II
MANUSCRIPT EVIDENCE

There are a number of books on this subject available, and one of the best is F.F. Bruce's New Testament Documents. He gives an excellent comparison of scriptural and secular historical documents: "Perhaps we can appreciate **how wealthy the New Testament is in manuscript attestation** *if we compare the textural material for other ancient historical works. For Caesar's Gaelic War (composed between 58 and 50 B.C.) there are several extant MSS, but only nine or ten are good, and the oldest is some 900 years later than Caesar's day. Of the 142 books of the Roman History of Livy (59 B.C. - A.D. 17) only thirty-five survive...The extant MSS of his minor works (Dialogue de Oratoribus, Agaicola, Germania) all descend from a codex of the tenth century. The History earliest belonging to c. A.D. 900, and a few papyrus scraps, belonging to about the beginning of the Christian era. The same is true of the History of Hereodotus (c. 480-425 B.C.)"*[136] *To perhaps help you better understand and appreciate the significance of that quotation, let me share a chart that I think will be helpful.*

---

[136] F. F. Bruce, *The New Testament Documents: Are They Reliable?* Downers Grove, IL: InterVarsity Press, 1960, p. 16.

Chart of Secular Historical Documents

Author	Date Written	Earliest Copy	Time Span	No. of Copies
Caesar's *Gallic War*	c. 58-50 B.C.	900 A.D.	1,000 years	10
Roman *History of Livy*	c. 59 B.C. – A.D. 17	?	?	35 (of 142 books) survive
Plato (*Tetralogies*)	427 – 347 B.C.	900 A.D.	1,200 years	7
Annals of Tacitus	100 A.D.	1,000 A.D.	900 years	1
History of Pliny the Younger	61 – 113 A.D.	850 A.D.	750 years	7
History of Thucydides	460 – 400 A.D.	900 A.D.	1,300 years	8
Syetonius (*De Vita Caesarun*)	75 – 160 A.D.	950 A.D.	800 years	8
History of Herodotus	480 – 425 B.C.	900 A.D.	1,300 years	8
Sophocles	496 – 406 B.C.	1,000 A.D.	1,400 years	100
Euripides	480 – 406 B.C.	1,100 A.D.	1,500 years	9
Catullus	54 B.C.	1,550 A.D.	1,600 years	3
Demosthenes	383 – 322 B.C.	1,100 A.D.	1,300 years	200
Aristotle	384 – 322 B.C.	1,100 A.D.	1,400 years	5[137]

---

137 All from one copy

| Aristophanes | 450 – 385 B.C. | 900 A.D. | 1,200 years | 10[138] |

(The above was taken from F.W. Hall, "MS Authorities for the Text of the Chief Classical Writers," *Companion to Classical Text*, Oxford, Clarendon Press, 1913)

In spite of the skimpy number of existing manuscripts – all of which are hundreds of years later than the historic event – no one would dare doubt their trustworthiness! F.F. Bruce concludes: *"No classical scholar would listen to an argument that the authenticity of Herodotus or Thucydides is in doubt because the earliest MSS of their works which are of any use to us are over 1,300 years later than the originals."* [139]

However, even though no classical scholar would either make or listen to an argument based on the long time span that exists between the existing manuscripts and the originals – *theologians and other scholars do it all the time in regard to the New Testament documents!* F.F. Bruce concludes it is because of the nature of the claims made by the Bible:

> *"The evidence for our New Testament writings is ever so much greater than the evidence for many writings of classical authors, the authenticity of which no one dreams of questioning. And if the New Testament were a collection of secular writings, their authenticity would generally be regarded as beyond all doubt. It is a curious fact that historians have often been much readier to trust the New Testament records than have many theologians. Somehow or other, there are people who regard a 'sacred book' as ipso facto under suspicion, and demand much more corroborative evidence for such a work than they would for an ordinary secular or pagan writing. From the viewpoint of the historian, the same standards must be applied to both. But we do not quarrel with those who want more evidence for the New Testament than for other writings; firstly because* **the universal claims which the New Testament makes upon mankind are so absolute, and the character and works of its chief Figure so unparalleled,** *that we*

---

[138] Of any one work
[139] F. F. Bruce, *The New Testament Documents: Are They Reliable?* Downers Grove, IL: InterVarsity Press, 1960, pp. 16-17.

want to be as sure of its truth as we possibly can; and secondly, because in point of fact **there is much more evidence for the New Testament than for other ancient writings of comparable date**." [140]

The Greek Scholar, J. Harold Greenlee, writes in *his Introduction to New Testament Textual Criticism:*

"...*the number of available MSS of the New Testament is overwhelmingly greater than those of any other work of ancient literature...the earliest extant MSS of the N.T. were written much closer to the date of the original writing than is the case in almost any other piece of ancient literature... The oldest known MSS of most of the Greek classical authors are dated a thousand years or more after the author's death. The time interval for the Latin authors is somewhat less, varying down to a minimum of three centuries in the case of Virgil. In the case of the N.T., however,* **two of the most important MSS were written within 300 years after the N.T. was completed**, *and some virtually complete N.T. books as well as extensive fragmentary MSS of many parts of the N.T. date back to one century from the original writings...Since scholars accept as generally trustworthy the writings of the ancient classics even though the earliest MSS were written so long after the original writings and the number of extant MSS is in many instances so small, it is clear that* **the reliability of the text of the N.T. is likewise assured**." [141]

The conclusions are obvious! When you compare the often few and fragmentary manuscripts of classical writers – most of which date hundreds to a thousand or more years from the originals – you see that **the New Testament writings truly are the most documented manuscripts of history!**

In order to help you better appreciate the **comparison between classical and New Testament writings**, let me share the following chart with you. Please carefully compare the very early dates of these Biblical

---
140 Ibid., p. 15.
141 J. Harold Greenlee, *Introduction to New Testament Textual Criticism*, Grand Rapids: W. B. Eerdmans Publishing Co., 1964, pp. 15-16.

manuscripts with the very late ones on the preceding pages for the classical manuscripts.

Chronology of New Testament Manuscripts

Name of Manuscript	Date	Significance
John Ryland MSS	130 A.D.	It is called such because it is housed in the John Ryland Library of Manchester, England. It is the oldest fragment of the N.T. It would strongly contend that the Gospel of John was not a second century writing as the German professor Baur said.
Chester Beatty Papyri	200 A.D.	Located in the Chester Beatty Museum in Dublin. It contains major portions of the N.T.
Bodmer Papyrus II	150 – 200 A.D.	Housed in the Bodmer Library of World Literature. It contains most of the Gospel of John.
Diatessaron	160 A.D.	It means "a harmony of four parts" and was the first harmony of the Gospels. It was done by Tatian.
Codex Sinaiticus	350 A.D.	Contains almost all of the N.T. and over half of the O.T. It was found in a wastebasket in the Mount Sinai Monastery in 1844.
Codex Vaticanus	325 – 350 A.D.	It contains almost the entire Bible.
Codex Alexandrinus	400 A.D.	It also contains almost the entire Bible.
Codex Ephraemi	400's A.D.	Every book except II Thessalonians and II John
Codex Bezae	450 A.D. plus	Cambridge Library. It contains the Gospels and Acts in both Greek and Latin.
Codex Washingtonensis or *Codex Freericanus*	450 – 550 A.D.	It contains the four Gospels in the following order: Matthew, John, Luke, Mark.
Codex Claromontanus	500's A.D.	It also is a bilingual MSS that contains the Pauline Epistles.

At about this point you might be saying: *"Why does it matter how many manuscripts we have of the New Testament and how early they are?"* The point is just this: *The shorter the time period between the original autographs* (the writings by the N.T. writers themselves which we do not have) *and the earliest copies we have, the better* **historical confirmation of their accuracy.** *Conversely, the longer the time lapse the more problematic because of the increased potential for corruption of the text.*

Illustration:

Original Autographs

↓

copy "B"   copy "C"   copy "D"   copy "E"

By using this illustration to compare classical and Biblical writings we can see the difference.

CLASSICAL WRITINGS
Original Autographs

"A"

copy "B"   copy "C"

A very short period of time

A long period of time

BIBLICAL WRITINGS
Original Autographs

"A"

copy "B"   copy "C"

When you stop to consider that all of the New Testament autographs or "A" were written between 50 and 100 A.D. – and the earliest manuscript we currently have, or "Copy B", is dated a 130 A.D. (John Ryland MSS), you can see *that the time span between the two is historically so small that it is insignificant!* However, the lapse between point "A" and "B" in classical writings is often a thousand or more years! And yet, their authenticity is not questioned – and the Biblical one is constantly challenged! How academically incongruous!

However, the time lapse between the original autographs and the earliest copies is not the only thing that is important. There is also the matter of the number of copies we have for the purpose of comparative study and textual criticism. *If you have copies of the original manuscript – the more copies you have, the better chance you have of reconstructing the original.*

Illustration:
Original Autographs [142]

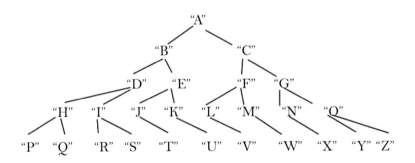

Starting with "P" through "Z" we can work back and better reconstruct "A". Remember that we now have over 13,000 manuscripts or portions of the New Testament – *literally thousands more than any classical writing!* Therefore, there is less than 1/1,1000th chance of error or variance – or about 1 word per page in the New Testament. And *there is no doctrine involved that is not somewhere else plainly given in the Word.* So *even though*

---

142 Adapted from Josh McDowell's book *Evidence that demands a Verdict*, p. 51.

only the original manuscripts (autographs) were inspired – the copies we have today are absolutely trustworthy!

Conclusions

Allow me to conclude this section with several cogent statements by renowned New Testament scholars: *"The works of several ancient authors are preserved for us by the thinnest possible thread of transmission...In contrast with these figures, the textural critic of the New Testament is embarrassed by the wealth of his material."* [143]

There is yet another vast resource of Biblical substantiation for the Christian – *the writings of the early church Fathers.* These are the ones who became the leaders of the church after the death of the original disciples of Christ. Like Paul, Luke, John and the other Biblical writers, these men were very prolific in their writing. Obviously, they constantly quoted the New Testament in their writings, sermons and defenses to the pagan world of their day.

The compilation of their writings is itself a vast storehouse of Scripture! Two Biblical scholars concluded that: *"...The quotations are so numerous and widespread that if no manuscripts of the New Testament were extant, the New Testament could be reproduced from the writings of the early Fathers alone."* [144]

Perhaps the following chart will help you appreciate the richness of this resource.

---

[143] Bruce M. Metzger, *The Text of the Old Testament*, New York: Oxford University Press, 1968, p. 34.
[144] Normal L. Geisler and William E. Nix, *A General Introduction to the Bible*, Chicago: Moody Press, 1968, p. 357.

Quotations of the New Testament By Early Church Fathers [145]

Church Father	Gospels	Acts	Paul's Epistles	General	Revelation	Total
Justin Martyr (A.D. 133)	268	10	43	6	3 (266 allusions)	330
Irenaeus (A.D. 170)	1,038	194	499	23	65	1,819
Clement of Alex-andria (A.D. 150-212)	1,107	44	1,127	207	11	2,406
Origen (A.D. 185-233/4)	9,231	349	7,778	399	165	17,922
Tertullian (A.D. 160-220)	3,822	502	2,609	120	205	7,258
Hippolytus (A.D. 170-235)	734	42	387	27	188	1,378
Eusebius (A.D. 260? – 340?)	3,258	211	1,592	88	27	5,176
Totals	19,368	1,352	14,035	870	664	36,289

One other scholar, after studying these early church Fathers, said that in them he had "...*found the entire New Testament, except eleven verses.*" As J. Harold Greenlee said, the Scripture quotations in these early Fathers "...*are so extensive that the New Testament could virtually be reconstructed from them without the use of New Testament manuscripts.*" [146]

---

145 Adapted from Geisler and Nix, *A General Introduction to the Bible.*
146 J. Harold Greenlee, *Introduction to New Testament Textual Criticism*, Grand Rapids: Wm. B. Eerdmans Publishing Co., 1964, pp. 15-16.

- *"There is no body of ancient literature in the world which enjoys such a wealth of good textual attestation as the New Testament."* [147]

- *"...In the variety and fullness of the evidence on which it rests the text of the New Testament stands absolutely and unapproachably alone among ancient prose writings."* [148]

- *"The net result (of all these early N.T. MSS)...is, in fact, to reduce the gap between the earlier manuscripts and the traditional dates of the New Testament books so far that it becomes negligible in any discussion of their authenticity. No other ancient book has anything like such early and plentiful testimony to its text, and no unbiased scholar would deny that the text that has come down to us is substantially sound."* [149]

Saint, rest assured that your faith in the New Testament and in the Christ that it so clearly sets forth is *absolutely sound!* The manuscript and historic evidence are overwhelming and indisputable!

---

[147] F. F. Bruce, *The Books and the Parchments*, Westwood: Fleming H. Revell Co., 1963, p. 178.

[148] Fenton J. A. Hort and Brooke F. Wescott, *The New Testament in Original Greek, Vol. 1*, New York: The Macmillan Co., 1881, p. 561.

[149] Frederic Kenyon, *The Bible and Modern Scholarship*, London: John Murray, 1948, p. 20.

Appendix III

THE DEAD SEA SCROLLS: CONTENTS OF ELEVEN CAVES

Cave #1	Cave #2	Cave #3
Complete Isaiah Scroll	100 fragments of Exodus, Leviticus, Numbers, Deuteronomy, Jeremiah, Job, Psalms and Ruth	A 12" copper scroll with directions to 60 sites containing hidden treasures – which have not yet been found.
A partial Isaiah Scroll		
The Habakkuk Commentary		
The Manual of Discipline (the rules for the members)		
Thanksgiving Hymns		
A Genesis Apocrypha (Apocryphal literature abounded at Qumran)		
Wars of the Sons of Light against the Sons of Darkness		
Plus thousands of jar and cloth fragments		

Cave #4	Cave #'s 5 – 10	Cave #11
40,000 fragments of an unknown number of manuscripts – about 400 of which have been identified	A wide assortment of scroll fragments too diverse to list here	Very good portions of Psalms and Leviticus
About 100 of these were Biblical scrolls, and represent all the O.T. books except Esther (however, allusions to Esther have been found in other books). The fragments were: • 13 scrolls of Deuteronomy • 12 of Isaiah • 10 of Psalms • 6 of Exodus • 5 of Genesis		
A fragment of Samuel, dating from the 3rd century B.C. was also found – now thought to be the oldest known piece of Biblical Hebrew		

Note: A very interesting "Temple Scroll" also came out of one of the caves but it is not known which one because it was obtained during the 6 Day War of 1967. It contains a large number of religious rules and regulations for sacrifices and offerings. And interestingly, it contains a detailed description of the Temple – not so much as it was but as it was to be in the future![150]

---

150 *Bible and Spade,* Winter, 1978, Vol. 7, No. 1, pp. 5-6).

Appendix IV

THE "KING JAMES VERSION ONLY" CONTROVERSY

While many accept newer translations, some wonderful Christians agonize over the "translation controversy!" *Which translation is the best? Which one is the most faithful to the original Hebrew and Greek manuscripts? Which one has the highest view of God...Jesus Christ...salvation...the blood, etc?"*

For those who were raised on the King James Translation, or Authorized Version – there is no more precious or revered Book! They love the lofty sounding words...the poetic flow...the majesty of the tone. Many were even taught that it is the only translation that is the inspired Word of God. Therefore, reading any other translation is heresy – and jeopardizes one's salvation! Many of the "King James Only" people defend that translation as if it were written by the very finger of God – in the same way the 10 Commandments were given by God to Moses on Mt. Sinai! They will not even use the New King James because they believe it has become corrupted. They will read only the 1611 KJV as the truly Authorized Version. While some of them may secretly read the NIV, NASV or even the NLT for clarity of understanding – they do so with fear, guilt and condemnation. They feel that they have apostatized and compromised their faith.

Why do some feel so strongly about modern translations? According to James White, *"the KJV was not the first English translation, nor the last. Hence, it is perfectly logical to ask, 'Why should I use it as the standard by which I am to test all others?' Yet the reason, almost always, is found in the equation, 'The King James Bible Alone = the Word of God Alone.'"* [151]

In America today, only "Fundamental Churches" and ultra conservative ones continue to utilize the KJV or NKJV in their services. Most have chosen the NIV. But for those who do use the KJV – it is a "fighting issue!" While I will not fight or argue with anyone who chooses to use the KJV or NKJV, I would suggest that there are some authentic issues that need to be honestly looked at. Some have to do with archaeological finds. Others have to do with archaic words and evolution of language. Still others have to do with exegesis, etc. While the purpose of this book is not to focus on the "King James Only" controversy, we do need to try and set emotions aside, and objectively look at some of the issues on the table. But we do need to clearly say up front that there are Godly people and good scholars on both sides of this issue. Therefore, whatever side of this issue we come down on, we should make our stand with a sense of humility before God and each other as brothers and sisters in Christ! At the end of the day, the important thing is that EVERY Christian gets into God's Word in a systematic and understandable way so they can be conformed to the image of Christ!

There are some, unfortunately, who not only maintain their right to choose the KJV as their translation of choice…but who *"…believe that God supernaturally inspired the King James Version in such a way that the English text itself is inerrant revelation. Basically, God 're-inspired' the Bible in 1611, rendering it in the English language. As a result, these folks go so far as to say that the Greek and Hebrew texts should be changed to fit the readings found in the KJV!"* [152] They believe that the 1611 KJV was "new revelation" from the Lord – but remember, God may give further illumination but He has not and will not send new revelation.

---

151 James White, *The King James Only Controversy*, Minneapolis, Minnesota: Bethany House Publishers, 1995. P. 3.
152 Ibid. P. 4.

> *"When we look at how God led His people to recognize the canon of Scripture, the listing of the books that were inspired over against those books which were not, we note that God did not engage in any celestial fireworks in the process. No angels showed up with golden tablets marked 'Divine Index.' Instead, God worked with His people over time, leading them to recognize what He had already done through the act of inspiration. It took time, and some might wish for a more 'spectacular' method, but **God did it in His way, in His time.**"* [153]

In the same way, God chose to enable the text of the Bible to be written in different forms, and located in different areas (Alexandrian, Western, Byzantine, and Caesarean). How did this actually help to protect and preserve the text of the Bible? *"By having the text of the New Testament in particular 'explode' across the known world, ending up in the far-flung corners of the Roman Empire in a relatively short period of time, God protected that text from the one thing that we could never detect: the wholesale change of doctrine or theology by one particular man or group who had full control over the text at any one point in its history. You see, because the New Testament books were written at various times, and were quickly copied and distributed as soon as they were written, there was never a time when any one man, or any group of men, could gather up all the manuscripts and make extensive changes in the text itself..."* [154]

Let's look at where the KJV fits in the progression through the years. As James White writes, *"...this is not the first time in history that people have argued that a particular text, a particular translation, should be used exclusively by those who would be faithful to God."* [155]

1. The Hebrew Old Testament was translated to Greek, known as the Septuagint, and *"...the only translation of the Scriptures the early Christians had ever known was...the Septuagint."* [156]

2. In the early fifth century (400 A.D.), the Hebrew Old Testament was translated by Jerome to Latin, known as the Vulgate. Why

---

153 Ibid., p. 47.
154 Ibid, pp. 47-48.
155 Ibid, p. 10.
156 Ibid., p. 11.

did he do that? Latin had superseded Greek as the "language of the people" in the West – people were no longer speaking Greek! Note that he didn't translate the *Septuagint*, but his work was based on the actual Hebrew Old Testament. This caused quite a stir! The Christians were disturbed at his variations from the standard Septuagint.

3. 1,100 years later, Jerome's Latin Vulgate was the most popular translation in Europe. *"By the early sixteenth century the Vulgate was 'everyone's Bible.' It held the position in the minds of Christians that the Septuagint had held a millennium before."*[157]

4. With the advent of the ability to print books, in 1516, Desiderius Erasmus, a Roman Catholic priest and great scholar, published a Greek New Testament. In one column was the Greek text, and in the other, a new Latin translation. *"Not only was he dabbling with the language of heretics, Greek, but he dared 'change' the ecclesiastical text, the Latin Vulgate!...One cannot but note the irony that faced Erasmus. Just as Jerome's work had received criticism for being 'new' or 'radical' back in the fifth century, so Erasmus was berated in the same manner for daring to 'change' Jerome! What was once new had become traditional...And so we see a second time in the history of the church where a translation of the Bible became the 'norm' after centuries of use. When a new translation appears, a violent reaction erupts."*[158]

Interestingly, in Erasmus' rush to get his translation to print, he actually copied entire passages *directly* from the Latin *Vulgate*.

5. Erasmus' shocking translation – in the form of the *Textus Receptus* – ultimately became the **basis of the New Testament of the King James Version**. Stephanus used Erasmus' text to publish his four editions. The third one (1522) was the most "received text" of that day – and in Latin, that is called *Textus Receptus*.

6. Theodore Beza used Stephanus' writing as a basis of his own.

---

[157] James White, *The King James Only Controversy*, Minneapolis, Minnesota: Bethany House Publishers, 1995. P. 13.
[158] Ibid. p. 16 - 17.

While he followed it closely, he did make some changes known as "conjectural emendations" – changes made to the text without any evidence from the manuscripts. For instance, Rev. 16:5 originally read "**who art and who wast, O Holy One**." Beza's change was incorporated into the KJV: "**O Lord, which art, and wast, and shalt be.**"

7. In 1611, the King James Version was completed, having used a combination of texts from Erasmus, Beza, and Stephanus. The motive of its editors and translators was to place the Word of God into more readable modern English – just like our modern translations. In fact, *"for eighty years after its publication in 1611, the King James Version endured bitter attacks. It was denounced as theologically unsound and ecclesiastically biased, as truckling to the king and unduly deferring to his belief in witchcraft, as untrue to the Hebrew text and relying too much on the Septuagint."*[159]

Also, *"the KJV translators did not utilize just one Greek text when working on the New Testament. Instead, they drew from a variety of sources, but mainly from Erasmus, Stephanus, and Beza. When these sources diverged, the decision lay with the KJV translators themselves..."*

The Textus Receptus Versus the Textus Receptus Different Versions

Luke 2:22	their purification Erasmus, Stephanus, Majority Text	her purification (Beza, KJV, Complutensian, 76 and a few Greek minuscules, *Vulgate*)

---

[159] John Ankerberg and John Wledon, *The Facts on The King James Only Debate*, Eugene, OR: Harvest House Publishers, 1996. P. 12.

Luke 17:36	Erasmus, Stephanus 1, 2, 3, and Majority Text omit this verse	**Two men shall be in the field; the one shall be taken, and the other left** Stephanus 4, Beza, KJV along with Codex Bezae and the Vulgate
John 1:28	**Bethabara beyond Jordan** Erasmus, Stephanus 3, 4 Beza, KJV	**Bethany beyond Jordan** Stphanus 1, 2, Majority Text, Papyrus 66, Papyrus 75, Codex Sinaiticus, Codex Vaticanus, *Vulgate*
John 16:33	**shall have tribulation** Beza, KJV, Codex Bezae, f1 Lake Group, f13 Ferrar Group, *Vulgate*	**have tribulation** Erasmus, Majority Text, Papyrus 66
Romans 8:11	**by His Spirit** Beza, KJV, Codex Sinaiticus, Codex Alexandrinus, Codex Ephraemi	**because of His Spirit** Erasmus, Stephanus, Majority Text, Codex Vaticanus, Codex Bezae, *Vulgate*
Romans 12:11	**serving the Lord** Erasmus 1, Beza, KJV, Majority Text, Papyrus 46, Codex Sinaiticus, Codex Alexandrinus, Codex Vaticanus, Vulgate	**serving the time** Erasmus 2, 3, 4, 5, Stephanus, Codex Bezae, Codez Herleianus
I Tim. 1:4	**Godly edifying** Erasmus, Beza, KJV, Codex Bezae, Vulgate	**dispensation of God** Sephanus, Majority Text, Codex Sinaiticus, Codex Alexandrinus, Codex Herleianus
Heb. 9:1	**first tabernacle** Stephanus, Majority Text, KJV omits "tabernacle" and regards covenant as implied	Omit **"tabernacle"** Erasmus, Beza, Luther, Calvin, Papyrus 46, Docex Sinaiticus, Codex Vaticanus, Codex Bezae, Codex Herleianus
James 2:18	**without Thy works** Calvin, Beza (last 3 editions), KJV, Doces Sinaiticus, Codex Alexandrinus, Codex Vaticanus, Vulgate	**by Thy works** Erasmus, Stephanus, Beza 1565, Majority Text

The most important thing to note here is that there are *no variations in our translations that significantly impact doctrine.*

KJV	NIV
"Take heed therefore unto yourselves, and to all the flock, over the which the Holy Ghost hath made you overseers, to feed the church of God, which He hath purchased with His own blood" (Acts 20:28).	"Keep watch over yourselves and all the flock of which the Holy Spirit has made you overseers. Be shepherds of the church of God, which He bought with His own blood" (Acts 20:28).

"In this case the KJV translates the word that literally means 'to shepherd' as 'to feed,' which, while acceptable, breaks up the connection between 'flock' and 'shepherd' in Paul's thought. At the same time, the KJV maintains the longer sentence structure of the passage, while the NIV simplifies it by breaking it into two sentences, which might cause a person to miss the fact that in Paul's speech to the Ephesian elders, shepherding God's flock was the purpose for which the elders had been appointed to their office. **Neither translation is 'wrong,' they are simply different in certain aspects. By comparison of the two one has a better idea of what Paul said than would a person relying solely on one translation or the other.**"[160]

Some people may feel very uncomfortable with modern versions of the Bible, because they have been told that certain words, phrases, and even verses in the KJV are "omitted"…"deleted"…"left out" of the newer translations. In other words, did the NIV (for example) translators deliberately or even accidentally "forget" certain passages or text? No – but where they found that copyists or scribes had repeated or inserted a phrase *found elsewhere in Scripture*, they carefully checked several manuscripts to see if they were consistent with one another. Here are a few examples[161]:

---

160 James White, *The King James Only Controversy*, Minneapolis, Minnesota: Bethany House Publishers, 1995, pp. 129-130.
161 Ibid., pp. 157-158.

KJV	NIV	Background
"And knew her not till she had brought forth her firstborn son; and he called His name JESUS" (Matt. 1:25).	"But he had no union with her until she gave birth to a son. And he gave Him the name Jesus" (Matt. 1:25).	"Firstborn" borrowed from Luke 2:7: "and she gave birth to her firstborn, a son."
"And, behold, they cried out, saying, 'What have we to do with Thee, Jesus, Thou Son of God? Art Thou come hither to torment us before the time?'" (Matt. 8:29).	"'What do You want with us, Son of God?' they shouted. 'Have You come here to torture us before the appointed time?'" (Matt. 8:29).	"Jesus" is borrowed from the similar passage in Mark 1:24: "What do You want with us, Jesus of Nazareth? Have You come to destroy us?"
"So the last shall be first, and the first last: for many be called, but few chosen" (Matt. 20:16).	"So the last will be first, and the first will be last" (Matt. 20:16).	Phrase is borrowed from Matthew 22:14: "For many are invited, but few are chosen."
"Watch therefore, for ye know neither the day nor the hour wherein the Son of man cometh" (Matt. 25:13).	"Therefore keep watch, because you do not know the day or the hour" (Matt. 25:13).	Phrase is found in Matt. 24:44: "because the Son of Man will come at an hour when you do not expect Him."
"And they crucified Him, and parted His garments, casting lots: that it might be fulfilled which was spoken by the prophet, They parted my garments among them, and upon my vesture did they cast lots" (Matt. 27:35).	"When they had crucified Him, they divided up His clothes by casting lots" (Matt. 27:35).	Quotation borrowed from parallel passage in John 19:24: "This happened that the scripture might be fulfilled which said, 'They divided my garments among them and cast lots for my clothing.'"

> "...we have here [Matt. 1:25] another example of parallel influence that caused a scribe, undoubtedly zealous for orthodox doctrine, to insert the term "**firstborn**" here so as to protect a sacred truth and bring this passage into line with Luke's account. Modern translations, far from seeking to denigrate such divine truths, are simply seeking to give us what was written by the original authors."

This may help you understand reasons there are variances in the modern translations. It is not the purpose of this book to painstakingly detail all the scholarly research throughout Christian history. There are many resources available – and every Christian can be enriched by a study of Christian history. Please prayerfully consider the quotations below:

- *In the end, **the truth of Romans 8:28 will remain**...the end result of divisions like the KJO controversy will be to spur Christians who love God to a fair and honest study of the issues. This will result in an understanding of God's Word that honors God, upholds the trustworthiness of Scripture, and recognizes the importance of the facts surrounding the origin and inspiration, text, transmission and translation of the Bible.* [162]

- *Let's be grateful for what we do have. Both KJO [King James only] promoters and those who use modern translations have been more than blessed by God as far as His Word is concerned. They are privileged to have the Word of God more complete than the vast majority of God's people throughout history...Christians of today are immeasurably richer – not only to have the King James translation, but to also have reliable modern versions.* ***All believers should give thanks for the great wealth they do have*** *rather than bickering over relatively minor differences among translations. If you are a Christian who uses the King James Version – if you understand what you read and are comfortable with it – then by all means continue to use it. If you are a Christian who uses a good modern translation, you should also feel free to continue to use it.* [163]

---

[162] John Ankerberg and John Wledon, *The Facts on The King James Only Debate*, Eugene, OR: Harvest House Publishers, 1996. P. 40.
[163] Ibid, p. 42.

Appendix V

DATES OF THE NEW TESTAMENT DOCUMENTS

"*...in assessing the trustworthiness of ancient historical writings, one of the most important questions is: 'How soon after the events took place were they recorded?'*" (48, p. 14). If the time lapse was too great – there would be a larger margin for error. Let's look at the **dates that the N.T. books and letters were written** – and compare those dates with the ones I have listed on the preceding pages.

EARLY DATE (Conservative)[164]   **LATE DATE** (Liberal)[165]

Gospels

	Early Date	Late Date
Mark	c. 55-65	c. 64 - 70
Luke	c. 60 – 70	c. 70 - 90
Matthew	c. 60 – 70	c. 80 - 100
John	c. 80 – 100	c. 90 - 110

---

[164] F.F. Bruce, Rylands, Professor of Biblical Criticism and Exegesis at the University of Manchester, England.

[165] W. G. Kummel, Professor of New Testament, University of Marburg, Germany. If his dates are correct then much of the N.T. was not written by contemporary eyewitnesses of the events they record but reflect the views of the later church.

Pauline Epistles

Written from:

Galatians	c. 48 or 58	c. 56	Ephesus
I & II Thessalonians	c. 50	c. 55 – 56	(I) Ephesus (II) Macedonia
Philippians	c. (delivered by Tychicus)	c. 80 – 100	Rome
I & II Corinthians	c. 54 – 56 (delivered by Titus)	c. 50	Corinth (2nd journey)
Romans	c. 57	c. 56 – 58	Rome or Ephesus
Ephesians	c. 60	c. 55 – 56	Corinth (during last 3-month stay)
Colossians	c. 60 (delivered by Epaphras)	c. 56 – 60	Rome
Philemon	c. 60	c. 56 – 60	Rome
Titus	c. 63 – 64	c. 100 – 110	Possibly Rome
I & II Timothy	c. 63 – 64	c. 100 – 110	Possibly Rome

General

Acts	c. 60 - 70	c. 80 – 90
I & II Peter	c. 62	c. 90 – 95
James	c. 75	c. 70 – 100
Hebrews	c. 68	c. 80 – 90
Jude	c. 70	c. 95
I, II, III John	c. 85	c. 90 – 110
Revelation	c. 90	c. 90 - 110

Appendix VI
BIBLICAL TIMELINE

Biblical historians have tried to determine the dates for the creation of the world by counting backward from the birth of Abraham, which they estimate as 1995 B.C. With the detailed information that the Bible provides in the genealogies (in Genesis 1-11, 1,946 years are accounted for!), historians are able to place the creation of Adam in about 3941 B.C. How then do we explain where *Biblical dates* and *nonbiblical chronologies* differ? For instance, archaeologists date the ruins of a tower in the town of Jericho to at least 7000 B.C. – more than 3,000 years before Adam! In ancient times, different nations used different systems of dating. And even ancient versions of Genesis differ in the ages provided for the patriarchs.

Text   **Years from Adam to the birth of Abraham**

Text	Years
Hebrew Bible	1,946
Samaritan Pentateuch	2,247
Greek Septuagint	3,312

Since the early 1600's, when Archbishop James Ussher[166] determined the sum of the ages of all the patriarchs, the King James Version of the Bible has indicated as margin notes, not Bible text:

---
166 F Ussher was Archbishop of Armagh, Primate of All Ireland, and Vice-Chancellor of Trinity College in Dublin

Date of creation	4004 B.C.	
The Flood	2348 B.C.	2,008 years from Adam to Abraham
Abraham's birth	1996 B.C.	

Much of the information on this timeline prior to Abraham is still being studied by scholars – uncertain and not able to be verified. But we are simply concerned here with looking at what was happening in the world while the Biblical events were taking place. Please bear in mind that no timeline is perfectly accurate, as this one certainly does not claim to be! There are hundreds of wonderful Christians and scholars who would offer very good data and reasons why this chart might be contested or altered at certain points. But on the broad outline, there would be basic agreement. We are only trying to show broad general representations of what was happening in the world at *roughly* the time of Biblical events. If we wait until we have perfect information, with which everyone is in perfect agreement – the Lord will probably have returned!

Where you see a date preceded by the letter "c" it means that date is approximate. B.C. stands for "Before Christ". A.D. stands for *Anno Domini* – which is Latin for "Year of the Lord". In non-Christian writings, you will frequently see B.C.E. or C.E. instead of B.C. or A.D. They stand for "Before Common Era" or "Common Era" respectively. Why? Many other religions – as well as Jewish people who do not believe that the Messiah has yet come – feel the use of B.C. and A.D. imply their belief in and acceptance of Christ.

DATE B.C.	BIBLICAL EVENTS	GLOBAL/HISTORICAL EVENTS
c. 4000	c. 4000 Creation – Adam and Eve placed in the Garden of	3700 Wheel invented * Mesopotamia: Sumerian

Appendix VI

c. 4000	Eden (some sources state 3941) c. 3880 Cain murders Abel	civilization; cuneiform writing
c. 3000	c. 2500 – 2285 Evil increases c. 2285 The Flood – Noah c. 2284 The ark comes to rest on a mountain on the Ararat range, after 1 year and 10 days	c. 3000 World population 100 million * Egypt: Nile valley civilization; hieroglyphic writing; first pyramid built 2670; papyrus formed and Sphinx built 2550-2500 * China: Concept of yin and yang developed, herbal medicine and acupuncture are first used, silkworms are first cultivated
c. 2000	c. 2160 Tower of Babel (Babylon) c. 2000 Abraham	* Bronze Age * Egypt: Old Kingdom * No. America: early Inuit society * Greece: Indoor bathroom plumbing * Britain: Stonehenge built
c. 1900	c. 1950 Abram and Sarai (Genesis 17:8)	
c. 1800	1896 Abram becomes Abraham; Sodom and Gomorrah destroyed 1882 God commands Abraham to sacrifice Isaac c. 1835 Jacob and Esau are born to Isaac and Rebekah; Esau sells his birthright to Jacob for a bowl of beans (1805)	

c. 1700	1763 Jacob wrestles with an angel, and God changes his name to Israel 1727 Joseph, at 17, is sold into slavery in Egypt	* Egypt: Age of Pharaohs * Mesopotamia: Epic of Gilgamesh written (c. 1750); detailed astronomical observation begins * Crete: Minoan civilization
c. 1600		
c. 1500		
c. 1400		* China: Shang dynasty (c. 1480-1050)
c. 1300	1355 Moses is born 1321 Joshua is born 1315 Moses kills an Egyptian and flees into the Sinai Desert	* Egypt: Aton the sun god is worshiped; c. 1370 Nerfertiti marries her brother; c. 1360 Tutankhamen (King Tut) reigns as boy king; c. 1320 – 1237 Rameses I and II rule
c. 1200	1276 Moses sees a burning bush, and Moses and Aaron are commissioned to lead the Israelites out of slavery 1275 God inflicts the Ten Plagues on Egypt; Israelites eat the first Passover meal and depart the next day; three months after the Exodus, they arrive at Mt. Sinai, where God gave Moses the Ten Commandments 1273 Israelites arrive at Kadesh-Barnea, but are afraid to enter Canaan 1235 Balaam, a Mesopotamian prophet, is rebuked by his donkey 1234 Joshua leads the Israelites invading Canaan;	

	Israelite males circumcised; the walls of Jericho fall 1210 Joshua dies	
c. 1100	1196 Eglon of Moab takes Jericho 1178 Ehud assassinates obese Eglon 1156 Deborah, the judge, defeats Jabin 1140 Gideon defeats Midianites c. 1120-1115 Ruth, a Moabite widow, accompanies her widowed mother-in-law back to Israel, and marries Boaz – she is King David's great-grandmother 1105 Abimelech (Gideon's son) tries to make himself king of Israel, and reigns for 3 years	* Rise of India's civilizations * Egypt: Rameses III battles an invasion of the "Sea Peoples", who settle in southern Canaan and become known as Philistines
c. 1000	1086 Samuel is born to Hannah, and is raised by Eli at the sanctuary 1045 Samson dies by pulling down a temple on himself and a Philistine crowd c. 1025-1004 Saul, king of Israel 1016 David is anointed by Samuel 1015 David kills Goliath 1004 Saul commits suicide to avoid capture by the Philistines; his son Jonathan slain 1004 – 965 David reigns	* Greece: Trojan War * China: Chou dynasty * Babylon: Nebuchadne-zzar I * Italy: Asian tribes invade Italy The use of iron tools and weapons spreads from the Middle East to the Mediterranean region. * Central America: founding of Mayan dynasties * China: Refrigeration is developed using block ice cut in winter and stored

c. 900	991 David commits adultery with Bathsheba, and has her husband killed in battle	* Greece: Temple of Hera built at Olympia (975)
	989 Solomon is born to David and Bathsheba	* North Africa: founding of Carthage by Phoenicians
	978 David's son Absalom leads a rebellion against David; Absalom is killed in 976.	
	After David's death in 965, Solomon reigns	
	926 Solomon dies, and his son Rehoboam is crowned king	
	924 Pharoah Shishak invades and strips the Temple	
c. 800	870 King Ahab marries Jezebel, a devoted Baal worshiper	* Greece: first Olympic Games; Homeric epics *The Iliad* and The Odyssey
	862 Elijah challenges all of Baal's prophets to a contest on Mt. Carmel – they are defeated and executed; Jezebel swears to kill Elijah, and he flees	* Phoenicia: Ethbaal, Jezebel's father, is king of Tyre and Sidon (873 – 842)
	861 Elijah appoints Elisha his successor as prophet	
	850 Elijah is taken to heaven in a whirlwind	
	846 Elisha heals Naaman's leprosy	
c. 700	757 King Uzziah enters the holy area of the temple, and is afflicted with leprosy as a punishment	775 Greek script develops
		772 Asia Minor: Work begins on the Temple of Artemis at Ephesus, one of the seven wonders of the ancient world
	742 Isaiah sees a vision of God in the Temple c. 740 Hosea marries Gomer	763: (June 15th) Eclipse of the sun visible in Mesopotamia

APPENDIX VI

	734 Isaiah declares, "Behold a virgin shall conceive and bear a son" 722 Fall of Samaria	* Italy: founding of Rome. The principal Roman dating system begins from 753. 731-721 Babylon under Assyrian rule * China: Peking is begun as a settlement * Egypt: (712-663) Dominated by Ethiopian rulers
c. 600	698 Hezekiah cuts a 1,777-ft tunnel through solid rock from inside the walls to a spring outside, to secure water for Jerusalem 621 Hilkiah finds the book of the Law of Moses (probably Deuteronomy, newly put into writing) in the Temple 609 Egypt takes control of Palestine (Jewish independence lost for more than four centuries)	* Persia: Zoroaster * Greece: Aesop's Fables; Sappho; laws of Solon. 621 Draco authors Greeks' first written laws, which are "draconian" in their severity. 689 Sennacherib destroys Babylon 626 Babylon gains independence from Assyria, and dominates Mesopotamia. It destroys Nineveh, and the Assyrian empire is destroyed. (605 – 562) Nebuchadnezzar II * Egypt: (609 – 593) Pharaoh Necho II * China: Lao-tsu, the founder of Taoism, lives (604 – 531)
c. 500	597 Babylonians conquer Judah, destroy Temple, deport people to Babylon 594 Daniel interprets Nebuchadnezzar's dream 586 Fall of Jerusalem	575 Babylon: Nebuchadnezzar builds the Hanging Gardens, one of the seven wonders of the ancient world 568 Nebuchadnezzar of Babylon invades Egypt

	539 Daniel interprets the handwriting on the wall at Belshazzar's feast	* India: Siddhartha Gautama (the Buddha, "the enlightened one") lives 563 - 483
	538 Cyrus allows Israelites to return to Jerusalem; Judah a Persian province	* Asia Minor: King Croesus of Lydia invents metal coinage – an official mark or image stamped on a piece of precious metal of a specific weight (555)
	521 Haggai and Zechariah begin to prophecy, calling for the Temple to be built	
	516 The building of the Temple is complete	* China: Confucius (K'ung Fu-tsu) lives (c. 551-479)
		* Greece: Archaic period
		* India: Gautama Buddha experiences enlightenment after 5 years of asceticism and founds Buddhism (528)
		* Persia: Darius has a 125-mile-long canal dug between the Nile and the Gulf of Suez, opening travel between the Mediterranean and the Red Sea.
c. 400	480 Esther becomes Queen of Persia	* Greece: Persian Wars; Classical Age; Socrates, Plato, Euripides, etc.
	474 Esther exposes Haman's plan to kill all the Jews, and the king permits the Jews to destroy their enemies in Persia. (Feast of Purim)	* Greece: Sophocles and Aeschylus are leading playwrights. Pericles rises to power in Athens (461). The Parthenon temple to Athena is built in Athens (447-432). The Peloponnesian War between Athens and Sparta ends when Athens surrenders (431-404).
	458 Ezra sent to Judah, urging radical religious reform	
	444 Nehemiah, butler to Artaxerxes I of Persia, is allowed to rebuild the walls of Jerusalem	
	443 Nehemiah reappointed governor of Judah, enforcing tithing, the	

	Sabbath, and banning marriage to non-Jews	
	400 Book of Job written	
c. 300	397 Prophecy of Malachi	399 Greece: Socrates the philosopher is executed in Athens for undermining traditional Greek values.
	380 The prophet Joel foresees a time of restoration for Judah, in a time of locust plague.	397 – 347 Greece: Plato is active as a philosopher in Athens, and in 387 founds a philosophical school known as the Academy.
	332 Alexander the Great conquers Palestine	
	331 Samaria rebels against Alexander and is destroyed. Samaria is refounded as a Greek military colony.	371 – 289 China: Mencius (Meng-tzu), a teacher of Confucius' doctrines, lives.
	323 – 198 After Alexander's death, Palestine is controlled by Ptolemy, governor of Egypt. It is briefly ruled by Antigonus, then Ptolemy regained control, and it remained under Egyptian rule for the next century.	335 Greece: Aristotle founds a philosophical school near Athens.
		333 Alexander the Great conquers Persian Empire; Hellenization begins
		* Rise of Roman Republic. In 350 Roman armies develop the battle tactics of the Roman legion.
		323 Ptolemy, one of Alexander's generals, becomes governor of Egypt.
		322 Greece: Aristotle dies in Athens.
		312 Greece: Zeno, a Phoenician philosopher, comes to Athens and founds the Stoic school of philosophy.
		312 Rome: Engineers begin building the Appian Way, a Roman highway.
		300 France: The Parisi tribe founds a small fishing village called Lutece on an island

			in the Seine River – the origin of the city of Paris.
c. 200		285-246 Septuagint translated in Alexandria. This translation became the Bible of Greek-speaking Jews and later of early Christians.	* Rome conquers Carthage, Greece, and Asia Minor
			294 Egypt: The Library and Museum at Alexandria are established.
			270 – 232 India: Asoka becomes emperor and makes Buddhism the state religion.
			264 Rome: Mortal combat between gladiators is displayed for the first time in Rome.
			221 China: The country is unified under the Ch'in dynasty, founded by Shi Huang-ti.
			218 – 201 Rome: The Carthaginian general Hannibal crosses the Alps before being stopped.
			214 China: Shi Huang-ti begins construction of the Great Wall to block Mongol tribes.
			213 China: Shi Huang-ti orders Confucian classics burned.
			202 BC – AD 220 China: Han dynasty
c. 100		198 Antiochus III of Syria takes Palestine. Jewish governing classes are divided into pro-Egyptian and pro-Syrian factions. 174 Jerusalem is renamed Antioch at Jerusalem and given a Greek city government and Greek school (gymnasion). 167 Antiochus IV bans obedience to the Jewish Law. He devotes the Temple in Jerusalem to Olympian Zeus, and burns copies	185 India: The Maurya empire falls. Hinduism expands again. 179 Rome: The first stone bridge is built in the city. 170 Rome: Streets are paved. 169 - 168 Egypt: Antiochus IV invades Egypt, but a Roman ultimatum forces

of the Torah. Many Jews die rather than break their ancestral laws.

167 – 142 The Maccabean Revolt seeks Jewish independence from the Seleucids (heirs of Alexander).

164 Judas Maccabeus' forces recapture the Temple and begin to purify it for rededication. Antiochus V rescinds his father's prohibition of the Jewish Law.

163 A new Syrian army equipped with war elephants attacks and defeats the Jewish forces. The Syrians recapture the Temple and destroy its fortifications.

140 A faction of devout Hasideans is so scandalized by the appointment of the high priest they found a monastery at Qumran near the Dead Sea. They are well-known as the Essene sect, especially through the discovery of the Dead Sea Scrolls.

Another faction of the Hasideans who are more interested in teaching the law reconcile themselves to the appointed High Priest – and become the Pharisees.

134 Rome renews its treaty with the Jews.

107 Some of the Pharisees, whom the High Priest had supported, urge him to give up the high priesthood. He rejects the Pharisees and supports the more aristocratic sect of the Sadducees.

him to withdraw.

146 Greece: Roman armies destroy Corinth.

136 China: The emperor Wu Ti founds a state religion of Confucianism.

124 China: Wu Ti begins a university for Confucian studies and examinations for all civil servants. These continue until 1905.

116-107 Egypt: Ptolemy IX with Cleopatra III

107 – 101 Egypt: Ptolemy X Alexander with Cleopatra III

102 Italy: Julius Caesar is born.

101 – 88 Egypt: Ptolemy X with Cleopatra Berenice

100 China: Ships from China reach India for the first time

c. 50	94 – 88 The Pharisees lead a six-year civil war against the High Priest and self-proclaimed king, Alexander Jannaeus. 50,000 Jews are killed. After the revolt, 800 of the leaders (mostly Pharisees) are forced to watch their families being killed, and then they were crucified.	90 Rome: Vitruvius publishes his work On Architecture
		64 – 63 Syria: The Roman general Pompey conquers Syria and Palestine, ending the Seleucid empire.
		63 Rome: Cicero is consul; Julius Caesar is Pontifex Maximus (chief priest).
	76 – 68 Under the reign of the queen, Salome Alexandra, the Pharisees exercise great political power. The nobility and the Saducees resent the power of the Pharisees.	60 Rome: Julius Caesar, Pompey, and M. Crassus form the first Triumvirate to share power over the empire.
		58 – 51 Europe: Julius Caesar conquers Gaul.
	72 Herod is born to Antipater, a powerful Idumean Jew, whose father had been forcibly converted to Judaism.	
	63 The Roman general Pompey is asked by two Hasmoneans struggling for power to assist them each in claiming the office of High Priest. At the same time, a delegation of the Jewish people ask Pompey to overthrow both of them – and restore the historic government of priests. Pompey visits Jerusalem, captures the Temple, and enters the Holy of Holies. Hundreds of Jews are sent as slaves to Rome. Judea becomes subject to Rome.	
	50 The Pharisees interpret Pompey's conquest as God's punishment, and anticipate the coming of the Messiah, a king who will restore Israel and rule all nations.	

c. 40	48-47 Julius Caesar confirms the High Priest, and Antipater, Herod's father, as chief administrator of Judea. Antipater appoints his son Herod as governor of Galilee. 42-41 After his father is assassinated, Herod gives his allegiance to Mark Antony and is appointed a regional governor. 40 Herod goes to Rome, and the Senate appoints him king of the Jews, but he most overthrow Antigonus, high priest and king.	49 Italy: Civil war begins as Julius Caesar invades Italy against the forces of Pompey 48 Greece: Caesar defeats Pompey at Pharsalus. 48 Egypt: Pompey is murdered. Julius Caesar invades Egypt, defeats Ptolemy XIII, and installs Cleopatra VII and her brother Ptolemy XIV as Egyptian rulers. 44 Rome: Julius Caesar is proclaimed dictator for life, but is assassinated in a conspiracy led by C. Cassius and M. Brutus. Octavian, Julius Caesar's nephew and adopted son, arrives in Rome. 42 Rome: Julius Caesar is counted as a god of the state. Octavian is styled "son of god."
c. 30	39-37 Herod, supported by Roman troops, lands in Palestine and gradually conquers the land. Jerusalem falls after a bloody siege. 37-34 At 35 years old, Herod "the Great" is king of the Jews, and executes many who had opposed him. He changes high priests repeatedly throughout his reign. 30 After Octavian defeats Mark Antony and Cleopatra, Herod lays his crown before the victor, and Octavian confirms him as king of the Jews.	31 Greece: Octavian defeats Antony and Cleopatra in the battle of Actium. 30 Egypt: Antony and Cleopatra commit suicide in Alexandria.

c. 20	25 Herod builds a theater and amphitheater for Jerusalem. He inaugurates Roman-style festival games in honor of Augustus.	27 Rome: Octavian is officially given the title Augustus (Revered One) 25 BC – AD 14 Rome: Augustus' building projects in Rome transform it from a city of brick to a city of marble.
c. 10	13 – 4 Herod's family falls in to murderous intrigues over the succession. Herod descends into sickness and madness.	15 Europe: Roman conquests reach the Danube River
c. 1	8 Mary and Joseph are betrothed. The angel Gabriel visits Zechariah, a pious elderly priest, and promises that his wife Elizabeth will bear a son whose name will be John. 7 Herod has his two sons Alexander and Aristobulus executed for treason. 7 The angel Gabriel appears to Mary in Nazareth of Galilee to announce that she will bear a son to be named Jesus. 7 Mary visits Elizabeth, and stays until time for Elizabeth to bear her child. 7 Mary returns home. When Joseph learns that she is pregnant, he contemplates ending their betrothal, but he is told in a dream to take her as wife because her child is "of the Holy Spirit." 6 Mary and Joseph come to Bethlehem for tax registration, but find no place to stay. 6 Jesus is born in a stable in Bethlehem.	7 Bethlehem: A conjunction of Saturn and Jupiter makes a brilliant "star" in the sky. Some have speculated that this conjunction may be the Star of Bethlehem. 1 World population is about 250 million

Perhaps this helps you better understand not only the timeline of Biblical events, but the intrigue at the time of Jesus' birth! When you understand the heavy Roman hand on the area, and the hopes of the Pharisees and the Jewish people for a Messiah who would assume political power – perhaps you can sadly grasp their dismissal of the "suffering Servant"!

You may notice that other world religions are indicated, while Islam is not on this chart. This is because Muhammad the Prophet lived in 570-632 AD. Islam is the youngest of the very large religions (although their belief is that their precepts go back to creation), having been founded in 622 AD.

Sources:
Halley's Bible Handbook

The Bible Timeline by Thomas Robinson, Nashville: Thomas Nelson Publishers, 1992. Note that this resource utilizes material from Apocryphal as well as Biblical and historic information (i.e. 1, 2 and 3 Maccabees)

www.historychannel.com

Information on Islam, Hinduism, Confucianism, and Buddhism confirmed by information on www.religioustolerance.org

United Methodist Women in Mission website: http://gbgm-umc.org/umw/bible/timebce.stm

Appendix VII

New Testament References to Old Testament Events [167]

Old Testament Event	New Testament Reference
1. Creation of the universe (Gen. 1)	John 1:3; Col. 1:16
2. Creation of Adam and Eve (Gen. 1-2)	I Tim. 2:13, 14
3. Marriage of Adam and Eve (Gen. 1-2)	I Tim. 2:13
4. Temptation of the woman (Gen. 3)	I Tim. 2:14
5. Disobedience and sin of Adam (Gen. 3)	Rom. 5:12; I Cor. 15:22
6. Sacrifices of Abel and Cain (Gen. 4)	Heb. 11:4
7. Murder of Abel by Cain (Gen. 4)	I John 3:12
8. Birth of Seth (Gen. 4)	Luke 3:38
9. Translation of Enoch (Gen. 5)	Heb. 11:5
10. Marriage before the Flood (Gen. 6)	Luke 17:27
11. The Flood and destruction of man (Gen. 7)	Matt. 24:39
12. Preservation of Noah and his family (Gen. 8-9)	II Pet. 2:5
13. Genealogy of Shem (Gen. 10)	Luke 3:35-36
14. Birth of Abraham (Gen. 12-13)	Luke 3:34

---

167 Josh McDowell, *The New Evidence that Demands a Verdict*, Nashville: Thomas Nelson Publishers, 1999, p. 116.

15. Call of Abraham (Gen. 12-13)	Heb. 11:8
16. Tithes to Melchizedek (Gen. 14)	Heb. 7:1-3
17. Justification of Abraham (Gen. 15)	Rom. 4:3
18. Ishmael (Gen. 16)	Gal. 4:21-24
19. Promise of Isaac (Gen. 17)	Heb. 11:18
20. Lot and Sodom (Gen. 18-19)	Luke 17:29
21. Birth of Isaac (Gen. 21)	Acts 7:9-10
22. Offering of Isaac (Gen. 22)	Heb. 11:17
23. The burning bush (Ex. 3:6)	Luke 20:32
24. Exodus through the Red Sea (Ex. 14:22)	I Cor. 10:1-2
25. Provision of water and manna (Ex. 16:4; 17:6)	I Cor. 10:3-5
26. Lifting up serpent in wilderness (Num. 21:9)	John 3:14
27. Fall of Jericho (Josh. 6:22-25)	Heb. 11:30
28. Miracles of Elijah (I Kings 17:1; 18:1)	James 5:17
29. Jonah in the great fish (Jon. 2)	Matt. 12:40
30. Three Hebrew youths in furnace (Dan. 3)	Heb. 11:34
31. Daniel in lion's den (Dan. 6)	Heb. 11:33
32. Slaying of Zechariah (II Chr. 24:20-22)	Matt. 23:35

Appendix VIII
The Error of the Documentary Hypothesis

Archaeology, as I have previously pointed out, is an exciting science for the world of biblical studies. As young as it still is as a scientific discipline, it has still cast much light upon the background of the Bible, and confirmed much of Bible history. Tragically, many people are not aware of the results of archaeological excavations. **Many theological theories and false beliefs would have to be set aside if more people would consider the evidence before they set forth their hypothesis.**

The history of theology – especially the theology of the last hundred years or so – reveals that there is a high mortality rate for theological theories that have been based more upon presuppositions than upon evidence. The subject of this chapter is one such theological theory. Tragically, it has not been set aside – but persists in its popularity in spite of the overwhelming, evidence that disproves it! It is variously referred to as the *"Documentary Theory"* or the *"Graf-Weahausen Theory"* or the *"JEDP Theory."*

Variations of this theory have been with us for over a hundred years now – and its influence is very current and contemporary. It is still taught today as "fact" in almost every college, university, graduate school and seminary classroom. It was taught to me in both a Methodist College and Seminary. Most of the students I work with still confront some form of the theory in the classroom every year in basic Old Testament Courses. And yet, ***the evidence does not support the theory!*** It is based far more upon the anti-supernatural presuppositions of its proponents than upon fact. ***The evidence of archaeology does not support the theory at all*** – and yet it is still being taught as though it is beyond question, and represents *"the consensus of scholarly research and opinion"*. However, to paraphrase Bishop Robinson, it is really based upon the *"tyranny of unexamined assumptions!"* (see page 149). It seems that once a theory/hypothesis is printed up in a textbook and popularized through repetition in the classroom it soon evolves up the academic scale from hypothesis to fact! As Josh McDowell said: *"What begins as a very tentative guess becomes by repetition an assumed fact and represents 'the consensus of scholarly opinion'"* (68, p. v).

A proper study of this theory and its many variations and modifications would fill many long, tedious chapters. I will therefore, only seek to give you a very basic overview of the theory. I hope you will come to realize the fallacies and dangers in this theory – and that it is just that – theory and not fact! Let me then begin with a very brief summary of the history of the theory.

A Brief History of the Theory

- In the early part of the 18th century a Protestant priest, H. B. Witter, asserted that there were 2 parallel accounts of creation (Gen. 1:1-2:4; 2:S-3:24) – and these accounts were distinguishable by the use of different divine names. He was the first, in so far as it is known, to suggest the divine names as a criteria for distinguishing the different documents.

- His theory was picked up and expanded by a French physician, Jean Astruc. He also believed that the different documents in Genesis were distinguishable by the different divine names – but he also pointed to repetition of events (creation, flood stories, etc.) as proof of different documents. However, he still believed Moses was the compiler of the documents. These were the earliest forms of the *"Documentary Hypothesis"*.

- The theory of Astruc was introduced into Germany by J. C. Eichhorn. He added that literary style (diversity in style, words, etc.), should also be a factor in discerning the various documents.

- Many others followed with their own variation of this theory: A Scottish Roman Catholic priest, A. Geddes, in 1800; in 1802 a German named Johann Vater further developed Geddes' theory. These were called the *"Fragmentary Hypothesis"*. In 1853, Herman Hupfield came up with a "Modified Documentary Theory". He said there were 4 basic documents discernable in the Pentateuch: P,E,J,D – and in that order.

- In the 1860's Karl H. Graf revised Hupfield's order to J,E,D,P. It was then picked up and popularized in Europe (and later America) by Julius Wellhausen (1844-1918), who had finished his variation of the hypothesis by 1895. Because of his role in popularizing the theory, Wellhausen has won a place in biblical studies comparable to the place held by Darwin in the field of biology!

All of the above information was gleaned from E. J. Young's book, *An Introduction to the Old Testament*, William B. Eerdmans, Grand Rapids, MI, 1963, pp. 125-164.

A Synopsis of the Theory

Wellhausen's theory is based largely on two basic assumptions:

1. That a literary analysis of the Pentateuch reveals *four basic documents* (called "J,E,D,P") and thus at least that many or more writers or compilers.

2. *The Religion of Israel evolved from animism into monotheism.* According to the theory, Israel's history was divided into 3 periods that reflect an evolution in their religious beliefs:

    A.   Preprophetic period;
    B.   Prophetic period;
    C.   Priestly period.

According to this theory then, t*he law came after the prophets* – rather than before them! This theory also says that the Pentateuch (Genesis to Deuteronomy[168]) was not written by Moses, as the Bible claims, but was completed years after his death – so these first 5 books of the Bible were written close to 1,000 years after Moses died. Rather than being written by Moses or by his supervision, this theory says that the Pentateuch came about through the process of oral transmission, writing, rewriting, editing and compiling by various anonymous redactors or editors. The reasons Wellhausen believed this was because of the different use of divine names, repetition of accounts, etc., used in the Pentateuch. He believed that these differences must mean different writers and compilers – thus J,E,D,P. But by now you are no doubt wondering what the letters JEDP mean or stand for! Let me explain them according to the theory.

JEDP

J   Stands for the divine name YHWH – which is the name for God commonly used by the "J" writer. (Note: it was called "J" because the German scholars who first "discovered" this writer spelled "*Yahweh*" with a "J".) He was the first or earliest writer to bring together the legend, myths, poems, stories, etc., – and even materials from other peoples such as the Babylonians into one great history. Some of the "J" sources were oral and some were *written*. This "J" writer lived about the time of King David

---

168 *Pentateuch comes from the Greek word for "5 volumes".* It was first called such by Origen in the 3rd century A.D. The Jews call these 5 books of Moses the "Torah" – from the Hebrew word meaning instruction.

or Solomon (c. 1,000-900 B.C.). When Israel was beginning to become a nation this writer desired to save the old traditions and so reduced them to writing.

E   Stands for the divine name *"Elohim"* because the "E" writer commonly used that name for God. He was the 2nd writer and he wrote about 700 B.C. – perhaps when the Northern Kingdom of Israel was in a time of danger from its enemies. The "E" writer was an especially good storyteller/writer and therefore preserved some of the best ones (ex. the story of Joseph). The "J" and "E" writers are often difficult to separate in the text so they are often referred to together as "JE". These two were put together about 650 B.C.

D   Stands for the *Deutetonomic Code*. It was primarily interested in reform in religious practices. According to the theory, it was probably written in the 7th century B.C. and perhaps made public during the reform of Josiah in 621 B.C.

P   Stands for the *Priestly writer* or writers. He/they were *the last writers to compile their materials* – or put the finishing touches on what the other writers (JED) had done. This probably took place during the Babylonian exile. These writers developed a *"holiness code"* for their people to observe, i.e., w*ays to worship, sacrifice, laws to observe,* etc. They were also the ones who were interested in genealogies, specific locations, dates, measurements, etc. They stressed God's intervention – even to the degree of the magical (miracles).

A Summary of the Theory

1. *Moses was not the writer of the Pentateuch.* The things that the Pentateuch records are post-Exilic instead of pre-Kingdom.

2. The literary analysis of the Pentateuch reveals *4 basic documents* – J,E,D,P.

3. It postulates therefore a late date for the composition of the Pentateuch – composed in its present form c. 400 B.C. – as opposed to the conservative/Biblical view is that it was written by Moses who lived 1,400/1,300 B.C. It should also be pointed that **the Mosaic authorship was also advocated by Jesus and the Apostles** in the New Testament (see below).

A Few Implications of the Theory

1. First, by *denying the Mosaic authorship of the Pentateuch*, the theory calls into question:

   a. The credibility of the entire Bible;
   b. The integrity of Moses;
   c. The trustworthiness of Jesus and Apostles.

   "*If this theory is correct then the entire Old Testament is a gigantic literary fraud.*"[169]

2. Secondly, this theory implies that *within the religious history of Israel we have a perfect example of the evolution of religion*. Wellhausen based his theory upon the then current **evolutionary philosophy/hypothesis** that assumed that an evolution from simple to complex or primitive to advanced has occurred in the religious realm, like they believed had in the physical realm. According to the theory then, the people of Moses' day were polytheistic and not monotheistic, until perhaps the time of Amos. Israelite monotheism came about, they believe, as a result of the purifying effects of the Babylonian exile. This theory then believes that the religion of Israel – and thus Christianity – has evolved from animism into monotheism.

---

169 Josh McDowell, *More Evidence that Demands a Verdict*, Arrowhead Springs, CA: Campus Crusade for Christ, Inc., 1975, 31.

spiritism/animism ⟶ polytheism ⟶ monotheism
(Judaism/Christianity)

As Gleason Archer says of the evolutionary theory of that day: *"An evolutionary understanding of history and an anthropocentric view of religion dominated the 19th century. The prevailing thinkers viewed religion as devoid of any divine intervention, explaining it is a natural development produced by man's subjective needs. Their verdict was that the Hebrew religion, as its neighbor religions, certainly must have begun with animism and then evolved through the stages of polydemonism, polytheism, menolatry, and finally monotheism."*[170]

3. Thirdly, *most who accept the theory hold that the people mentioned in the Pentateuch were not historical people* – but at the very most only *"idealized heroes"*. The Pentateuch then does not give us a true picture of the times they *report*, but a *romanticized religious history*. Also, since these people were not really historic, they obviously could not have had a physical tabernacle as recorded in Exodus.

4. Fourthly, *God never really spoke to* any individual in ancient times – not intervened in human affairs. The priests only give that impression through their writings. So if God did not really communicate to man then He did not speak to Moses! Besides, the law could not have been written in Moses time, since it represents a too advanced level for that age. After all, those people back then were not that civilized or educated (Don't forget the findings at Ebla in regard to this!).

5. Fifthly, *God never really acted redemptively on behalf of Israel* as Exodus reports.

---

170 Gleason Archer, *A Survey of the Old Testament*, Chicago: Moody Press, 1964, pp. 132-133.

Logical Consequences of Theory

The Pentateuch is relatively useless for us today as far as accurate history or trustworthy theology!

A General Refutation of the Theory

Even though Wellhausen's theory fits together well after you accept his basic presupposition – the cumulative result is still the same: 0 + 0 + 0 + 0 = 0! If the foundation is wrong so is the superstructure!

As we have already seen, Wellhausen begins with an anti-supernatural bias that makes *his conclusions pre-determined* – i.e., *"God does not intervene in the affairs of man."* Thus we live in a closed system! As C.S. Lewis said, their presupposition: *'If miraculous, unhistorical' is just not academic objectivity."*[171]

Then there is the problem one must face concerning the "redactor" or "interpolater" – *"Wellhausen's villainous ghosts"* as one writer called them! *Any time the recorded facts do not seem to fit Wellhausen's presuppositions – as when the variation of divine names are out of his documentary order – he falls back on the work of a redactor!* These anonymous gap-filling individuals are to Wellhausen what *time* is to the evolutionary hypothesis. In the evolutionary theory, any time there are gaps in their evolutionary chain (and there are more gaps than links!) – the evolutionists simply drop in a couple million years of time and say *"it evolved during this time."* No solid facts, objective controls, observable phenomena, etc., – but give the theory enough time and all gaps can be filled. Just so with the Documentary Hypothesis! Anytime the written scriptural records do not fit his preconceived pattern – Wellhausen calls in *his ever-faithful redactor and his editorial work* to explain the variance!

---

171 C. S. Lewis, "Faulting the Bible Critics," *Christianity Today*, June 9, 1967, p. 8.

However, the variation in divine names – particularly in the early chapters of Genesis (*Elohim, Jehovah*) – can be explained on **theological grounds**. The two divine names are not synonymous and were not randomly chosen by Moses. ***He chose whichever name for God that best fit his purpose and message.***

Comparison of Divine Names

YHWH[172]   ELOHIM

1. YHWH is a proper noun and is thus the more specific name that God uses when He reveals Himself specifically to man; It is what we might call the "proper name" for God.

1. Elohim is a common noun; the most frequent Hebrew Word for God – over 2,500 times in O.T. Plural in form; Christ used a form of it from the cross: "Eli, Eli, lama sabachthani". It was used both for the One God of Israel and for the heathen gods. It is the more general name for God without reference to His personality or moral qualities.

---

[172] The earliest MSS of the Hebrew Bible contain no vowels so the sacred name appears simply as YHWM (the "Tetragrammaton" or "tetragram"). The name was so sacred that a Jew would not even pronounce it – but would substitute "my Lord" (Adonai) for it. The Masorites later added the vowels – thus "Yahweh". The word means: "He who is", "*He who is present*", "*He who causes to be*". The English spelling for it – "*Jehovah*" was introduced by Tyndale.

2. This name expresses more of God's inner nature, essence and character; since these are only known through His self-revelation. Jehovah stresses God's imminence – His involvement in the affairs of His people – His Divine Presence. "Emmanuel" – God with us!

2. Elohim would have a tendency to stress the transcendence of God – His obscurity: "out there", "above, "outside" the physical universe He created.

3. This is the name of God used between Himself and His covenant people; the specific name for the God of Israel – the God of Abraham, Isaac and Jacob.

3. This is the divine name of God used with those who are not in a covenant relationship with Him.

- God revealed to the Jews that He is One: "**YHWH, He is Elohim**" (I Kings 18:39).

- So the common word "**Elohim**" came to hold the significance of the proper noun, "**YHWH**" or Elohim became synonymous with the name *YHWH*.

Finally we note to note that for Wellhausen, Abraham was a "free creation of unconscious art". However, archaeology as we have already seen, has demonstrated that the cities mentioned in relation to Abraham really existed – so if the cities really existed, why not Abraham?

A Biblical Refutation of the Theory

Jesus Himself over and over again in the New Testament affirmed the historicity of Moses as well as his authorship of the Pentateuch (see: Matt. 8:4; 19:3-9; 22:24-33; 23:2; Mk. 7:10; 10:3-9; 12:24-27; Lk. 16:29-31; 20:34-38; 24:44; Jn. 3:14; 5:45-56; 6:32; 7:10-23). For anyone who accepts the authority of Jesus, **His testimony is final!**

Also, the other New Testament writers likewise affirmed the same belief (see: Acts 3:22; 7:20-44; 13:39; 16:22; 28:23; Rom. 5:14; 9:15; 10:5, 19; I Cor. 9:9; 10:2; II Cor. 3:7-15; II Tim. 3:8; Heb. 3:2-5, 16; 7:14; 8:5; 9:19; 10:28; 11:23-24; 12:21; Jude 9; Rev. 15:3).

Finally, there is also no record through the 1st and 2nd centuries of the Christian era where the Mosaic authorship or the Pentateuch was denied. Both Apostolic and ante-Nicene (Council of Nicea, 325 A.D.) Fathers believed it.

A Brief Archaeological Refutation

One of the greatest problems with the theory is that it almost completely ignores the findings of archaeology – most of which were discovered after *Wellhausen formulated his theory*. As one writer said: *"Wellhausen took almost no note whatever of the progress in the field of oriental scholarship, and once having arrived at his conclusions, he never troubled to revise his opinion in the light of subsequent research in the general field."*[173]

Harrison further said: *"Whatever else may be adduced in criticism of Wellhausen and his school **it is quite evident that his theory of Pentateuchal origins** would have been vastly different (if, indeed, it had been formulated at all) **had Wellhausen chosen to take account of the archaeological material available for study in his day, and had he subordinated his philosophical and theoretical considerations to a sober and rational assessment of the factual evidence as a whole**. While he and his followers drew to some extent upon the philological (study of literature) discoveries of the day and manifested a degree of interest in the origins of late Arabic culture in relation to Semitic procurers, they depended almost exclusively upon their own view of the culture and religious history of the Hebrews for purposes of Biblical interpretation."* [174]

---

173 R. K. Harrison, *Introduction to the Old Testament*, Grand Rapids: Wm. B. Eerdmans Publishing Co., 1970, p. 509.
174 Ibid.

As the great Biblical Archaeologist and Scholar, William Albright, said: *"Wellhausen's structure was so brilliant and afforded such a simple, apparently uniform interpretation that it was adopted almost universally by liberal Protestant scholars, and even largely by Catholic and Jewish scholars. There were, or course, some exceptions, but in nearly all places where men were thoroughly schooled by learning Hebrew and Greek and absorbing the critical method, they also learned Wellhausenian principles. Unfortunately all of this developed in the infancy of archaeology, and was of very little value in interpreting history."* [175]

Over and over again in the last 75 years, archaeological discoveries have buried some of the previously held *"assured results of modern scholarship."* As A. H. Saycer renowned British Assyriologist, put it: *"Time after time the most positive assertions of a skeptical criticism have been disproved by archaeological discovery, events and personages that were confidently pronounced to be mythical have been shown to be historical, and the older writers have turned out to have been better acquainted with what they were describing than the modern critic who has flouted them."* [176]

The theory that Moses could not possibly have written the Pentateuch is based on the widely held theory of that day that before the time of David writing was uncommon and limited to specialists. However, contrary to this opinion, archaeology has now proven that writing was not only in existence – but abounded and was almost universally used in the Ancient Near East! Since Wellhausen postulated his theory, archaeology has proven that at least 6 scripts were in wide use in the Biblical world of Moses' day:

---

175 William F. Albright, *Archaeology and the Region of Israel*, Baltimore: John Hopkins Press, 1942, p. 15.
176 A. H. Sayce, Monument Facts and Higher Critical Fancies, London: *The Religious Tract Society*, 1904, p. 23.

> (a) Egyptian hieroglyphs
> (b) Sinaitic pictographs
> (c) Babylonian alphabet
> (d) Akhadian cuneiform
> (e) Ugaritic alphabetic cuneiform
> (f) And now "Ebaite" (see section on Archaeology).

The British Assyriologist A. H. Sayce, said this about this theory of the late appearance of writing in the ancient world: *"This supposed late use of writing for literary purposes was merely an assumption, with nothing more solid to rest upon than the critic's own theories and presuppositions. And as soon as it could be tested by solid fact it crumbled into dust. First Egyptotogy, then Assyriology, showed that the art of writing in the ancient East, so far from being of modern growth, was vast antiquity, and that the two great powers which divided the civilized world between them were each emphatically a nation of scribes and readers. Centuries before Abraham was born Egypt and Babylon were alike full of schools and libraries of teachers and pupils, of poets and prose-writers and of the literary works which they had composed."* [177]

Contrary to much popular "scholarly" opinion – everything in the ancient world was not left to oral tradition. Archaeologists have unearthed too many cuneiforms and archives to believe that theory any longer. Moses then was far from being illiterate! Dr. Donald Wiseman said that Moses *"...probably read eight languages. From the biblical account, he was raised in the court of Pharaoh, and was well educated."* [178]

Archaeology then continues to pull the ground from beneath Wellhausen! As another Biblical scholar said: "The vast resources of archaeology made available since the turn of the century have revolutionized the attitude of many biblical scholars and have led to a questioning of the two basic tenants of the Wellhausen theory." [179]

---

177 Ibid., pp. 28-29.
178 David Virtue, *"Archaeologist Finds Bible Best Historical Source,"* North Carolina Christian Advocate, October 22, 1978, p. 3.
179 Samuel Schultz, "Did Moses Write Deuteronomy?" *Christianity Today,* August 29, 1975, p. 12.

It is true that oral tradition was popularly used to spread information from the written source to the common people since there were no means of mass printing or communication. *"But to see oral tradition as the means of transmitting important materials from generation to generation seems unwarranted."*[180]

Also, since Deuteronomy presented a God-man communication, it is even more probable that Moses would have put it into written form for later generations. "Wouldn't you if God had spoken to you as He did to Moses?"

Not only does archaeology disprove the theory of the late appearance of writing, it also does not tend to substantiate the theory of the gradual *"evolution of religion"* from polytheism to monotheism. As Ronald Youngblood said: *"It cannot be shown that there is a universal tendency on the part of polytheistic religions to gradually reduce the numbers of deities until finally arriving at one deity. In some instance, in fact, such religion may even add more deities as its adherents become aware of more and more phenomena to deify! At any rate, the Old Testament teaches that monotheism, far from having evolved through the centuries of Israel's history, is one of the inspired insights revealed to the covenant people by the one true God Himself."*[181]

Of the many archaeological discoveries that would tend to support the Mosiac authorship of the Law, the discovery of the Code of Hammurabi (c. 2000-1700 B.C.) by itself is decisive – to say nothing of the legal codes found at Ebla! It was written several hundred years before the time of Moses (c. 1500-1400 B.C.), and contained some laws that are similar to those recorded by Moses. The Code of Hammurabi was a civil code as opposed to that recorded by Moses, which contained largely religious laws. Concerning the discovery of that Code, Joseph Free has said: *"In the light of this, the liberal has no right to say that the laws of Moses are too advanced for his time, and could not have been written by him."*[182]

---

180 Ibid., p. 15.
181 Ronald Youngblood, *The Heart of the Old Testament*, Grand Rapids: Baker Book House, 1971, p. 9.
182 Joseph Free, *Archaeology and Bible History*, Wheaton, IL: Scripture Press, 1969, p. 121.

Appendix VIII

Summary Evaluation of the Theory

1. First, archaeological discoveries have proven that the Graf-Wellhausen theory in reality was based far more on *subjective presuppositions and prior beliefs than objective facts!*

2. Secondly, the theory does not represent the *"consensus of scholarly opinion!"* Let me share a few statements by reputable scholars to underscore this:

    - *"It is very doubtful whether the Wellhausen hypothesis is entitled to the status of scientific respectability. There is so much of special pleading, circular, reasoning, questionable deductions from unsubstantiated premises that it is absolutely certain that its methodology would never stand up in a court of law. Scarcely any of the laws of evidence respected in legal proceedings are honored by the architects of this Documentary Theory. Any attorney who attempted to interpret a will or statute or deed of conveyance in the bizarre and irresponsible fashion of the source-critics of the Pentateuch would find his case thrown out of the court without delay."* [183]

One writer studied the basic premises of the Documentary Hypothesis and likened them to the pillars, which hold up a house. Concerning these theoretical pillars that hold up Wellhausen's theory, this writer said:

- *"I did not prove that the pillars were weak or that each one failed to give decisive support, but I established that they were not pillars at all, that they did not exist, that they were purely imaginary. In view of this, my final conclusion that the documentary hypothesis is null and void is justified."* [184]

Another Jewish scholar said:

- *"...we must reject the Documentary Theory as an explanation of*

---

183 Archer Gleason, *A Survey of the Old Testament*, Chicago: Moody Press, 1964, p. 99.
184 Umberto Cassuto, *The Documentary Hypothesis, Jerusalem:* Magnes Press, 1961, pp. 100-101.

the composition of the Pentateuch. The Theory is complicated, artificial and anomalous. It is based on unproven assumptions. It uses unthinkable criteria for the separation of the text into component documents."[185]

Conclusions

It can probably safely be assumed that much of current biblical study and criticism will continue to blindly cling to the Documentary Hypothesis and teach it as "fact". The Jewish scholar Cyrus Gordon has commented on this attitude as follows:

"When I speak of a 'commitment to JEDP', I mean it in the deepest sense of the word. I have heard professors of Old Testament refer to the integrity of JEDP as their 'conviction'. They are willing to countenance modifications in detail. They permit you to subdivide (D1, D2, D3, and so forth) or combine (JE) or add a new document designated by another capitol letter but they will not tolerate any questioning of the basic JEDP structure...I am at a loss to explain this kind of 'conviction' on any grounds other than intellectual laziness or inability or reappraise."[186]

In spite of the fact that archaeology has literally dug the ground out from under them – most "scholars" will continue to perpetrate the theory. As one Jewish scholar put it, *"Wellhausen's arguments complemented each other nicely, and offered what seemed to be a solid foundation upon which to build the house of biblical criticism. Since then, however, both the evidence and the arguments supporting this structure have been called into question and, to some extent, even rejected. Yet biblical scholarship, while admitting that the grounds have crumbled away, nevertheless continues to adhere to the conclusions."*[187]

---

[185] M. H. Segel, *The Pentateuch – Its Composition and Its Authorship*, Jerusalem: Magnes Press, 1967, p. 22.
[186] "Higher Critics and Forbidden Fruit," *Christianity Today*, Nov. 23, 1959, pp. 131-133.
[187] Yehezkel, Kaufman, *The Religion of Israel*, Chicago: University of Chicago Press, 1960, p. 1.

It seems increasingly evident to the objective student that the Documentary Hypothesis – like that of its progenitor, evolution – is in reality more of a religion than a science! George Mendenhall said: *"It is at least a justified suspicion that a scholarly piety toward the past, rather than historical evidence, is the main foundation for their position."* [188]

In spite of all their talk about "academic objectivity" – it appears that there is just too much loss of face involved, for most theologians to come out and admit that the theory is wrong! As the Jewish author and playwright, Herman Wouk, said: *"It is a hard thing for men who have given their lives to a theory, and taught it to younger men, to see it fall apart."* [189]

Perhaps a quotation by C.S. Lewis would be helpful. Even though he is here not speaking directly about the Documentary Hypothesis – his point is still very relevant to this discussion.

> *"...whatever these men may be as biblical critics, I distrust them as critics. They seem to me to lack literary judgement, to be imperceptive about the very quality of the texts they are reading. It sounds a strange charge to bring against men who have been steeped in those books all their lives. But that might be just the trouble. A man who has spent his youth and manhood in the minute study of New Testament texts and of other people's studies of them, whose literary experiences of those texts lacks any standard of comparison such as can only grow from a wide and deep and genial experience of literature in general, is I should think very likely to miss the obvious things about them. If he tells me that something in a gospel is legend or romance, I want to know how many legends, and romances he has read, how well his palate is trained in detecting them by the flavor; not how many years he has spent on that Gospel...I have been reading poems, romances, vision literature, legend, myths all my life. I know what they are like. I know that not one of them is like this (the Bible)."* [190]

---

188 G. E. Wright, ed., *Biblical History in Transition, the Bible and the Ancient Near East*, New York: Doubleday and Co., 1961, p. 36.
189 Herman Wouk, *This is My God*, New York: Doubleday and Co., 1959, p. 318.
190 C. S. Lewis, "Faulting the Bible Critics," *Christianity Today*, June 9, 1967, p. 7.

Lewis summarizes his argument:

> "...The men ask me to believe they can read between the lines of the old texts; the evidence is their obvious inability to read (in any sense worth discussing) the lines themselves. They claim to see fern-seed and can't see an elephant ten yards away in broad daylight...while I respect the learning of the great biblical critics, I am not yet persuaded that their judgement is equally to be respected."[191]

So sound biblical criticism must be based on objective fact more than subjective literary opinions or interpretations! William F. Albright said: "*The ultimate historicity of a given datum is never conclusively established nor disproved by the literary framework in which it is imbedded: there must always be external evidence.*"[192]

I concur then with the Biblical scholarship that says the "external evidence" is just not there to support Wellhausen's theory! As the renowned Biblical archaeologist, William Albright concluded: "...*Wellhausen's Hegelian method was utterly unsuited to become the master key which scholars might enter the sanctuary of Israelite religion and acquire a satisfying understanding of it.*"[193]

Contrary then to the Wellhausen theory, we believe and affirm that **God does and has intervened in human history revelatory and redemptively!** And, we believe that the Bible – both Old and New Testaments – accurately record that intervention and revelation!

---

191 Ibid., pp. 7-9.
192 "The Israelite Conquest of Canaan in the Light of Archaeology," *The Bulletin of the American Schools of Oriental Research*, 74, 1939, p. 12.
193 William F. Albright, *Archaeology and the History of Israel*, Baltimore: John Hopkins Press, 1942, p. 3.

Appendix IX
POSTMODERNISM AND THE WORD

What is postmodernism? What is relativism? What do they have to do with studying the Bible? Postmodernism refers both to an era and to a worldview or philosophy.

Definition of Postmodernism:

1. **The Era following Modernism**

    The era that followed the Medieval Age is known as the Age of Modernity. From 1470, the Italian Renaissance, to 1700 and the Industrial Revolution – man thought that his salvation would come through the march of progress. He would gain control of his own destiny once superstition was replaced by science and reason.

    From 1789, the French Revolution, to 1989 and the fall of the Berlin Wall – the Age of Enlightenment continued to reflect the elevation of reason over the bondage of superstition via philosophy and science.

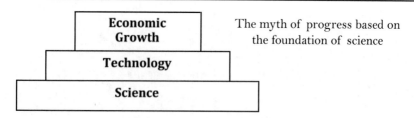

Murli Menon from India is an eloquent and passionate Christian who has taught all over the world, speaking about Eastern religions and the New Age Movement. In his book *The Challenges to Christian Mission in the Contemporary World*, he articulately answers the question: "What happened?"

> *In the 21st century, it has dawned on us that the humanistic vision of modernity was a pipe dream. The two World Wars and the Great Depression of the last century burst the bubble of the progress myth... The walls of modernity are crumbling...Indeed, the progress myth was a grand dream, which has turned into a nightmare for many. The confidence of modernism has turned into suspicion in postmodernity. The very concept of reality has totally changed.*

We surrounded ourselves with appliances...conveniences... technological marvels – and yet we did not find ourselves in Utopia!

2. **The Philosophy or Mindset of Postmodernism**

How have we reacted to this disappointment? Webster's defines "postmodern" as: *"any of several movements that are **reactions against** the philosophy and practices of modern movements..."* As you research Christian writers on the subject of postmodernism, you find that it is the only *"ism"* that *"isn't"*! It does not stand for a particular philosophy, but is characterized by what it refutes.

According to George Barna in Real Teens: *A Contemporary Snapshot of Youth Culture*, Chuck Colson once described the postmodern philosophy as one that could be summed up in a single word: **"whatever"**.
(Regal Books, California, 2001, pp. 94–96).

Chuck Colson writes: "*The only remaining 'ism' is postmodernism, which is not an ideology but a **repudiation of all ideologies**. Its relativism is the admission that every attempt to construct a comprehensive, utopian worldview has failed. It is a formalized expression of despair.*[194] *Oprahism and Donahuism represent a form of materialism that is very seductive because it is pervasive. It makes people believe that they'll find happiness. It appeals to the '**imperial republic of the self**,' as George Weigel called it, and therefore is very insidious.*"[195]

A. As Mr. Colson indicated, the postmodern worldview is characterized by **relativism**. This means "*a view that ethical truths depend on the individuals and groups holding them.*" You may frequently hear someone say "What's true for you isn't true for me" or "There is no absolute truth." Truth becomes a consensus of values — a social construct — and therefore *relative*, and it welcomes plurality.

(1) **Religious Pluralism** is the view that all religions are equally valid – in other words, "all roads lead to Rome." Salvation can be found in all religions and faiths, including Christianity.

(2) According to Rev. Dan Kimball of Santa Cruz, CA, America is the *5th largest unchurched country in the world* – and 75% of our children are being raised in non-church attending homes! With the emergence of relativism as an attractive option, and an emphasis on freedom of choice, supermarket religion emerges. We pick out the parts we want…

- Eternal life in heaven from Christianity
- Eastern mysticism from Zen Buddhism
- Foreknowledge and predictions from astrology
- Empowerment from sorcery and witchcraft
- Lack of consequences of sin from atheism/agnosticism

(3) With the rapid increase in choices and changes, there is a corresponding decrease in commitment, continuity and

---

194 Chuck Colson, "The Sky Isn't Falling", *Christianity Today*, January 11, 1999
195 Interview with Chuck Colson, May 19, 2003

conviction. According to Murli Menon, the result is a faith that is shallow and transient – *even among professing Christians!*

(4) The definition of Christian spirituality is "the practice of Christian life." For the postmodern, spirituality is defined as "the way individuals seek to renew spirit and soul in their lonely lives."

B. How is postmodernism reflected in our culture?

(1) Murli Menon visualizes ours as a **carnival culture**.

- Entertainment values dominate
- The market defines reality
- Images and visuals have great power
- Faith is superficial, weightless, and inauthentic

(2) Modernity said *"I want it all."* Postmodernity says *"I'm paralyzed in the face of it all."* There is a sense of homelessness, anxiety, and a sense of betrayal. People are unstable and de-centered.

(3) **Detachment** is a characteristic and symptom of our culture.

(a) Soong-Chan Rah is senior pastor of Cambridge Community Fellowship Church in Cambridge, Massachusetts. He writes: "The Internet is both a metaphor for and a contributor to our detached culture. Constantly shifting from one screen to another at such high speed, you have little time to make lasting human connection. The Internet exacerbates our short attention span. When we move from screen to screen, nothing impacts us. This is true with television as well, but it has become even more so with the Internet.

"A lot of people find it difficult to believe that we want them in heaven if we don't want them in our living room."

– Ralph Neighbor

This has shaped the way we view life. It's easy to switch off reality, to click through other people's pain...Like Jesus, we must connect with and care for the people around us.

In our postmodern setting, we have to almost re-teach social skills and re-teach human contact. So our goal as a church is...to offer what the high-tech culture does not provide. We're out to re-establish **genuine human connection**...ultimately, the gospel is about incarnational outreach – the human touch."[196]

(b) Reverend Rah further writes: "As a child, I read books about kids growing up in colonial New England. On Sundays, they would sit on hard, splintery wooden benches. They were uncomfortable and built to be that way, so that they would keep the kids alert as they learned about God... In its most rudimentary sense, comfort is not so much about feeling good – it's about feeling nothing...**Comfort** is yet another value of our postmodern culture that goes against incarnational ministry. We don't want to have our La-Z-Boy lives interrupted by people in pain, because we have worked so hard to make ourselves comfortable.

This postmodern desire to "*feel nothing*" is contrary to what the Scriptures teach. Christ opened Himself freely to the pain. "**For the joy set before Him,**" says the writer of Hebrews, "**Jesus suffered the pain of the cross**" (12:2). As a church, we're trying to recover the biblical motif of the suffering body of Christ in order to minister to the suffering body of a postmodern culture made passive by motion, comfort, and individualism."[197]

(4) **Pessimism** is also characteristic of the culture. The confidence in humanity that was prevalent in the Age of Enlightenment

---

196 Soong-Chan Rah, "Navigating Cultural Currents", *Leadership Journal*, Fall 2000.
197 Ibid.

has been diffused by Hitler, Idi Amin, Hussein, bin Laden, Khaddafi, etc.

(5) Dr. Uwe Siemen-Netto, the religion reporter for UPI, said, "There is a desperate need for intelligent, articulate Christians to instruct journalists in a **media-driven age**..." Erwin McManus addressed a Promise Keeper's convention, and said, "The church must engage the culture...The church must be relevant and germane..."

3. **Postmodernism and Tolerance**

Josh McDowell has spent many years researching and teaching apologetics (remember this means to *defend not apologize*) in the public arena. In an article on the Focus on the Family website, he talked about the new cultural climate. [198]

"For decades, I have addressed millions of high school and college students about Jesus Christ and the historical evidence for His life and resurrection. As might be expected, I would often be heckled by people saying such things as, *"Prove it!"* and *"I don't believe you."* But recently I have witnessed a startling shift. Now my attacker invariably says, *"How dare you say that?"* or *"Who do you think you are?"* The issue is no longer the truth of the message, but the right to proclaim it.

Tolerance has become the cardinal virtue, the sole absolute of our society, and our children hear it preached every day in school and from government and the media. Yet few of us understand what society really means by tolerance, nor do we realize that **it is the central doctrine of an entire cultural movement**. As a result, few of us recognize the threat it poses to us, our children, our churches and our very faith.

---

[198] Josh McDowell has co-authored with Bob Hostetler the book *The New Tolerance: How a Cultural Movement Threatens to Destroy You, Your Faith and Your Children.* (Tyndale House, 1998)

The traditional definition of tolerance means simply to recognize and respect others' beliefs, practices, and so forth without necessarily agreeing or sympathizing with them. This attitude, that everyone has a right to his own opinion, is what tolerance means to most of us.

But today's definition is vastly different. This new tolerance means to consider every individual's beliefs, values, lifestyle and truth claims as equally valid. So not only does everyone have an equal right to his beliefs, but all beliefs are equal. **The new tolerance goes beyond respecting a person's rights; it demands praise and endorsement of that person's beliefs, values and lifestyle.** I believe that fundamental change in meaning – and thinking – represents one of the greatest shifts in history, and most people are missing it.

We must humbly pursue truth. It may be difficult to speak the truth in today's climate, but Jesus said, "The truth will set you free." Pursuing truth in this context means countering the new doctrine of tolerance...We must always remember, however, that when the apostle Peter told us, "**Always be prepared to give an answer to everyone who asks you to give the reason for the hope that you have,**" he added, "**But do this with gentleness and respect**" (1 Peter 3:15).

We must aggressively practice love. Everyone loves love, it seems, but few recognize how incompatible love is with the new tolerance. Tolerance simply avoids offending someone; we must help our children live in love, which actively seeks to promote the good of another person.

Tolerance says, "You must approve of what I do." Love responds, "I must do something harder; I will love you, even when your behavior offends me."

Tolerance says, "You must agree with me." Love responds, "I must do something harder; I will tell you the truth, because I am convinced **'the truth will set you free.'"**

Tolerance says, "You must allow me to have my way." Love responds, "I must do something harder; I will plead with you to follow the right way, because I believe you are worth the risk."

Tolerance seeks to be inoffensive; love takes risks. Tolerance glorifies division; love seeks unity. Tolerance costs nothing; love costs everything.

I believe the dreadful potential of the new tolerance can be averted, but only with a renewed commitment to truth, justice and love."

Where is that truth? In the Bible! Perhaps you are studying the Bible for the first time. Perhaps you come from a background that taught you that the Gospel is irrelevant to your daily life. You are in for a life-changing surprise!

Further, there are great opportunities and responsibilities in this postmodern culture! As Murli Menon writes: *"In a highly consumer-oriented society, the Spirit-formed community will be a living and covenantal alternative to the disoriented and fragmented people of the postmodern world… the Gospel is the answer to the longings of the postmodern generation. Our task is to live out, proclaim and articulate the Gospel faithfully."*

The postmodern mind likes mystical things – they are very accepting of taking things in the Bible on faith. That differs from the baby-boomer mentality that everything must relate to what's happening today. Rev. Dan Kimball says: *"The young generations desire a spiritual encounter with the living God – not a worship service that feels like a business seminar, or information packages. They want reverence, holiness, mystery, transcendence. Quit trying to be cutting edge, move back to the center and unapologetically present Jesus!"*

David Edwards said, "***Postmodernism is no more an enemy of the Gospel than any other human philosophy*** – *we just need to develop the ability to communicate, to connect.*" Dr. Siemen-Netto said, "*Jesus can eliminate the confusion, distortion and relativism of the postmodern spiritual chaos. Postmodernity has opened the minds of young people to the Gospel, but on the condition that lifestyle reflects belief. Christians must model exemplary behavior.*" Murli Menon agrees: "*In a postmodern world, our communities must reflect exemplary character and conduct…that is the only hermeneutic of the Gospel.*"

The economic and military status in America will offer many opportunities for each of us to present the Gospel. As unemployment and underemployment continues, many unbelievers will lose the arrogant self-sufficiency that kept their hearts hardened to the Word. As St. Francis of Assisi said, "Preach the gospel at all times. If necessary, use words."

"**Your word I have hidden in my heart…Your word is a lamp to my feet and a light to my path…The entrance of Your words gives light; it gives understanding to the simple**" (Ps. 119:11, 105, 130 NKJV).

Quotes for Further Reflection

- *For let us make no mistake. If the end of the world appeared in all the literal trappings of the Apocalypse, if the modern materialist saw with his own eyes the heavens rolled up and the great white throne appearing, if he had the sensation of being himself hurled into the Lake of Fire, he would continue forever, in that lake itself, to regard his experience as an illusion and to find the explanation of it in psychoanalysis, or cerebral pathology. – C.S. Lewis, God in the Dock*

- *What is dangerous today is the postmodern vacuum in which we amuse ourselves to death with Oprah and we substitute feeling better – the therapeutic model – for really facing ourselves…there is a deepening hunger for orthodoxy….We have to do more than just give people* biblical knowledge. We have to figure out how to carry it to the heart. — Interview with Chuck Colson, May 19, 2003, Christianity Today

- *Pluralism is not just recognition that there is a plurality of faiths in the world today. That is an obvious fact. No, pluralism is itself an ideology. It affirms the independent validity of all faiths. It therefore rejects as arrogant and wholly unacceptable every attempt to convert anybody (let alone everybody) to our opinions...The reason we must reject this increasingly popular position is that we are committed to the uniqueness of Jesus (He has no competitors) and His finality (He has no successors). It is not the uniqueness of "Christianity" as a system that we defend, but the uniqueness of Christ. He is unique in His incarnation (which is quite different from the ahistorical and plural "avatars" of Hinduism); in His atonement (dying once for all for our sins); in His resurrection (breaking the power of death); and in His gift of the Spirit (to indwell and transform us). So, because in no other person but Jesus of Nazareth did God first become human (in His birth), then bear our sins (in His death), then conquer death (in His resurrection) and then enter His people (by His Spirit), He is uniquely able to save sinners. Nobody else has His qualifications..."Nothing commends the Gospel more eloquently than a transformed life, and nothing brings it into disrepute so much as personal inconsistency" (Manila Manifesto). — John Stott, "Why Don't They Listen?"* www.christianitytoday.com [September 8, 2003]

Appendix X

Further Resources
Online Degree Opportunities

Some yearn deeply for an opportunity to further their theological training, or attain a degree – yet they cannot. Many brothers overseas pray fervently for an opportunity to come to America and attend a college or seminary. But just as God has been pleased to provide the technology to offer this writing online, there are many resources available to attain an education online.

I do not encourage or sponsor nationals to come to America or Europe for further studies for several reasons: First, it is too disruptive to their family life – and causes prolonged separation, emotional pain and financial expense. Secondly, it causes a disruption in their local ministry – and by the time they return, they have become "Americanized" or "Westernized," and lost touch with their own country and culture. Thirdly, there are now excellent Bible Colleges, Seminaries and Graduate Schools in Africa, Asia and South America where they can study, and stay closer to home… to their ministries…to their country and culture.

I am listing several Websites here, but this is not intended to be inclusive – just representative. Also, I cannot endorse or recommend any of them – you should investigate and find the one that best answers your questions:

- Do they believe that the Bible is the infallible, inspired very Word of God? Do they believe that Jesus is the Son of God – and fully God as Son?

- Are they accredited? Are they reputable? Will they offer references?

- Do they offer financial aid? Is the cost reasonable or roughly the same as others for the education you are seeking?

- Do they offer online assistance if you have questions?

- Are advisors and counselors available to you? Are they concerned about understanding your goals, and helping you attain them?

- Are many of the books you will need available to read online?

- Can you finish the requirements completely online? What degree will you have when you finish? Will it further your ministry to God's glory?

Luther Rice Seminary	www.lrs.edu
Trinity Evangelical Divinity School	www.tiu.edu
The King's College and Seminary	www.kingsseminary.edu
Trinity College of the Bible Theol. Seminary	www.trinitysem.edu
Liberty Home Bible Institute (Jerry Falwell)	www.lhbi.org
Gordon-Conwell Theological Seminary	www.gordonconwell.edu
Fuller Theological Seminary	www.fuller.edu

Non-Degree Study Resources

Biblical Training — www.biblicaltraining.org
BTCP (Bible Training Centre for Pastors) www.bibletraining.com
Charles Stanley Institute for Christian Living www.intouch.org
Billy Graham Bible Study — www.billygraham.org/BibleStudy
Carolina Evangelical Divinity School, www.ceds.edu

BIBLIOGRAPHY

Articles

1. "A New Third World." *Time*, Oct. 18, 1976.

2. Barker, Kenneth L. "An Insider Talks About the NIV." *Kindred Spirit*, Fall 1978.

3. Bruce, F. F., "Are the New Testament Documents Still Reliable?" *Christianity Today*, Oct. 20, 1978.

4. Cauffiel, Lowell. "Archaeological Find Lends Credibility to Bible History." *National Courier*, November 26, 1976.

5. DeVaux, Roland. "The Bible and the Ancient Near East." Quoted in Howard Vos, "Archaeology and the Text of the Old Testament." *Bible and Spade*, Winter 1978.

6. Geisler, Normal L. "The Nature of Scripture." *Christianity Today*, Feb. 24, 1978.

7. Graham, Billy. "Biblical Authority in Evangelism." *Christianity Today*, Oct. 22, 1976.

8. Gundry, Stanley N. "Which Version is Best?" *Moody Monthly*, Jan., 1979.

9. "Higher Critics and Forbidden Fruit." *Christianity Today*, Nov. 23, 1959.

10. "Inerrancy Matters." *Christianity Today*, Oct., 1978.

11. "Justin Martyr, Dialogue with Trypho 7." Quoted in William Barclay, *The Making of the Bible*, New York: Abingdon Press, 1965.

12. LaFay, Howard. "Splendor of an unknown Empire, *National Geographic*, Dec., 1978.

13. LaSor, William S. "Major Archaeological Discoveries at Tell Mardikh." *Christianity Today*, Sept. 24, 1976.

14. "Letters of St. Augustine LXXXII," No. 3. Quoted in Harold Lindsell, "The Infallible Word." *Christianity Today*, Sept. 15, 1972.

15. Lewis, C.S. "Faulting the Bible Critics." *Christianity Today*, June 9, 1967.

16. Lindsell, Harold. "The Infallible Word." *Christianity Today*, Sept. 15, 1972.

17. Maloney, Paul G. "Assessing Ebla." *Biblical Archaeology Review*, March, 1978.

18. Martin, Walter. *The Christian Research Institute Newsletter*. Third Quarter, 1977.

19. "Melodyland School of Theology's Doctrinal Statement. Quoted in John Warwick Montgomery "Whither Biblical Inerrancy?" *Christianity Today*, July 29, 1977.

20. Mikaya, Adam. "The Politics of Ebla." *Biblical Archaeology Review*, Sept./Oct., 1978.

21. Mill, John Stuart. "Three Essays on Religion." Quoted in J.N.D. Anderson, *Christianity: The Witness of History*. London: The Tyndale Press, 1969.

22. Montgomery, John Warwick. "History and Christianity." His, Jan., 1965.

24. Oliver, Connie. "Pinnock Speaks on Biblical Inerrancy." *Perspective*, May/June, 1976.

25. Oliver, Kay. "Summit '78 Takes Stand on Inerrancy." *Moody Monthly*, Dec., 1978.

26. Pache, Rene. "The Inspiration and Authority of Scripture." *Moody Monthly*.

27. Ramm, Bernard. His, Oct., 1975.

28. Schaeffer, Francis. "Schaeffer on Scripture." *Christianity Today*, August 29, 1975.

29. "Scholars Agree." *Christianity Today*, June 9, 1972.

30. Schultz, Samuel. "Did Moses Write Deuteronomy?" *Christianity Today*, August 29, 1975.

31. "Tatians Address to the Greeks 29." Quoted in William Barclay, *The Making of the Bible*, New York: Abingdon Press, 1965.

32. *Time*, December 30, 1974.

33. "The New Testament Dating Game." *Time*, March 21, 1977.

34. "The Israelite Conquest of Canaan in the Light of Archaeology." *The Bulletin of the American Schools of Oriental Research*, 74 (1939).

35. Virtue, David. "Archaeologist Finds Bible Best Historical Source." *North Carolina Christian Advocate*, October 22, 1978.

36. Vos, Howard F. "Archaeology and the Text of the Old Testament." *Bible and Spade*, Winter 1978.

37. Wiseman, Donald J. "Archaeology and Scripture." *The Westminster Theological Journal*, May, 1971.

38. Yamauchi, Edwin. "Ebla: A Spectacular Discovery." *Evangelical Newsletter*, December 1, 1978.

39. Yamauchi, Edwin. "The Word from Nag Hammadi." *Christianity Today*, January 13, 1978.

Books and Other References:

40. Albright, William F. *Archaeology and the History of Israel*, Baltimore: Johns Hopkins Press, 1942.

41. Albright, William F. *Archaeology and the Region of Israel*, Baltimore: Johns Hopkins Press, 1942.

42. Albright, William F. *Archaeology, Historical Analogy and Early Biblical Tradition*, Baton Rouge: Louisiana State University Press, 1966.

43. Albright, William F. History, *Archaeology, and Christian Humanism*, New York: McGraw-Hill Book Co., 1964.

44. Anderson, J.N.D. Christianity: *The Witness of History*, London: The Tyndale Press, 1969.

45. Archer, Gleason. *A Survey of the Old Testament*, Chicago: Moody Press, 1964.

46. Barnhouse, Donald Grey. *The Invisible War*, Grand Rapids: Zondervan Publishing House, 1965.

47. Bruce, F.F. *The Books and the Parchments*, Westwood: Fleming H. Revell Co., 1963.

48. Bruce, F.F. *The New Testament Documents: Are They Reliable?* Downers Grove, Ill., InterVarsity Press, 1960.

49. Burrows, Millar. *What Mean These Stones?* Quoted in Paul Little, *Know Why You Believe*, Chicago: InterVarsity Press, 1968.

50. Cassuto, Umberto. *The Documentary Hypothesis*, Jerusalem: Magnes Press, 1961.

51. Free, Joseph. *Archaeology and Bible History*, Wheaton, Ill., Scripture Press, 1969.

52. Geisler, Normal L. and Nix, William E. *A General Introduction to the Bible*. Chicago: Moody Press, 1968.

53. Geisler, Normal L. and Nix, William E. *From God to Us: How We Got Our Bible.* Quoted in Wally Kroeker, "How We Got The Bible." *Moody Monthly*, April, 1975.

54. Getz, Gene. *The Measure of a Church.*

55. Greenlee, J. Harold. *Introduction to New Testament Textual Criticism*, Grand Rapids: Wm. B. Eerdmans Publishing Co., 1964.

56. Harris, R. Laird. "How Reliable is the Old Testament Text?" *Can l Trust My Bible.* Quoted in Paul Little, *Know Why You Believe.* Chicago: InterVarsity Press, 1968.

57. Harrison, R.K. *Introduction to the Old Testament.* Grand Rapids: Wm. B. Eerdmans Publishing Co., 1970.

58. Hodge, Charles. *Systematic Theology, vol. 1.* Grand Rapids: Wm. B. Eerdmans Publishing Co., 1975 (reprint edition).

59. Hort, Fenton J.A. and Wescott, Brooke F. *The New Testament in Original Greek, vol. 1.* New York: The Macmillan Co., 1881.

60. Jeremias, Joachim. *Unknown Sayings of Jesus*, Alec R. Allenson, 1964.

61. Kaufman, Yehezkel, *The Religion of Israel.* Chicago: University of Chicago Press, 1960.

62. Kenyon, Frederic. *Journal of Transactions of the Victoria Institute.* Quoted in Paul Little, *Know Why You Believe.* Chicago: InterVarsity Press, 1968.

63. Kenyon, Frederic. *Our Bible and the Ancient Manuscripts*, New York: Harper and Brothers, 1941.

64. Kenyon, Frederic. *The Bible and Modern Scholarship*, London: John Murray, 1948.

65. Kilby, Clyde S., ed. *A Mind Awake, An Anthology of C.S. Lewis*, New York: Harcourt, Brace, and World, Inc., 1968.

66. Kilby, Clyde S. *The Christian World of C. S. Lewis,* Grand Rapids: Wm. B. Eerdmans Publishing Co., 1964.

67. McDowell, Josh. *Evidence that Demands a Verdict, vol. I,* Arrowhead Springs, California: Campus Crusade for Christ, Inc., 1972.

68. McDowell, Josh. *More Evidence that Demands a Verdict,* Arrowhead Springs, California: Campus Crusade for Christ, Inc., 1975.

69. Mears, Henrietta. *What the Bible is all About,* Glendale, California: Gospel Light Publications, 1966.

70. Metzger, Bruce M. *The Text of the Old Testament,* New York: Oxford University Press, 1968.

71. Montgomery, John Warwick. *History and Christianity,* Downers Grove, Ill.: InterVarsity Press, 1971.

72. Nee, Watchman, *Ye Search the Scriptures,* New York: Christian Fellowship Publishers, Inc., 1974.

73. Phillips, J.B. *New Testament Christianity,* New York: The Macmillan Co., 1957.

74. Phillips, J.B. *The Ring of Truth,* New York: The Macmillan Co., 1967.

75. Putnam, Roy. "Traversing the Text." A lecture given at the Good News Convocation, 1978.

76. Radmacher, Earl. "Inspiration of Scriptures." tape series, Conservative Baptist Theological Seminary, Denver, Colorado.

77. Sayce, A.H. *Monument Facts and Higher Critical Fancies,* London: The Religious Tract Society, 1904.

78. Segel, M.H. *The Pentateuch – Its Composition and Its Authorship.* Jerusalem: Magnes Press, 1967.

79. Schaff, Philip. "The Person of Christ." American Tract Society, 1913.

80. Stoner, Peter W. *Science Speaks,* Chicago: Moody Press, 1963.

81. Stott, John. Understanding the Bible. Glendale, California: Regal Books, 1972.

82. Unger, Merrill F. *Unger's Bible Dictionary,* Chicago: Moody Press, 1971.

83. White, John. *Eros Defiled,* Downers Grove, Illinois: InterVarsity Press, 1977.

84. Wouk, Herman. This is My God, New York: Doubleday and Co., 1959.

85. Wright, G.E., ed. *Biblical History in Transition., the Bible and the Ancient Near East,* New York: Doubleday and Co.,.1961.

86. Youngblood, Ronald. *The Heart of the Old Testament,* Grand Rapids: Baker Book House, 1971.